# GREAT 2x4
# Projects for
# Outdoor Living

# GREAT 2x4
# Projects for
# Outdoor Living

## Making Stylish Furniture from Standard Lumber

### Stevie Henderson & Mark Baldwin

STERLING INNOVATION
An imprint of Sterling Publishing Co., Inc.

New York / London
www.sterlingpublishing.com

**Library of Congress Cataloging-in-Publication Data**

Henderson, Stevie, 1943-2007
Great 2 x 4 projects for outdoor living / Stevie Henderson and Mark Baldwin.
p. cm.
Includes index.
ISBN-13: 978-1-4027-5337-4
ISBN-10: 1-4027-5337-3
1. Outdoor furniture. 2. Furniture making. 3. Garden ornaments and furniture--Design and construction.
I. Baldwin, Mark, 1975- II. Title. III. Title: Great two by four projects for outdoor living. IV. Title: 2x4 projects
for outdoor living.

TT197.5.O9H454 2008
684.1'8--dc22

2007032211


2  4  6  8  10  9  7  5  3  1


Published 2008 by Sterling Publishing Co., Inc.
387 Park Avenue South, New York, NY 10016

© 2008 by Stevie Henderson and Mark Baldwin

This book is comprised of materials from the following Sterling/Lark books:
*Great Outdoor 2x4 Furniture* © 1998 by Stevie Henderson
*2x4 Projects for Outdoor Living* © 2000 by Stevie Henderson and Mark Baldwin

Distributed in Canada by Sterling Publishing
c/o Canadian Manda Group, 165 Dufferin Street
Toronto, Ontario, Canada M6K 3H6
Distributed in the United Kingdom by GMC Distribution Services
Castle Place, 166 High Street, Lewes, East Sussex, England BN7 1XU
Distributed in Australia by Capricorn Link (Australia) Pty. Ltd.
P.O. Box 704, Windsor, NSW 2756, Australia

Sterling ISBN-13: 978-1-4027-5337-4
ISBN-10: 1-4027-5337-3


Design by StarGraphics Studio


For information about custom editions, special sales, premium and
corporate purchases, please contact Sterling Special Sales
Department at 800-805-5489 or specialsales@sterlingpublishing.com.

In Loving Memory of
Stevie P. Henderson
1943-2007

# Contents

# Seating 77

# Accessories 155

# Introduction

More and more we find ourselves living out-of-doors. In years past, we might have grilled burgers on Saturday afternoon or picnicked during the day on Sunday, but now we find ourselves sitting on the deck with friends on a weeknight and holding most of our parties in the backyard. Perhaps it is a return to the days when grandma and grandpa sat on the front porch and visited with neighbors, or perhaps today we cherish a more casual way of living. Whatever the reason, our backyards have become extended living areas.

To make our new living area "liveable" requires a whole new list of desirable additions to the yard and garden. And those additions are very costly if you purchase them in specialty stores. Not having shopped for outdoor furniture and fixtures in a number of years, we were appalled at the prices for tables, swings, deck chairs, and fountains. Rather than settle for four plastic chairs and a matching plastic table, we decided to build our outdoor living furniture and fixtures. We are thrilled with the results. Not only did we save money, but our new outdoor rooms are filled with practical and attractive pieces that fit our outdoor living lifestyle.

Even if you have never picked up a hammer and nails, this book is for you. We have simplified the construction of every project with the beginner in mind. Browse through the book, pick out a project, and read through the instructions. We will bet you'll agree that you can do it. There is something for everyone, and even the largest projects, such as the Mini Gazebo, will take just a couple of weekends to complete. There's plenty of variety, including a garden chair, a dining table, a potting bench, different types of planters, a lawn bench, a privacy screen, and a hammock stand. Build a small project to get started, and, after that success, you'll be tackling everything in the book. We hope that you will find just the right project for your lawn, garden, deck, or dock. Because we live in Florida, we are outdoors year 'round, and our lawn furniture gets as much use as our indoor furniture. For that reason, we know it's important to build practical and sturdy projects that will last. No matter where you live, we think you'll enjoy building and using the designs in this book.

*Happy outdoor living!*

# Materials, Tools, & Techniques

This book is written for beginning woodworkers who want to build sturdy, good-looking, and practical furniture and accessories for their patio, garden, or lawn. If you have ever held a hammer and know what a nail is, you can build the projects in this book. There is nothing mystical about working with wood. Like any endeavor, it requires some patience and a little introductory knowledge to get started. We suggest that you read through this section before beginning any project.

If you are an accomplished woodworker who works in a fully equipped shop of stationary power tools, please bear in mind that these instructions are geared to the beginner. Many of the procedures in this book don't translate logically or safely to large, stationary power tools. We suggest, therefore, that you alter the instructions to accommodate your more advanced tools and knowledge. Know the capabilities of your tools and don't exceed them.

## Materials

By definition, building outdoor furniture requires using materials and finishes that will stand up to the elements. There are lots of options in woods, adhesives, fasteners, and finishes. With a little information, you will be able to make informed choices about the materials that are available. These choices become easier if you start by defining your personal needs in terms of location, budget, and appearance.

The first thing to consider is where you plan to place your finished project. All outdoor sites are not the same. Will the bench you are building be placed on a covered porch in a moderate climate, or will it sit in the middle of a yard during a Montana snowstorm? Do you want to build an heirloom piece that will last for years—no matter what the cost? Are you building a piece that will be grouped with existing furniture that you would like to match? The answers to questions like these will determine the appropriate wood, adhesive, fasteners, and finish for each woodworking project you undertake.

## Adhesives

Since this book deals with exterior projects that will be exposed to the weather much of the time, a weatherproof glue is mandatory. Ordinary interior glue will dissolve when exposed to the elements. The easiest glue to use is an exterior-formulated version of ordinary straw-colored carpenter's glue. Look for the words "exterior use" on the container. You may also use the more costly two part resorcinol, though it takes about 12 hours to set and at least another 12 hours to cure completely.

Don't overdo the amount of glue you use. If too much is applied, the glue will be squeezed out of the joint and drip all over your project when pressure is applied. Just apply a small ribbon of glue down the center of one surface, then rub the adjoining surface against the ribbon to distribute the glue evenly. Your objective is to coat both surfaces with a uniform, thin coating. If you do encounter drips, wipe them off quickly with a damp cloth. It is easy to do at the moment, but if you let the glue dry, it can be very difficult to remove. If it dries, it will have to be sanded off, since it will not accept most stains.

## Fasteners

The projects in this book are designed for exterior use, so any fastener you use to construct them must also be weatherproof—or at least weather resistant. There are several different kinds of materials and coatings that make a nail or screw suitable for exterior use. The basic rule is that the longer the coating or material is expected to last, the more you can expect to pay for it.

The most popular choices for nails and screws used for outdoor woodworking are described below.

**Galvanized** fasteners are coated with zinc, are inexpensive, and are the most widely used type of coated fastener. Over time, they may stain redwood and cedar, and corrode in pressure-treated wood.

**Anodized** fasteners are roughly equivalent to galvanized in quality and performance.

**Zinc-plated** fasteners are somewhat more weather resistant but difficult to find outside specialty stores.

**Brass** fasteners are lovely to look at and resistant to weather but lack strength.

**Stainless steel** fasteners are highly resistant to corrosion and extremely strong but extremely expensive.

Another note about galvanized products: It may be worth the extra trouble to look for what are known as "hot-dipped" or mechanically galvanized nails or screws rather than the somewhat less-expensive products that use an electrical plating technique. The dipping process more effectively deposits zinc on the surface of the metal.

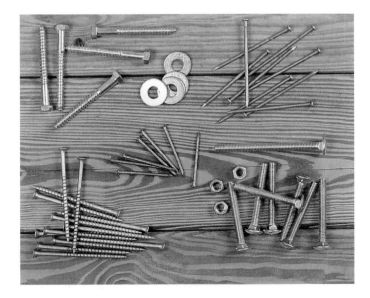

Ultimately, we tend to match the quality of the fasteners we choose to the quality of the wood. For example, if you are building a project out of expensive teak, it makes sense to purchase stainless steel screws. If you are using inexpensive pressure-treated pine, galvanized decking screws are probably the logical choice.

## Nails

Although there are many different types of nails (common, large flathead, duplex head, oval head, and so forth), the one most commonly used in woodworking is a finish nail. It has a much smaller head than the common

*An assortment of nails, screws, brads, washers, and nuts*

nail, making it easy to recess below the surface of the wood, or countersink. The small hole remaining on the surface is easily concealed with wood filler.

Nail sizes are designated by "penny" (abbreviated as "d"). Penny size directly corresponds to length, although the diameter is larger for longer nails. They range in length from 1 inch to 6 inches. Confused? To determine the penny size of a particular nail length, the following method works well for lengths up to 3 inches (10d). Take the length of the nail you need, subtract $1/2$ inch, and multiply by four. For example, if you need a $2^1/_2$-inch nail, subtract $1/2$ inch, and multiply by four. What you need is an 8-penny nail (8d). Some of the more commonly used nail sizes are listed below.

| Penny Size | Length |
|:----------:|:------:|
| 2d | 1″ |
| 3d | 1-$^1/_4$″ |
| 4d | 1-$^1/_2$″ |
| 5d | 1-$^3/_4$″ |
| 6d | 2″ |
| 7d | 2-$^1/_4$″ |
| 8d | 2-$^1/_2$″ |
| 9d | 2-$^3/_4$″ |
| 10d | 3″ |
| 12d | 3-$^1/_4$″ |
| 16d | 3-$^1/_2$″ |
| 20d | 4″ |

As a general rule, when joining two pieces of wood, use a nail length that will provide the greatest amount of holding power without penetrating the opposite surface. For example, if you are joining two 1x4s, each piece of wood is $^3/_4$ inch thick—a total of $1^1/_2$ inches of wood. To maximize your holding power, you should choose a $1^1/_4$-inch nail.

Nails driven in at an angle provide more holding power than those that are driven straight into the work. *Toenailing* refers to the process of driving a nail into the wood at an extreme angle to secure two pieces together.

The most difficult part of toenailing comes when the nail is nearly all the way into

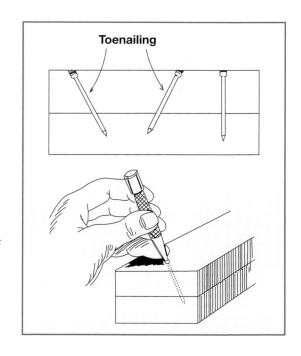

the wood and only the head and a bit of the shank are visible. To avoid making hammer marks on your wood, hammer the nail into the piece until the head is still slightly above the surface. Then use a nail set to finish the job and countersink the nail.

In fact, the best way to prevent hammer marks on all of your work is to use a nail set. The trick to using a nail set effectively is to hold it in the proper manner. It should be steadied with the hand by gripping it firmly with all four fingers and your thumb. Rest your little finger on the surface of the wood for added stability.

If you are working with hardwood, a very narrow piece of softwood, or any wood that has a tendency to split when you nail into it, it is wise to predrill the nail hole. Choose a drill bit that is just barely smaller than the diameter of the nail, and drill a pilot hole about two-thirds the length of the nail.

## Brads

Wire brads are used for attaching trim or for very small projects. They are just a smaller and thinner version of finish nails. They are designated in length in inches and wire gauge numbers from 11 to 0. The lower the gauge number, the larger the diameter.

## Screws

The advantage of screws over nails is their holding power and the fact that (when used without glue) they can be removed easily at a later date. Their disadvantage is that they are not as easy to insert. Almost all of the projects in the book use screws in the construction.

As with nails, there are many kinds of screws. The one most often used in woodworking is a flathead Phillips screw. As the name implies, it has a flat head that can be countersunk below the surface. It is most often labeled as a "drywall screw" and can be driven with a power drill.

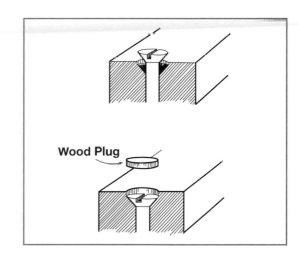

Wood Plug

Screws are designated by length and diameter. In general, as with nails, you want to use the longest screw possible that will not penetrate the opposite surface. The diameter of a screw is described by its gauge number.

Common sizes range from #2 to #16, with larger diameters having higher gauge numbers.

When you are working on very soft wood, it is possible to countersink a screw simply by driving it with a power drill. However, the resulting surface hole may be covered only by using wood filler. An alternate method is to predrill the screw hole and insert a wood plug over the top of the countersunk screw head.

Predrilling is normally a two-step operation. First drill the larger, countersunk portion deep enough and at a diameter just slightly larger than the diameter of the screw head (or the depth and diameter to accommodate the screw and the wood plug you are using).

Then drill the pilot hole in the center of the larger hole, using a drill bit the same diameter as the solid portion of the screw (minus the threads). If you use the same size screws on a regular basis, you may wish to invest in a combination pilot-countersink bit for your drill, which will perform both operations at the same time.

You can purchase wood plugs, or you can cut your own. It is easy to slice a wooden dowel rod into many wood plugs. The only disadvantage to this plug is that it will show the end grain and will be visible if you stain the wood. The alternative is to cut your own plugs using a plug cutter, but that method requires a drill press.

Screws can be inserted at an angle, the same way that nails are, to toenail two pieces of wood together. After some practice, you will be able to start a screw at any angle with very little or no effort. If you find it difficult, simply use a drill or a screw starter to begin your screw hole.

Although you do not want to add so many screws to your project that the metal outweighs the wood, do not be stingy with them. If there is the slightest chance that the joint could be shaky, add a couple of extra screws. Remember that the project you are making will probably be subjected to several moves over the course of the years—either to a different room or a different house—which will place additional strain on the joints.

## Wood

The two basic classifications of wood are softwood and hardwood. As the name implies, softwood is usually softer and therefore easier to work with than hardwood. It is also much less expensive. Because of this, softwood is usually a good choice for beginning woodworkers. We built all of the projects in this book with softwood, but, of course, they can be built with hardwood. We have specified pine in the instructions, but use whatever softwood is most plentiful (and least expensive) in your area.

Softwood is cut from coniferous trees (evergreens) such as pine, redwood, and cedar. Hardwood comes from deciduous trees such as maple, cherry, and walnut, which shed their leaves each year.

Because these projects are designed for outdoor use (which does not mean you have to use them outdoors), you will most likely want to use wood that will stand up to life in the great outdoors. Damp weather, insects, and fungi cause wood to deteriorate. Heartwood, the dense, dead wood from the inner core of a tree, repels moisture and insects far more effectively than the sapwood that surrounds it. However, this core wood takes years to develop, and most old-growth trees were harvested years ago. Today, most commercial lumber consists of second-growth timber that lacks any substantial amount of heartwood.

Some species are naturally resistant to decay and insects. They include white cedar, redwood, black locust, cypress, hemlock, and oak. Douglas fir and Southern yellow pine, although they are not as resistant to damage, are good choices for outdoor projects. They are reasonably priced, hard, and durable. They also do well when chemically treated.

You can use untreated pine for smaller projects, as long as the lumber is thoroughly sealed, painted, and sealed again. If the piece you are building will be exposed to the elements for any length of time, we recommend that you use a treated pine.

## Treated Wood

There are two general categories of preservatives used to treat wood: oils, such as creosote and pentachlorophenol solutions in petroleum, and chemical salts that are applied as waterborne solutions. The lumber you purchase will probably be treated with the second method, and is known as pressure-treated, or "PT," wood. The name is apt, as the preservatives are forced under pressure into the cells of the wood to protect it from destructive organisms. Lumber treated in this way will last five to 10 times longer than untreated lumber.

Pressure-treated lumber is classified by how it will be used: above ground or in contact with the ground. If any portion of the project will come in contact with the ground, use the latter classification, even though it is more expensive. Just to make things more complicated, there is also a difference between pressure-treated wood used for decks and buildings and pressure-treated wood used for general purposes. This information should be printed on a tag stapled to the end grain of the lumber you buy. If not, ask the salesperson to help you determine whether you are buying the best treated lumber for your needs. Ratings may simply be LP-2 for above-ground use and LP-22 for below-ground use. If you plan to build a trellis and place it directly on the lawn, we recommend that you purchase below-ground treated wood.

Please keep in mind that there are chemicals in treated lumber. Always wear a dust mask when you cut treated lumber. Never burn treated-wood scraps. And, if you are concerned about possible skin sensitivities to treated lumber, you may want to wear leather gloves. After handling treated lumber, be sure to wash your hands before eating, and wash your work clothes separately from other laundry.

The ultimate choice of wood will probably be driven by your budget. For each of the materials required for exterior projects, the cost goes up relative to its ability to withstand the onslaught of Mother Nature. Untreated pine will work when correctly finished and placed in a protected area; above-ground treated pine will be fine for projects placed on a patio or deck; and below-ground treated pine will work for projects placed directly on the ground. Moving up in expense, redwood or cypress work well for all projects and can be placed directly on the ground.

## Softwood

Softwood is sold in most building supply stores in dimensional sizes—1x4s, 2x4s, and so forth. And it is sold in specific foot lengths. So you can buy a 1x4x6, or a 1x4x8, or a 1x4x10, and so forth. This would seem to make it simple. And it would be if a 1x4 was actually 1 inch thick and 4 inches wide. But such is not the case. Apparently the sawmills, lumberyards, and building supply stores have conspired in a huge plot to confuse us, because a 1x4 is actually

$^3/_4$ inch thick and $3^1/_2$ inches wide. There is a reason for this. When the board was cut originally, it was 1 inch thick and 4 inches wide. But when it is surfaced on all four sides, its actual dimensions are less. Listed below are the nominal sizes and the actual dimensions.

| Nominal Size | Actual Dimensions |
|:---:|:---:|
| 1x2 | $^3/_4" \times 1^1/_2"$ |
| 1x3 | $^3/_4" \times 2^1/_2"$ |
| 1x4 | $^3/_4" \times 3^1/_2"$ |
| 1x6 | $^3/_4" \times 5^1/_2"$ |
| 1x8 | $^3/_4" \times 7^1/_4"$ |
| 1x10 | $^3/_4" \times 9^1/_4"$ |
| 1x12 | $^3/_4" \times 11^1/_4"$ |
| 2x2 | $1^1/_2" \times 1^1/_2"$ |
| 2x4 | $1^1/_2" \times 3^1/_2"$ |
| 2x6 | $1^1/_2" \times 5^1/_2"$ |
| 2x8 | $1^1/_2" \times 7^1/_4"$ |
| 2x10 | $1^1/_2" \times 9^1/_4"$ |
| 2x12 | $1^1/_2" \times 11^1/_4"$ |
| 4x4 | $3^1/_2" \times 3^1/_2"$ |
| 4x6 | $3^1/_2" \times 5^1/_2"$ |
| 6x6 | $5^1/_2" \times 5^1/_2"$ |
| 8x8 | $7^1/_2" \times 7^1/_2"$ |

Softwood is also graded according to its quality. And, as with anything else, the better the quality, the higher the price. Do not buy a better quality than you need for the project you are building. A few imperfections may even make your project look more rustic (if that is the look you are after). The softwood grades are as follows.

## Common Grades

**No. 1 common** contains knots and a few imperfections but should have no knotholes.
**No. 2 common** is free of knotholes but contains some knots.
**No. 3 common** contains larger knots and small knotholes.
**No. 4 common** is used for construction only and contains large knotholes.
**No. 5 common** is the lowest grade of lumber and is used only when strength and appearance are not important.

## Select Grades

**B and better (or 1 and 2 clear)** are the best and most expensive grades used for the finest furniture projects.

**C select** may have a few small blemishes.

**D select** is the lowest quality of the better board grades. It has imperfections that can be concealed with paint.

Clear boards (those that are nearly free of imperfections) come from the center section (heartwood) of the tree, and **sapwood** (wood that have more knots and other flaws) comes from the outer sections.

Consider the type of finish that you want to apply to the completed project. If you plan to stain the finished piece, pay particular attention to the grain of the wood, and choose boards that have fewer imperfections and similar grain patterns. If you are going to paint the finished piece, you can purchase a lower grade of wood and cover the defects with wood filler and paint.

No matter what grade you purchase, you should inspect each and every board for defects and imperfections. A little extra inspection time in the store will save you hours of frustration later and will be well worth the effort. Some stores will not allow you to hand-select individual boards—take your business elsewhere. Although it is possible (but extremely time-consuming) to correct some defects in wood, it is simply easier to purchase blemish-free boards in the first place. There is no point in buying wood that is unusable, no matter how cheap the price.

Many large building supply stores purchase their wood from different suppliers, and that means that even in the same bin at the same store, the board widths may vary slightly. On the surface (no pun intended), that may not seem like a big deal. But even a difference of $1/64$th of an inch in width between two boards will mean that your project will not fit together correctly. So when you purchase wood for a specific project, place the boards together to make certain that they are all exactly the same width.

While you are checking, examine the board for warping and/or bowing. Warpage occurs over the length of the board, and bowing occurs across the width of the board. If you will be cutting only very short pieces of wood and the warpage is very slight, it probably will not affect your finished project. But if you need longer lengths, search until you find boards that are straight along the entire length. A good method to check for warping or bowing before you buy is to place one end of the board on the floor, and look down its length. Then turn the board and look down the edge. Your own eye is the best test.

Also check for knots. Small, tight knots are usually okay—especially for furniture that you plan to paint. But large knots may become a problem, as they are tough to cut through and also may fall out, leaving you with an unattractive hole in your finished project. Some imperfections can simply be eliminated. If a board is otherwise acceptable, but has a knothole on the end, it is easy enough to simply cut it off. But be sure to purchase extra material to compensate for the loss.

**Warp**

**Cup**

**Split**

**Knot**

Avoid buying boards that contain splits. Splits have a nasty habit of growing lengthwise, ultimately resulting in two narrow and unusable boards. If the split occurs only at one end, you can cut it off; but again, allow extra material for the waste.

## Selecting Wood

For purposes of clarity, this book refers to each surface of a board by a specific name. The broadest part of the board is called a *face*, and the narrow surface along the length of the board is an *edge*. The *ends*, as the name suggests, are the smallest surfaces occurring on the extremities of each board.

It will be time well spent to read through the instructions and cutting list of an individual project before shopping for your materials. Each materials list specifies the total number of linear feet of a particular wood required to make the project. So if the total linear feet required is 40 feet, you can purchase five 8-foot lengths, four 10-foot lengths, and so on. When you arrive at the lumberyard or store, you may find that the 8-foot lengths of wood are of lesser quality than the 6-foot lengths. So you could then buy seven 6-foot lengths and have a little left over. But you must first check to make certain that no single piece required by the project is over 6-feet long.

It is also wise to keep transportation abilities in mind. If you own (or can borrow) a pickup truck to transport your materials, board lengths are not a factor. But it is pretty difficult to get a 12-foot length of wood into a Corvette for the trip home. Most building supply stores will be happy to give you one free cut on an individual piece of lumber, but some charge a fee.

Unless you have chosen a very expensive wood to build your project, it makes sense to slightly overbuy your materials. That way if you do make a mistake, you have a "reserve" board to bail you out. Returning to the store for just one more board is frustrating, time-consuming, and (depending upon how far you have to drive) sometimes more expensive than if you had purchased an extra one on the original trip. We have built some overage into the materials list to accommodate squaring-off the piece and allowing for the width of saw cuts.

### Hardwood

You can also use hardwood to build any of the projects in this book. Hardwood, as the name implies, will resist dents and scratches much better than softwood. The downside is that it is more difficult to work with and is extremely expensive.

If you decide to use a hardwood for your project, it will take some calculating on your part, since hardwood is normally sold in random widths and lengths. Each board is cut from the log as wide and as long as possible.

Consequently, hardwood is sold by a measure called the *board foot*. A board foot represents a piece of lumber 1 inch (or less) thick, 12 inches wide, and 1 foot long. Hardwood thicknesses are measured in quarter inches. The standard thicknesses are $3/4$, $4/4$, $5/4$, $6/4$ and $8/4$.

## Plywood

As you might guess, plywood is made from several plies of wood that are glued together. It is sold in sheets measuring 4 feet by 8 feet. In some supply stores you can also purchase half-sheets measuring 4 feet by 4 feet. Plywood comes in standard thicknesses of $1/8$, $1/4$, $3/8$, $1/2$, $5/8$, and $3/4$ inch.

There are two principal kinds of plywood: veneer-core and lumber-core. Lumber-core is the higher quality material; its edges can be worked as you would work solid wood. The exposed cut edges of veneer-core plywood must be either filled or covered because they are unsightly.

Plywood is also graded according to the quality of the outer veneer. The grades are A through D, with A representing the best quality. A piece of plywood has two designations, one for each face. For example, an A-D piece has one veneered surface that is A quality and one that is D quality.

Any outdoor project should be built using only exterior-rated plywood. This designation means that the glue between the plies is waterproof. Interior-grade plywood should not be used to construct outdoor projects, as it will warp and split apart when exposed to the elements for even a very short period of time.

## Paints & Stains

The finish that you apply to your completed project is extremely important when building anything that will be used outdoors. It goes without saying that you must choose an exterior-rated finish for any project that will be exposed to the elements. Your choice of finishes, and the care with which you apply it, will make a considerable difference in the look of your finished project. The better the finish, the longer you will be enjoying your handiwork.

There are hundreds of products on the market, but the first choice is whether to stain, paint, or simply seal your project. The advantages and disadvantages of each choice follow.

### Paint

Paint will cover a multitude of flaws. It is possible to take wood that is not at all attractive in appearance, apply a flawless coat of paint, and produce an extremely good-looking piece of furniture. The disadvantage is that it must be thoroughly filled, sanded, and primed, all of which takes time and effort. Then it must be given two coats of paint, and at least one coat of sealer should be applied.

*Clockwise from bottom left: a natural-bristle brush; wood filler and putty knife; wood glue; an assortment of finishes, stains, paints, and sealant; and disposable foam brushes*

When shopping for paint, look for special characteristics that protect against local weather problems. For example, here in Florida, many paints are treated with special additives that protect against mildew, which occurs in our high humidity. Also look to see how long a warranty the paint has.

### Stain

Stains used to come in brown (or brown). True, there were gray-browns and yellow-browns and red-browns—but they were all brown nonetheless. And it used to be very difficult to apply them evenly. How times have changed! These days stains come in a terrific variety of colors—from the palest white to the darkest black. And they also range from extremely translucent to nearly opaque. They have an additional advantage of being extremely easy to apply and usually require only one coat.

Make certain that your stain is rated for exterior use. Although most manufacturers recommend that you apply their product with a brush, we have found that a plain old rag gives a very smooth and even appearance to most stains. (We do not guarantee best results with every type of stain, so we recommend you try it either on a scrap piece of wood or on a surface that will not show before attacking the entire project with our method.)

## Sealer

The finish that will affect the wood's appearance the least is a clear wood finish, often referred to as a water sealer. It is most commonly used on decks and railings. Clear wood finish is available as an oil-based or as a waterborne product. Its actual appearance can range from a muted, almost invisible finish to a smooth, semigloss sheen. Make sure you buy a finish sealer, not a clear sanding sealer, which is used under paints and stains to prime the wood. You can apply a wood finish sealer with a brush or roller, or you can spray it on.

## Brushes

Although most professionals swear by very expensive brushes, we use them only when there is absolutely no choice in the matter. We much prefer sponge brushes, which are extremely inexpensive and can be thrown in the trash after use. Look for the ones that have a smooth surface (like a cosmetic sponge) and a wooden handle. If you are interrupted in mid-coat, and the sponge brush is not yet ready for tossing, just pop your brush in an airtight sandwich bag. You can leave it there for a day or so, and it will remain pliable and ready to use.

## Tools

If you are just beginning in woodworking, you may think you'll need to spend thousands of dollars on tools. Not true! Unless they are independently wealthy, most woodworkers start using hand tools and gradually add to their shop over time. Obviously, there were not many power tools when Louis XV's furniture craftsmen were at work—all of history's magnificent furniture was built using only hand tools.

The obvious reason for using power tools is that they get the job done faster. Our goal is to create a good-looking piece of furniture in the least amount of time. So over the years we have added power tools that cut the time required to complete the job and require a lot less physical effort. We use a power drill rather than a screwdriver and a circular saw rather than a hand saw. A good approach is to add a tool to your workshop each time you build a large project. You will still save a substantial amount of money (compared to purchasing the project in a store) and will then have the tool for the next project.

The projects in this book require some basic tools that, if you do not already own them, would make useful additions to any household. Some tools, such as a saw and a set of screwdrivers, are needed for every project, but others are required only for a few pieces. You may want to choose your first project according to the tools you have available. So it is a good idea to read through the instructions before starting a project, to determine which tools you will need. The tools required for the projects in this book make a good starting set of woodworking equipment.

If you are starting from scratch, buy the best tools you can afford. A bargain screwdriver that falls apart after inserting three screws is not much of a bargain, and the resulting frustration is not worth the two-dollar savings. Look for the manufacturer's warranty when purchasing tools. If they offer a lifetime guarantee, it's a safe bet that you'll be purchasing a good tool.

As with most hobbies, when you purchase your equipment, you should consider your physical size and ability. A golf club or a tennis racquet must be matched to the person using it. In the same way, a physically large person may be able to use a very large hammer. Although it is true that the larger hammer will drive the nail into the wood faster, it does not mean very much if you are able to swing a heavier hammer only twice before you feel your arm going weak from the strain. So try before you buy! Lift the tool a number of times before you purchase it. The same philosophy applies to power tools. It requires a great deal of strength to control a 4-inch-wide belt sander, but almost anyone can use a 2-inch-wide sander.

The following is our recommended list of tools to help you begin working with wood.

*From lower right: claw hammer, tack hammer and nail sets, and rubber mallet*

*Battery-operated power drills (right), electric drill (lower left), and drill bits (upper left)*

## Basic Tools

- **Work surface:** smooth and level
- **Measuring tools:** tape measure, level, and combination square
- **Hammers:** two hammers (large and small), tack hammer, and nail set
- **Screwdrivers:** an assortment of flathead and Phillips sizes
- **Saws:** combination saw (or rip saw and crosscut saw), circular saw, and a selection of blades
- **Drill:** hand or power drill and a variety of bits
- **Clamps:** two "quick clamps" and two wood hand clamps
- **Sanding tools:** sanding block and assortment of sandpaper (from the coarse)
- **Safety equipment:** goggles and dust mask (use with power tools)

## Optional Tools

- **Measuring tools:** framing square
- **Clamps:** two C clamps, a web clamp, and two bar clamps
- **Saws:** saber saw, circular saw, and a selection of blades
- **Chisels:** 1/4-inch, 3/4-inch, and 1-inch-wide
- **Finishing sander**
- **Router**

## Advanced Tools

- **Belt sander**
- **Table saw**
- **Band saw**
- **Drill press**
- **Laser level**

A hammer and saw probably come to mind when discussing woodworking. However, other tools are just as important. A solid work surface, a ready supply of clamps, and the right sanding equipment can make woodworking an enjoyable pursuit—and the lack of such tools can spell complete frustration.

## Work Surface

Although most people would not put it at the top of the list, one of the most important tools in woodworking is a work

*An assortment of screwdrivers*

surface that is smooth and level. If you construct a project on an uneven work surface, chances are that your table legs will be uneven or the cabinet top will slope downhill. Your work surface does not have to be a professional-quality mahogany workbench—it just has to be level and even. It can be as simple as an old door (flush not paneled) or a piece of thick plywood supported by sawhorses.

To level your work surface, simply set a fairly long level in various places on the surface, turning it so that it faces in several directions. If necessary, shim the surface with thicknesses of wood to lift the surface enough to make it perfectly level. Be sure to attach the shim with glue and nails or screws to make certain that it stays in place while you work.

## Clamps

Clamps are an absolute must for woodworking. They are used to apply pressure and hold joints together until the glue sets, and they are valuable aids when assembling a project. A single person can assemble a large project by using clamps—a job that otherwise requires the concerted effort of two or more people. When you buy clamps, it is advisable to get two clamps of the same type. This is because you almost always use them in pairs to provide even pressure on the work.

When you apply clamps, always insert a scrap piece of wood between the clamp and your work to act as a cushion. That way, you will avoid leaving clamp marks on the surface of your project.

There have been some fairly recent improvements in woodworking clamps. A new type looks like a regular clamp, but instead of a screw mechanism for tightening, they have a trigger much like a caulk gun. This makes them especially useful, since they can be operated with one hand. They also have a quick-release mechanism. We recommend them for a beginner, since they are easy to use, work well, and come in a variety of lengths.

Old-fashioned **wood clamps** are a nice addition to your workshop. They are extremely versatile, since they can be adjusted to clamp offsetting surfaces.

**C clamps** are inexpensive and useful for many woodworking applications. One end of their C-shaped frame is fixed; the other end is fitted with a threaded rod and swivel pad that can be clamped tightly across an opening ranging from zero to several inches or more, depending on the size of the clamp. They can hold two thicknesses of wood together, secure a piece of wood to a work surface, and perform many other functions.

*Clamps. Clockwise from upper right: C clamps (in two sizes), bar clamp, pipe clamp, hand clamp, web clamp, and spring clamp*

*Clockwise from top left: small (torpedo) level, chalk line, laser level, 4-foot level, 6-foot level, and combination laser level with attachment*

**Bar clamps** and **pipe clamps** can be used to hold assemblies together temporarily while fasteners are added, as well as to apply pressure to laminates. Although they look very much alike and function the same way, pipe clamps are significantly less expensive than bar clamps. You buy the fittings separately, and they can be used with various lengths of pipe, depending upon the need. You can also buy rubber "shoes" that fit over the pipe clamp fittings, which will eliminate clamp marks on the wood.

**Web clamps** (or **band clamps**) are used for clamping such things as chairs or drawers, where a uniform pressure needs to be exerted completely around a project. It consists of a continuous band with an attached metal mechanism that can be ratcheted to pull the band tightly around the object.

**Spring clamps** are useful for quickly holding a piece of wood while you saw or for keeping two thin boards positioned. The 2-inch size is most useful because you can operate it with one hand.

## Measuring Tools

If you have been involved with woodworking at all, you have probably heard the expression "measure twice, cut once." And it is always worth repeating. If you measure accurately and cut carefully to that measurement, your project will fit together perfectly during final assembly. And accurate cutting depends on accurate measurements. So a quality measuring tool is a sound investment. A wide steel tape rule is a good choice for most projects. A narrow tape will bend more easily along the length of a board and will be less accurate.

Consistently use the same measuring device throughout the cutting process. Unless you have precise measuring tools, any two instruments may vary enough to give you slightly different measurements.

If you are cutting a length of wood to fit between two existing pieces in an assembly, there is an even more accurate method of measurement than a steel tape. After you square off the wood you are cutting, simply hold it up to the actual space, and mark it for cutting.

A straightedge is a handy woodworking tool for quick measurements. An ordinary steel ruler, 12 to 24 inches long, is sufficient.

A sliding T-bevel is valuable for establishing bevel angles. The steel blade pivots and slides within a handle and can be locked in position to form an angle. It is used to check and transfer bevels and mitered ends.

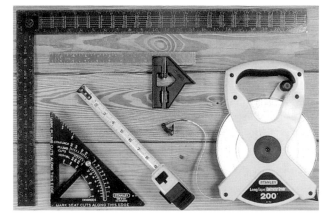

*Measuring tools. Clockwise from top left: carpenter's square, combination square, open-reel long tape, tape measure, and combination speed square*

Squares are versatile and essential tools in woodworking. The most commonly used types are the framing square (or carpenter's square) and the combination square. In addition to their obvious use for marking a cutting line on a board and obtaining a right angle, squares can be used to check the outer or inner squareness of a joint, to guide a saw through a cut, and much more.

## Cutting Tools

Keep in mind that every saw blade has a thickness (called a *kerf*) that is removed from the wood when you cut. (From whence cometh the gigantic amount of sawdust that accumulates when you make a project.) When you measure and mark a board, measure precisely. When you cut the board at your mark, set the saw so that the blade will exactly remove the mark. Cut so that you also remove the mark from the end of the board that will be waste.

A piece of wood may be either *ripped* (cut along the length of the board) or crosscut (cut across the width of the board). There are specific hand tools for each procedure. A **rip saw** has teeth designed for cutting along the length of board, with the grain. It comes with $4^{1}/_{2}$ through seven points per inch, the latter being the smoothest cut.

The **crosscut saw** is made to cut across the grain. Crosscut saws are available with seven through 12 points per inch, depending on how coarse or fine you wish the cut to be. The greater the number, the smoother the cut.

Probably the most popular power cutting tool is the **circular saw**. The blade can be adjusted to cut at a 90° or 45° angle or any angle in between. Although **saw blades** for power tools are available for both ripping and cross-cutting, the most practical blade for general woodworking is a combination blade. It rips and crosscuts with equal ease. Carbide-tipped blades are more expensive but well worth the cost, since they last much longer than regular blades.

The hand-held **jigsaw** or **saber saw** is used to cut curves, shapes, and large holes in panels or boards up to $1^{1}/_{2}$ inches in thickness. Its cutting action comes from a narrow reciprocating ìbayonetî blade that moves up and down very quickly. The best saber saws have a variable speed control and an orbital blade action, which swings the cutting edge forward into the work and back again during the blade's up-and-down cycle. A dust blower keeps the sawdust away from the cut.

A **power miter saw** is a favorite tool of ours. It can be used to efficiently cut boards to length and can be adjusted both horizontally from 90° to 1° and vertically from 45° to 1°. It is especially useful for cutting 45° miters.

When you are cutting either lumber or plywood, note the type of cut

*Cutting Tools. Clockwise from right: jigsaw and jigsaw blades, circular saw, router and bits*

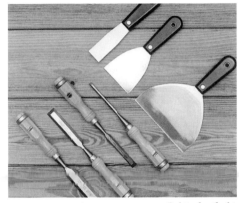

*An assortment of chisels (left) and scrapers (right)*

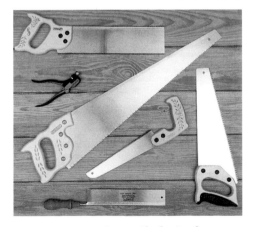

*Saws. Clockwise from top: back saw, crosscut saw (middle), miniature utility shortcut saw, tool-box saw (far right), finish saw (bottom), and saw-tooth set (below back saw)*

that your tool is making, and use it to your advantage. For example, circular saws and saber saws cut on the upstroke, so they may leave ragged edges on the upper surface of your wood. When using these saws, you should position the wood with the better surface facing down.

Certain types of cuts, such as hollowing out a section of wood, are done with **chisels**. Using a chisel well takes some practice, but it is worth the effort because chisels can perform unique woodworking tasks. Always work with sharp chisels. For your first

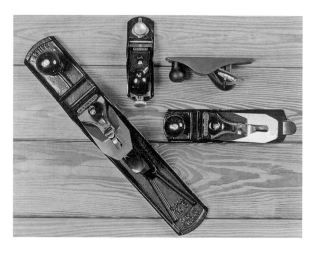

*An assortment of planes used to smooth wood surfaces*

purchase, choose two different sizes—one very narrow and one about an inch wide.

If you need to shave just a small portion of wood off the end or along the edge of a board, a plane is the appropriate tool. Again, buy a quality plane, and practice with it until you become fairly proficient.

## Sanding Tools

Of course, any project may be sanded by hand. An inexpensive plastic sanding block will do the job of sanding a level surface just fine. You can even wrap a block of wood with a piece of sandpaper. If you need to sand moldings or curves, try wrapping a pencil or other appropriately sized object with sandpaper.

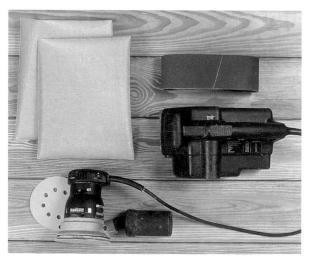

*Sanding Tools. Clockwise from upper left: sheets of sandpaper, belt sander with belt, and orbital sander with sandpaper disks*

The amount of sanding that you do on each project depends, in large part, on the intended use of the project and on what kind of finish you plan to use. Obviously, if you prefer a rustic look for your project, it need not be sanded completely smooth. However, a rustic chair requires more sanding than a rustic table—someone will be sitting on it.

An **orbital sander** does a good job of beginning the sanding process, but it may leave circular marks that must be subsequently sanded out by hand.

A **finishing sander** is probably the most practical power sander for furniture projects. It has the ability to smooth the surface quickly, and it does not leave circular marks.

A **belt sander** is often used for large jobs. It sands quickly, but it is difficult to control on softwood such as pine. Because of its power, a belt sander can easily gouge softwood, or if you do not watch carefully, it can remove more of the wood than you wish.

**Files**, which come in an assortment of shapes and sizes, are good tools for rough sanding work. No matter what tool you use, begin sanding with coarse grit and gradually progress to sandpaper with a fine grit.

# Techniques

## Wood Joints

There are hundreds of different kinds of wood joints. They range in complexity from the plainest butt joint to incredibly intricate and time-consuming ones. The projects in this book are constructed with only the simplest joints, secured with glue and either nails or screws.

*An assortment of files for rough sanding work*

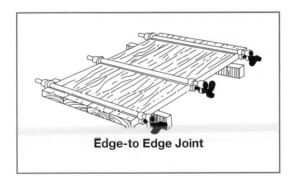

**Edge-to Edge Joint**

### Edge-to-Edge Joint

This joint is used when laminating boards together edge to edge to obtain a wider piece of wood. To ensure a perfect meeting between boards, a minuscule amount should be ripped from the first side of each board. Then flip the board widthwise to rip the second edge to ensure complementary angles and a flat glued surface. Then apply glue to the adjoining edges and clamp the boards together.

Apply even pressure along the length of the piece. The boards should be firmly clamped, but not so tightly that all of the glue is forced out or that the lamination starts to bow across its width. On a long lamination, extra boards may be placed above and below the lamination, across the width, then clamped with C clamps or wood clamps. It is a good idea to put a piece of plastic or waxed paper between the piece and any wood clamped across the joints. This will eliminate the clamped board becoming a permanent part of the finished lamination. Wipe off any excess glue that is squeezed out in the clamping process.

### Butt Joint

This is the simplest of joints, where one board abuts another at a right angle. This method offers the least holding power of any joint. It must be reinforced with some kind of fastener, usually screws.

**Butt Joints**

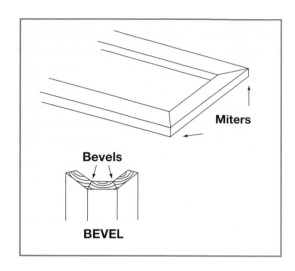

**Miters**

**Bevels**

**BEVEL**

## Miter

A miter is a angle cut across the width of a board. It is used to joint two pieces of wood without exposing the end grain of either piece. A mitered joint must also be reinforced with nails or screws. The angle most often cut is 45°, which is used to construct a right angle when two mitered boards are joined together. The difference between a perfect miter and a none-too-perfect miter is the care in the measurement. When cutting and applying molding, begin at one end, cut the first piece, and attach it. Then cut the first angle on the second piece, hold it in place, and mark the cut (and the direction of that cut) on the ether end. Since you are usually switching directions of 45° angles on each successive cut, this method avoids confusion. Attach the second piece, and continue the process for each subsequent piece. A helpful tip to make your miter joints look more perfect than they are is to firmly rub the length of the completed joint with the side of a pencil to smooth the two edges together.

A bevel is also an angular cut, but it refers to an angle cut along the length of a board, rather than across the width as in a miter.

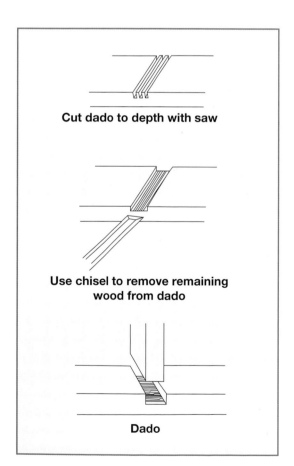

**Cut dado to depth with saw**

**Use chisel to remove remaining wood from dado**

**Dado**

## Dado

A dado is a groove cut in the face of one board to accommodate the thickness of another board. It can be cut with a hand saw and chisel (see below, right), with a router, or with a dado set on a table saw.

No matter what kind of joint you are making, it is advisable to use both glue and fasteners (nails or screws) whenever possible. The only exception, when you may want to omit the glue, is on joints that you wish to disassemble at a later time.

## Dry-Fitting

Particularly if you are a beginner, you may wish to *dry-fit* your project. This means that you can preassemble portions of the project without glue to make certain that all of the pieces were cut correctly and fit together tightly. You can use clamps to hold the pieces together temporarily, or simply hammer small nails into the surface just far enough to hold them in place. Leave a large portion of the nail head above the surface, so the nails are easy to remove at a later date. Check the fit and trim or adjust the pieces as necessary. Then remove the clamps and/or nails, apply glue, and reassemble the pieces.

## Measuring Lumber

Nothing is more frustrating than gathering the necessary materials and embarking upon a project only to find that inaccurate cutting has made it impossible for the pieces to fit together properly—and thus for the project to look right. Woodworking projects, regardless of the skill level, go much more smoothly if you follow the old adage "measure twice, cut once."

The best way to make good cuts is to measure accurately. There are a number of tools that will help with this: a wide steel tape rule, a square, and a variety of saws (see page 20 for more information on tools). It is essential that you buy or borrow quality tools. Whatever tools you choose, use the same measuring device throughout the project, as two instruments may vary enough to make a difference.

## Cutting Lumber

The most important rule of thumb in cutting lumber is to cut the longest piece first. If you botch the cut, then you can still cut smaller pieces from the remaining board. It is also important to re-examine each piece of lumber one last time before you cut; this is useful in spotting end splits or knots that can be cut off.

If you plan carefully, you can cut so that all the best sides of the wood are facing out—this makes for the best possible use of your wood and saves you from having to fill and sand any imperfections after the project is finished.

Every time you use a blade to cut wood, the blade removes an amount of wood equal to the width of its saw blade, called the kerf. After you have precisely measured for a cut and marked it with a sharp pencil, set the saw so that the blade will exactly remove the waste side of the mark. Cut along the mark, trying to remove just half of your pencil line.

There are two types of cuts that can be made to a piece of wood: a rip or a crosscut. A rip is a cut along the length of the board, and a crosscut is a cut across the width of the board. There are specific hand tools for each procedure; (see page 25 for detailed information on these cutting tools).

## Safety

Working with power tools can be dangerous. In a battle with a power saw, you will be the loser. And losing is extremely painful. We know many woodworkers, and many of them have missing digits. If that sounds scary, that is good. Read the instructions that are provided with every tool and follow them religiously. Again, we stress that these instructions are written for the beginner using hand tools; they must be altered when using power tools. Never attempt any woodworking

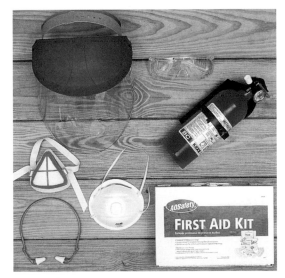

*Clockwise from top: face shield, safety goggles, fire extinguisher, first-aid kit, paper dust mask, ear plugs, and dust mask with replaceable filters*

maneuver that does not translate to power tools. Misuse of power tool equipment can lead to serious injury to yourself or damage to the tool.

Never take your eyes off the work; always concentrate on what you are doing, and take the necessary safety precautions. Just one moment of lost concentration or lack of adherence to safety rules can result in frightful consequences. Develop the habit of avoiding the path of the saw—do not stand directly behind it or directly in front of it. Power saws can flip a piece of wood back at you with incredible force.

Always wear safety goggles when working with wood. Avoiding just one splinter aimed at your eye makes this practice worth your while. A dust mask is a prudent accessory when working with wood. Sawdust can be very irritating to your lungs. You can choose from a number of different masks, from a simple paper mask to those with replaceable filters.

If you use power tools for extended periods—especially a power saw, which can be quite loud—a pair of ear plugs or protectors is a good investment. Prolonged exposure to loud noise can have harmful effects on your hearing.

Practicing all of these safety rules will keep you safe and make woodworking a pleasure.

# The Projects

Every project in this book includes lists of the materials, and hardware you need to build that project. Although we haven't listed every tool and every woodworking technique used, we do identify special tools and techniques required for certain projects. It's always a good idea to read the project lists and all the instructions at least once before deciding what project to undertake. That way, you'll know right away what to expect.

## Skill Level

This is a book designed for beginning woodworkers, although experienced woodworkers will enjoy building the projects, too. If we didn't think someone new to woodworking could handle all the projects, we wouldn't have included all of them in the book. But some of the projects demand more time, patience, and technique to accomplish than others. As is true of other skills, woodworking skills are developed with practice. We suggest that you begin by constructing one or two of the quick-to-build projects, such as the plant pedestal, footstool, or hurricane lamp. You will soon acquire the necessary skills and confidence to tackle projects that are more challenging.

## Special Tools & Techniques

This list lets you know that special tools and techniques are required, tools you may not own and skills you may not have. If you read "mitering" in this list and you've never cut a miter, look up miters in the index on page 255, and read the appropriate section. Then, take the time to practice cutting a few miters on scrap wood. Before you know it, you'll have the confidence to tackle miters and to successfully build that table or bench.

## Materials

This list identifies in linear feet the total amount of lumber you'll need to purchase. Softwood, such as pine, is sold in standard dimensional sizes, such as 2x4 and 1x2, and in specific lengths, such as 6-foot, 8-foot, etc. The bin labeled 2x4x8 at your local building-supply outlet contains 2x4 boards that are 8 feet long. If the Materials list specifies 23 linear feet of 1x4 pine, you can buy two 1x4s, each 12 feet long, or four 1x4s, each 6 feet long. It's important to read through the Cutting List and the instructions before deciding what lengths to buy.

## Hardware

Here you'll find listed every piece of hardware that you need for the project you've chosen.

## Cutting List

This list specifies the exact size of each piece of wood you'll need to cut from the lumber. Reviewing the linear feet quantities and the Cutting List information will tell you what lengths of a particular wood to purchase. You'll come up short if you buy all of your 1x4s in 6-foot lengths, and then discover that your project requires two pieces, each 7 feet long. When you get to the lumber outlet, carefully inspect the various lengths available. If you find that the 8-foot 2x4s are knotted and warped, while the 6-foot and 10-foot lengths are nearly perfect, it would make sense to purchase the required total linear feet in these boards.

It's a good idea to purchase 10 to 20 percent more lumber than you need. Having to return to the store to buy one more 2x4 because you miscut a board is far more expensive in terms of time and energy than a few extra feet of lumber. Remember, too, that the ends of boards aren't always square, so you need to allow for having to square them before you begin measuring. You can always use the leftover wood when you build the next project.

Don't cut the pieces of wood to size right away; the instructions will walk you through cutting each piece.

## One Final Note

All experienced woodworkers have their share of miscut boards, misdrilled holes, and mishaps with hammers landing on thumbs. If any of these missteps happen to you, it's probably time to take a break. The best safeguard against woodworking accidents, both minor and major, is a patient, content, and attentive mind. So when you start to make mistakes, go for a walk, take a nap, eat an apple—and then resume building.

# Tables

# Dining Table

*We love outdoor cooking and dining with friends and family, but we ran out of room at our pool side table. So we built a new one! Now we have ample space to accommodate the food off the grill—and lots of neighbors, too! The tile top allows you to coordinate the table color with the rest of your outdoor furnishings.*

## Special Tools & Techniques

- Dadoes
- Miters
- Metal trowel
- Rubber-surface trowel
- Tile cutter

## Materials

- 10 linear feet of 4x4 pine
- 24 linear feet of 2x4 pine
- 14 linear feet of 1x2 pine
- 20 linear feet of 1x8 pine
- 1 piece of $^3/_8$"-thick exterior plywood, measuring 52"x28"
- 4 wooden finials*
- Tile to cover an area 66$^1/_2$"x39$^1/_2$"*
- Tile grout
- Tile mastic
- Tile sealer

## Hardware

- 125 2$^1/_2$" screws
- 50 1$^1/_4$" screws

## *Notes on Materials

The wooden finials we used for the table "feet" are designed to be used on a fence post. They can be purchased at most building-supply stores, and have a large screw already attached in the center. The ones we used are 3 inches tall. You can substitute any exterior-rated finial you like, but if it's taller than 3 inches, be sure to adjust the length of your legs accordingly, or your completed table will not be the correct height.

When choosing tile for this table, consider that you must cover an area measuring 52"x28". If the tile you purchased doesn't fit within these dimensions, you can either alter the dimensions of the table or—use our much easier solution—simply cut the tiles into interesting shapes.

To install the tile, you need a plain, metal trowel for spreading the mastic and a rubber-surfaced trowel for applying the grout. If you need to trim the tile to fit the table, or want to cut them into pieces for a mosaic effect as we did with our table, you will also need a tile cutter.

## Cutting List

| Code | Description | Qty. | Materials | Dimensions |
|------|-------------|------|-----------|------------|
| A | Leg | 4 | 4x4 pine | 26" long |
| B | Long Side | 2 | 2x4 pine | 55" long |
| C | Short Sides | 2 | 2x4 pine | 31" long |
| D | Center Support | 3 | 2x4 pine | 8" long |
| E | Short Inner Support | 8 | 1x2 pine | 11$^7/_8$" long |
| F | Long Inner Support | 2 | 1x2 pine | 26$^1/_2$" long |
| G | Long Trim | 2 | 1x8 pine | 66$^1/_2$" long |
| H | Short Trim | 2 | 1x8 pine | 42$^1/_2$" long |
| I | Top | 1 | $^3/_8$" plywood | 52"x28" |

## Making the Legs

1 Cut four legs (A) from 4x4 pine, each measuring 26 inches long.

2 In order to properly support the table, the legs must be dadoed. Refer to *figure 1* on page 36 to dado the end of one leg (A). Note that the dado is 1¹/₂ inches deep on each side, and 3¹/₂ inches long.

3 Repeat step 2 to dado the ends of the remaining three legs (Λ).

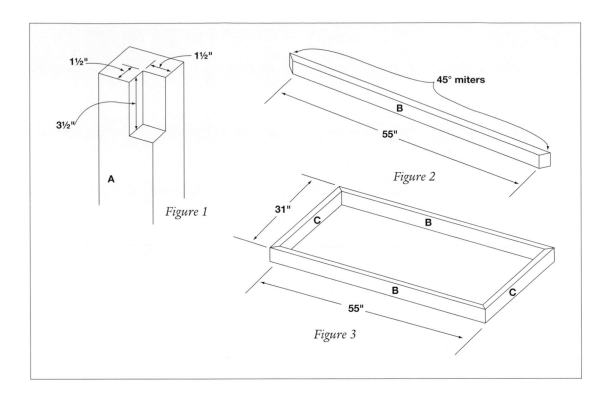

## Adding the Table Sides

1 Cut two long sides (B) from 2x4 pine, each measuring 55 inches long.

2 Miter each end of the long sides (B) at a 45-degree angle, as shown in *figure 2*. Note that the miters are mirror images of each other.

3 Cut two short sides (C) from 2x4 pine, each measuring 31 inches long.

4 Miter each end of the short sides (C) at a 45-degree angle, as you did for the long sides (B).

5 Place the long sides (B) parallel to each other on a level surface, with the miters facing in. Fit the short sides (C) between the long sides (B), matching miters on all four corners, as shown in *figure 3*. Apply glue to the meeting surfaces of the miters, and screw through each mitered joint, using a 2½-inch long screw on each side.

## Attaching the Legs

1 Turn one leg (A) dado-side down, and fit the dado over one corner of the side assembly, as shown in *figure 4* on page 37. Apply glue on the meeting surfaces, and screw through both the long side (B) and short side (C) into the leg (A). Use two 2½-inch-long screws on each joint.

2 Repeat step 1 three more times to attach the remaining three legs (A) to the three corners of the side assembly.

3 On the bottom of each leg, we attached a finial designed to top a fence post. Mark the center bottom of each of the legs (A), and screw in a finial.

## Adding the Inner Supports

1 Cut three center supports (D) from 2x4 pine, each measuring 28 inches long.

2 Fit the three center supports (D) between the two long sides (B), edge up, $11^7/_8$ inches apart, as shown in *figure 5*. Screw through the long sides (B) into the ends of the inner supports (D). Use two $2^1/_2$-inch-long screws on each joint.

3 Cut eight short inner supports (E) from 1x2 pine, each measuring $11^7/_8$ inches long.

4 Fit one short inner support (E) flush with the top of the long side (B), between the short side (C) and the center support (D), as shown in *figure 6*. Screw through the short inner support (E) into the long side (B), using three $1^1/_4$-inch-long screws. Repeat this process to attach the remaining seven short inner supports (E) to the long sides (B).

5 Cut two long inner supports (F) from 1x2 pine, each measuring $26^1/_2$ inches long.

6 Fit one long inner support (F) flush with the top of each short side (C), as shown in *figure 6*. Use four or five $1^1/_4$-inch-long screws to attach each of these supports (F) to the short sides (C).

## Adding the Trim

1 Cut two long trim pieces (G) from 1x8 pine, each measuring $66^1/_2$ inches long.

2 Miter both ends of each of the long trim pieces at opposing 45-degree angles, as shown in *figure 7* on page 38.

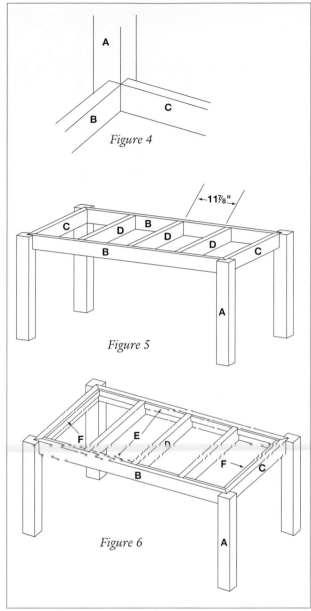

Figure 4

Figure 5

Figure 6

3 Cut two short trim pieces (H) from 1x8 pine, each measuring 42½ inches long.

4 Miter both ends of each of the short trim pieces (H) at opposing 45-degree angles, as shown in *figure 7*.

5 Fit the long trim pieces (G) over the long sides (B), exactly matching the miters, as shown in *figure 7*. Apply glue to the tops of the long sides (B) and screw through the long trim pieces (G) into the long sides (B), using 1¼-inch-long screws about every four inches.

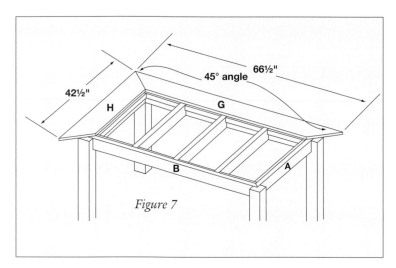

66½"

45° angle

42½"

H

G

B

A

*Figure 7*

6 Fit the short trim pieces (H) over the short sides (C), exactly matching the miters. Apply glue to the tops of the short sides (C) and to the miters. Screw through the short trim pieces (H) into the short sides (C), using 1¼-inch-long screws about every four inches. Finally, screw at an angle through the ends of the short trim pieces (G), using one 2½-inch-long screw on each joint.

## Adding the Plywood Top

1 Cut one top (I) from ⅜-inch-thick plywood, measuring 52x28 inches.

2 Fit the top (I) in the center of the table over the supports. The top sits ⅜ inch lower than the trim pieces (G and H) to allow enough depth for the tile and mastic. Screw through the top (I) into all of the supports (D, E, and F), using 1¼-inch-long screws spaced about every 5 inches.

## Adding the Tile

1 Following the manufacturer's directions, carefully spread an even coat of the tile mastic over the surface of the top (I) with a trowel.

2 Place the tiles on the mastic one at a time, making sure that they are positioned correctly. Don't slide the tiles, or the mastic will be forced up on the sides of the tile. Let the mastic dry overnight.

3 Mix the tile grout according to the manufacturer's directions (or use premixed grout).

4 Spread the grout over the tile using a rubber-surfaced trowel held at an angle so that the grout is forced evenly into the spaces between the tiles.

5 Use a damp rag to wipe the excess grout off the tiles and joints; if you let it dry, the hardened grout will be very difficult to remove. Try to use as little water as possible when removing the excess so that you don't thin the grout that remains. Let the grout dry overnight.

6 Rinse the remaining film from the tile and wipe it with an old towel.

7 Apply grout sealer, following the manufacturer's directions.

## Finishing

1 Fill all cracks, crevices, and screw holes with wood filler. Thoroughly sand all surfaces of the completed table.

2 We stained our table reddish brown to match our tile grout. You can stain yours a different color, or simply seal it with a waterproof sealer.

# Birdhouse Table

*This whimsical table is one of our favorite projects, because it never fails to produce a smile on the faces of our backyard guests. Not only is it cheerful to behold, but the glass top makes it a practical addition to any outdoor room. We hope you will enjoy having one in your backyard.*

### Special Tools & Techniques

- Miters

### Materials

- 4'x4' sheet of $\frac{1}{2}$" plywood
- 7 linear feet of 1x1 pine
- 4'x4' sheet of $\frac{1}{4}$" plywood
- 32 linear feet of $\frac{3}{4}$" screen molding
- 4 linear feet of $1\frac{1}{4}$" L-shaped molding
- 8 linear feet of 2x4 pine
- 2 linear feet of 2x2 pine
- 1 bundle of cedar shingles

### Hardware

- 70 $1\frac{1}{4}$" (3d) finish nails
- 40 $\frac{1}{2}$" wire brads
- 200 1" wire brads
- 2 small drawer pulls
- 10 $2\frac{1}{2}$" (8d) finish nails
- 8 3" wood screws
- 4 corrugated metal fasteners

### Cutting List

| Code | Description | Qty. | Materials | Dimensions |
|------|-------------|------|-----------|------------|
| A | Front/Back | 2 | $\frac{1}{2}$" plywood | 16"x24" |
| B | Corner Supports | 4 | 1x1 pine | 17" long |
| C | Side | 2 | $\frac{1}{2}$" plywood | 17"x18" |
| D | Outer Roof | 2 | $\frac{1}{4}$" plywood | 10"x$23\frac{1}{2}$" |
| E | Inner Roof | 2 | $\frac{1}{4}$" plywood | 8"x$23\frac{1}{2}$" |
| F | Side Trim | 4 | $\frac{3}{4}$" screen molding | $16\frac{1}{2}$" long |
| G | Center Trim | 1 | $\frac{3}{4}$" screen molding | 17" long |
| H | Outer Trim | 4 | $\frac{3}{4}$" screen molding | 18" long |
| I | Roof Trims | 8 | $\frac{3}{4}$" screen molding | cut to fit |
| J | Peak Cover | 2 | $1\frac{1}{4}$" L molding | $23\frac{1}{2}$" long |
| K | Doors | 2 | $\frac{1}{4}$" plywood | $8\frac{1}{2}$"x$4\frac{1}{2}$" |
| L | Horizontal Door Trim | 4 | $\frac{3}{4}$" screen molding | 3" long |
| M | Vertical Door Trim | 4 | $\frac{3}{4}$" screen molding | $8\frac{1}{2}$" long |
| N | Window | 4 | $\frac{1}{4}$" plywood | $4\frac{1}{2}$"x$4\frac{1}{2}$" |
| O | Horizontal Window Trim | 8 | $\frac{3}{4}$" screen molding | 3" long |
| P | Vertical Window Trim | 8 | $\frac{3}{4}$" screen molding | $4\frac{1}{2}$" long |
| Q | Long Base | 2 | 2x4 pine | $23\frac{1}{2}$" long |
| R | Short Base | 2 | 2x4 pine | 21" long |
| S | Chimney | 2 | 2x2 pine | 10" long |

## Building the Basic House

1 Following the pattern in *figure 1* on page 41, cut two Front/Backs (A) from $\frac{1}{2}$-inch plywood. Designate one as "Front" and one as "Back."

2 Drill four ¹/₄-inch-diameter holes in the Front (A), following the placement shown in *figure 1*. Do not drill any holes in the Back (A).

3 Cut four Corner Supports (B) from lxl pine, each measuring 17 inches.

4 Cut two Sides (C) from ¹/₂-inch plywood, each measuring 17x18 inches.

5 Position two Corner Supports (B) parallel to each other and 16¹/₂ inches apart. Place one Side (C) over the Corner Supports (B), matching the 17-inch edges, as shown in *figure 2*. Apply glue to the meeting surfaces, and nail through the Side (C) into the Corner Supports (B), using four evenly spaced 1¹/₂-inch finish nails.

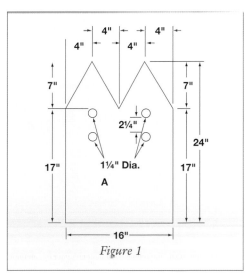

*Figure 1*

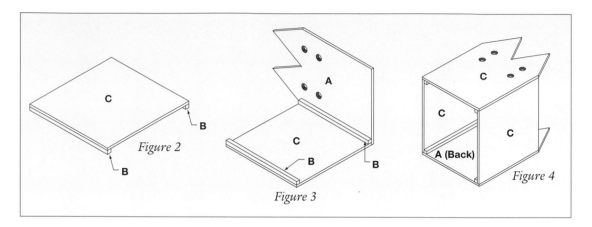

Figure 2

Figure 3

Figure 4

6 Repeat step 5 to attach the remaining two Corner Supports (B) to the remaining Side (C).

7 Place the Side (C) [with Corner Supports (B) on the top] on a level surface. Position the Front (A) perpendicular to the Side (C), matching the 17-inch edges, as shown in *figure 3*. Make certain that the outside edges are flush, then apply glue to the meeting surfaces, and nail through the Front (A) into the Corner Supports (B), using four evenly spaced 1¼-inch finish nails.

8 Repeat step 7 to attach the Back (A) to the opposite surface of the Side (C).

9 Position the remaining Side (C) over the assembly, aligning the 17-inch-long edges, as shown in *figure 4*. Apply glue to the meeting surfaces and nail through the Side (C) into the Corner Supports (B), using four evenly spaced 1½-inch finish nails on each joint.

## Adding the Roof

1 Cut two Outer Roofs (D) from ¼-inch plywood, each measuring 10x23½ inches.

2 Turn the assembly right side up, and fit one Outer Roof (D) over one top outer side of the assembly, over the edges of the Front (A), Back (A), and Side (C), as shown in *figure 5*. The Outer Roof (D) should be flush with the top points of the Front and Back (A), and should extend 2 inches past the Front (A), Back (A), and Side (C), as shown in *figure 5*. Apply glue to the meeting surfaces, and nail through the Outer Roof (D) into the edges of the Front (A), Back (A), and Side (C), using 1-inch wire brads spaced about 2 inches apart.

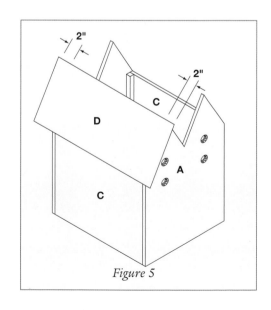

Figure 5

3 Repeat step 2 to attach the remaining Outer Roof (D) to the opposite side of the house.

4 Cut two Inner Roofs (E) from ¼-inch plywood, each measuring 8x23½ inches.

5 Place one Inner Roof (E) over the edges of the Front (A) and Back (A). Check to make certain that the Inner Roof (E) does not overlap the edge of the Outer Roof (D). Trim the width of the Inner Roof (E) if necessary. Apply glue to the meeting surfaces, and nail through the Inner Roof (E) into the Front (A) and Back (A), using four evenly spaced 1-inch wire brads on each joint.

6 Repeat step 5 to attach the remaining Inner Roof (E) to the opposite side of the assembly.

## Adding the Trim

1 The next step is to add trim pieces to the front, corners, and roof of the birdhouse. If you wish to paint your birdhouse and do not plan to paint the trim, it is a good idea to do it now, before the trim pieces are added.

2 Cut four Side Trims (F) from ¾-inch-wide screen molding, each measuring 16½ inches.

3 Attach one Side Trim (F) flush with the bottom edge of the Side (C), over the joint between the Front (A) and Side (C). The Side Trims (F) are ½ inch shorter than the Sides (C) to accommodate the pitch of the roof. Apply glue to the meeting surfaces, and nail through the Side Trim (F) into the edge of the Front (A), using 1-inch wire brads spaced 2 inches apart.

4 Repeat step 3 three times to attach the remaining Side Trims (F) to the remaining joints between the Sides (C) and the Front (A) and Back (A).

5 Cut one Center Trim (G) from ¾-inch-wide screen molding, measuring 17 inches.

6 Place the Center Trim (G) on the Front (A), centered horizontally, as shown in *figure 6*. Apply glue to the meeting surfaces, and nail through the Center Trim (G) into the Front (A), using 1-inch wire brads spaced 2 inches apart.

7 Cut four Outer Trims (H) from ¾-inch-wide screen molding, each measuring 18 inches. Place one Outer Trim (H) over the joint between the Side Trim (H) and the Front (A). Mark the angle and cut the top end of the Outer Trim (H) to the proper angle. Apply glue to the meeting surfaces, and nail through the Outer Trim (H) into the Front (A), using 1-inch wire brads spaced 2 inches apart.

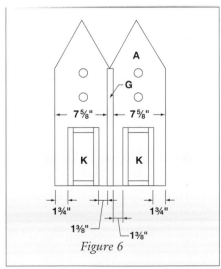

*Figure 6*

8  Refer to the photograph for the placement of the Roof Trims (I); measure and cut eight Roof Trims (I) from $^3/_4$-inch-wide screen molding that fit over the exposed edges of the Outer and Inner Roofs (D and E), mitering them as shown in the photograph.

## Adding the Shingles

1  We cut regular-size shingles into 6-inch lengths to match the reduced size of the birdhouse. It is better to work with the top portion of the original shingle, since that portion is thinner than the bottom edge. It is not difficult to shingle, and since the finished project should look somewhat rustic, the job is even easier.

2  Begin attaching the first row of shingles with 1-inch wire brads, just overlapping the bottom edge of one Outer Roof (D) with the first row of shingles. Each shingle should be nailed twice to prevent shifting. Shingles come in bundles containing random widths. Choose varying widths of shingles as you work across each row for a random look. A row of narrow shingles followed by a row of wide shingles will look odd. Add a second row, overlapping the first row, about $3^1/_2$ inches higher. Add a third row in the same manner. You may need to re-trim the length of the shingles on the third row, to make certain they don't extend past the roof's peak.

3  Repeat the application of shingles on the remaining Outer Roof (D).

4  Next, shingle the two Inner Roofs (E). These are shingled in the same manner, except that the Inner Roofs (E) are shorter, and therefore require only two rows of shingles. Try to match the rows of shingles on the Inner Roofs (E) to the rows on the Outer Roofs (D).

5  Cut two Peak Covers (J) from $1^1/_4$-inch L molding, each measuring $23^1/_2$ inches.

6  Apply glue to the meeting surfaces, and nail the Peak Covers (J) over the shingles on the roof peak, using $^1/_4$-inch finish nails spaced 2 inches apart.

## Adding the Doors

1  Cut two Doors (K) from $^1/_4$-inch-thick plywood, each measuring $8^1/_2$x$4^1/_2$ inches.

2  Cut four Horizontal Door Trims (L) from $^3/_4$-inch-wide screen molding, each measuring 3 inches.

3  Cut four Vertical Door Trims (M) from $^3/_4$-inch-wide screen molding, each measuring $8^1/_2$ inches.

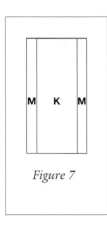

*Figure 7*

4   Lay one Door (K) on a flat surface, then place two Vertical Door Trims (M) flush with the outer 8½-inch edge of the Door (K), as shown in *figure 7*. Apply glue to the meeting surfaces, and nail through the Vertical Door Trims (M) into the Door (K), using four ½-inch wire brads on each joint.

5   Place the two Horizontal Door Trims (L) between the two Vertical Door Trims (M), flush with the 4½-inch edge of the Door (K). Apply glue to the meeting surfaces, and nail through the Horizontal Door Trims (L) into the Door (K), using two ½-inch wire brads on each joint.

6   Repeat steps 4 and 5 to assemble a second door.

7   Using *figure 6* as a guide, attach the two completed doors to the Front (A). Apply glue to the meeting surfaces, and nail through the assembled door into the Front (A), using a 1-inch wire brad in each corner of the door.

8   Attach a small drawer pull to each of the doors for door handles.

## Adding the Windows

1   Cut four Windows (N) from ¼-inch plywood, each measuring 4½ inches square.

2   Cut eight Horizontal Window Trims (O) from ¾-inch-wide screen molding, each measuring 3 inches.

3   Cut eight Vertical Window Trims (P) from ¾-inch-wide screen molding, each measuring 4½ inches.

4   Lay one Window (N) on a flat surface, and position two Vertical Window Trims (P) flush with the outer edges of the Window (N), in the same manner as for the door trims. Apply glue to the meeting surfaces, and nail through the Vertical Window Trims (P) into the Window (N), using four ½-inch wire brads on each joint.

5   Position the two Horizontal Window Trims (O) between the two Vertical Window Trims (P), flush with the edges of the Window (N). Apply glue to the meeting surfaces, and nail through the Horizontal Window Trims (O) into the Window (N), using two ½-inch wire brads on each joint.

6   Repeat steps 4 and 5 three times to assemble three additional windows.

**7** Using *figure 8* as a placement guide, attach two windows to each Side (C). Apply glue to the meeting surfaces, and nail through the completed window into the Side (C), using one 1-inch wire brad on each corner of the window.

## Adding the Base

**1** Cut two Long Bases (Q) from 2x4 pine, each measuring 23½ inches.

**2** Cut two Short Bases (R) from 2x4 pine, each measuring 21 inches.

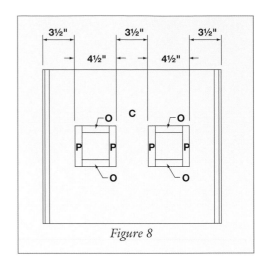

*Figure 8*

**3** Miter the ends of the Long and Short Bases (Q and R) at opposing 45° angles, as shown in *figure 9*.

**4** Position the two Long Bases (Q) on a flat surface, parallel to each other and 14 inches apart. Fit the two Short Bases (R) at the ends of the two Long Bases (Q) to form a 23½x21-inch rectangle, as shown in *figure 10*. Apply glue to the meeting surfaces, and screw through both sides of each corner, using two 3-inch screws on each corner. Reinforce each joint by adding a corrugated metal fastener across the inner corner of each joint.

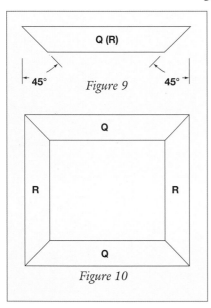

*Figure 9*

*Figure 10*

**5** Center the assembled birdhouse table over the base, making certain that the base extension is the same on all four sides. Toenail through the lower edges of the Front (A), Back (A), and Sides (C) into the base, using 2½-inch finish nails spaced about every 2 inches around the perimeter.

**6** An optional step at this point is to measure and miter ¾-inch-wide screen molding around the vertical trims at all four corners.

## Adding the Chimneys

**1** To help support the glass tabletop, we added two chimneys to the birdhouse. Cut two Chimneys (S) from 2x2 pine, each measuring 10 inches.

**2** Hold the Chimney (S) so that one end is level with the top of the birdhouse roofs, and mark the roof angle on the Chimney (S), so that the top of the Chimney (S) will sit level with the peak of the roof. Use the mark to trim the Chimney (S).

3 Repeat step 2 to trim the remaining Chimney (S).

4 Apply glue to the meeting surfaces, and attach both Chimneys (S) to the roof, halfway between the front and back of the birdhouse. Nail through the lower ends of the Chimney (S) into the shingled roof, using two 2½-inch finish nails on each Chimney (S).

## Finishing

1 Fill any cracks, crevices, and nail holes with wood filler.

2 Sand the wood filler and any other unsanded surfaces.

3 Paint or stain the remaining portions of the birdhouse table, or simply seal it with a clear varnish.

4 Place the circular glass tabletop on the completed birdhouse base.

# Occasional Table

*Small tables are always welcome in the garden or on the patio. This one is less than two feet square, so it will fit almost anywhere. Place one next to your favorite recliner, or make two of them and place them side by side to create a handy coffee table.*

### Special Tools & Techniques

- Web clamps
- Miters

### Materials

- 20 linear feet of 1x2 pine
- 15 linear feet of 1x4 pine
- 8 linear feet of 2x2 pine
- 2 linear feet of 2x4 pine

### Hardware

- 40 4px1$\frac{1}{4}$″ nails
- 15 1$\frac{1}{4}$″ screws
- 30 1$\frac{5}{8}$″ screws
- 10 2$\frac{1}{2}$″ screws
- 4 4″ screws

### Cutting List

| Code | Description | Qty. | Materials | Dimensions |
|------|-------------|------|-----------|------------|
| A | Long Center Support | 2 | 1x2 pine | 14$\frac{3}{4}$″ long |
| B | Short Center Support | 2 | 1x2 pine | 13$\frac{1}{4}$″ long |
| C | Slat | 8 | 1x2 pine | 14$\frac{3}{4}$″ long |
| D | Trim | 4 | 1x4 pine | 21$\frac{3}{4}$″ long |
| E | Side | 4 | 1x4 pine | 14$\frac{3}{4}$″ long |
| F | Leg | 4 | 2x2 pine | 20″ long |
| G | Triangular Support | 4 | 2x4 pine | 3$\frac{1}{2}$″ long |

## Constructing the Table Top

1  Cut two long center supports (A) from 1x2 pine, each measuring 14$\frac{3}{4}$ inches long.

2  Cut two short center supports (B) from 1x2 pine, each measuring 13$\frac{1}{4}$ inches long.

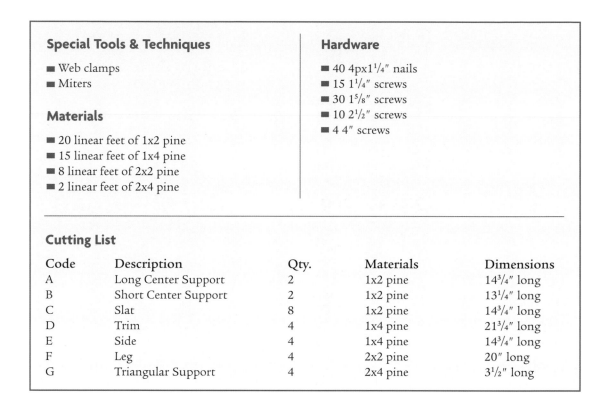

Figure 1

Figure 2

3 Place the two short center supports (B) between the ends of the long center supports (A), as shown in *figure 1* on page 48. Screw through the long center supports (A) into the ends of the short center supports (B), using two 1⁵/₈-inch-long screws on each joint.

4 Cut eight slats (C) from 1x2 pine, each measuring 14³/₄ inches long.

5 Place the eight slats (C) over the assembled center supports, as shown in *figure 2*. Space the slats (C) evenly across the width of the supports, leaving a little less than ¹/₄ inch between slats and the same amount on both sides, as shown in *figure 2* on page 48. The exact measurement is not critical—just make certain that all the spaces are equal and that the slats (C) are all straight. Nail through the ends of the slats (C) into the long center supports (A), using two 1¹/₄-inch-long nails on each end.

6 Cut four sides (E) from 1x4 pine, each measuring 14³/₄ inches.

**7** Attach the four sides (E) to the long and short center supports (B and C), as shown in *figure 3*, even with the corners of the box made with the center supports in step 3. The open corners will later accommodate the legs for the table. Apply glue to the meeting surfaces, and screw through the supports (A and B) into the four sides (E). Use three 1¼-inch screws to secure each side (E).

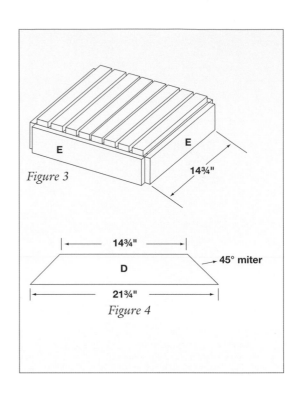

*Figure 3*

*Figure 4*

**8** The next step is to frame the slat assembly with the trim pieces (D). Cut four trims (D) from 1x4 pine, each measuring 21¾ inches long. Miter both ends of all four trim pieces at opposing 45-degree angles, as shown in *figure 4*. The long edge of each trim (D) should measure 21¾ inches and the short edge should measure 14¾ inches.

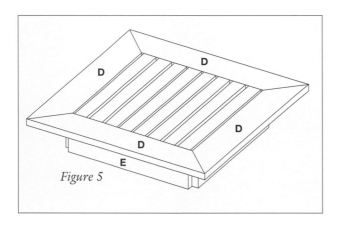

*Figure 5*

**9** Glue and clamp together the four trims (D) to form a four-sided picture frame. A web clamp is useful for this maneuver. Let the assembly dry overnight.

**10** Position the assembled trim frame over the sides (E) around the slat assembly, as shown in *figure 5*. It should be placed even with the inside edges of the four sides (E). Apply glue to the meeting surfaces, and nail through each of the trims (D) into the sides (E). Use four or five 1⅝-inch-long nails on each trim piece (D).

## Adding the Legs

**1** Cut four legs (F) from 2x2 pine, each measuring 20 inches long.

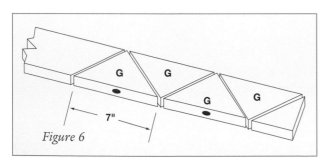

*Figure 6*

**2** Cut four triangular supports (G) at a 45-degree angle from 2x4 pine so that the grain runs with the long sides, as shown in *figure 6*.

**3** Predrill a ½-inch-diameter hole to a depth of 1 inch, beginning at the center of the long side of the triangular support (G) toward the 45-degree corner, as shown in *figure 6*.

4 Turn the assembled top upside down on a level surface. Apply glue to the short sides of the triangular supports (G), and place them in each of the four inside corners formed by the sides (E), on top of the top supports (A and B), as shown in *figure 7*. Screw through the ends of the triangular supports (G) into the top supports (A and B) and the sides (E). Use two 1⁵/₈-inch-long screws on each support.

5 Position each of the four legs (F) at the corners of the assembly, between the ends of the sides (E), as shown in *figure 7*. Make very certain that the legs are square to the assembly. Then insert a 4-inch-long screw into the predrilled hole in each triangular support (G), and screw it through the triangular support (G) and into each leg (F).

6 To further support the legs (F), carefully turn the entire assembly upside down. Again check to make certain that the legs are perfectly square and straight. Then screw through each of the trim pieces (D) down into the leg (F). Use two 2¹/₂-inch-long screws on each leg (F)—one through each trim piece (D).

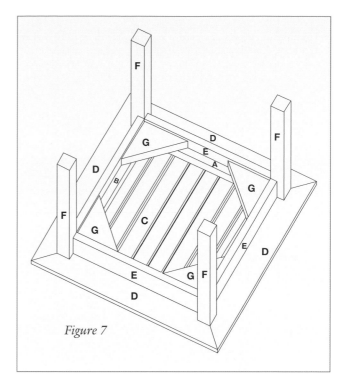

*Figure 7*

## Finishing

1 If you want a very finished look, fill any cracks, crevices, or screw holes with wood filler, and thoroughly sand all surfaces of the occasional table.

2 You can seal and paint or stain the completed occasional table the color of your choice, or— if you used treated lumber—simply leave it natural, as shown in the photograph on page 49.

# Barbecue Table

*If you have arrived at your barbecue with hands full of sauces, steaks, tongs, hot pads, and spatulas and had nowhere to put them, you'll want to build this barbecue table. It's perfectly sized to hold trays and bottles, and even has a place to hang your barbecue tools.*

### Materials

- 12 linear feet or 2x2 pine
- 30 linear feet of 1x4 pine
- 10 linear feet of $^5/_4$x6 pine

### Hardware

- 16 $1^5/_8$" wood screws
- 36 2" wood screws
- 50 $1^1/_4$" (3d) finish nails
- 3 cup hooks

### Cutting List

| Code | Description | Qty. | Materials | Dimensions |
|------|-------------|------|-----------|------------|
| A | Long Side | 4 | 1x4 pine | $34^1/_2$" long |
| B | Short Side | 4 | 1x4 pine | 15" long |
| C | Leg | 4 | 2x2 pine | 32" long |
| D | Support Trim | 2 | 1x1 pine | $32^3/_4$" long |
| E | Shelf Board | 8 | 1x4 pine | $13^1/_2$" long |
| F | Top Support | 1 | 1x4 pine | $13^1/_2$" long |
| G | Top Boards | 3 | $^5/_4$x6 pine | 38" long |

## Making the Frame

1 Cut four Long Sides (A) from 1x4 pine, each measuring $34^1/_2$ inches.

2 Cut four Short Sides (B) from 1x4 pine, each measuring 15 inches.

3 Place two of the Long Sides (A) on edge, parallel to each other, and $13^1/_2$ inches apart. Fit two of the Short Sides (B) over the ends of the Long Sides (A) to form a rectangle measuring 36x15 inches, as shown in *figure 1*. Apply glue to the meeting surfaces, and screw through the face of the Short Sides (B) into the ends of the Long Sides (A), using $1^5/_8$-inch wood screws.

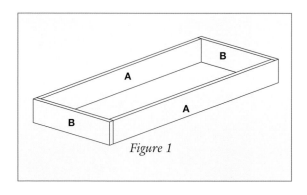

*Figure 1*

4 Repeat step 3 to form another rectangle with the remaining two Short and Long Sides (A and B). Designate one rectangle as the "Top" and the other as the "Bottom."

5 Cut four Legs (C) from 2x2 pine, each measuring 32 inches.

6 Place the four Legs (C) inside the corners of the assembled rectangle designated "Top," as shown in *figure 2* on page 54. Apply glue to the meeting surfaces, and screw through the Short and Long Sides (A and B) into both sides of each Leg (C), using two 2-inch wood screws on each joint.

7 Place the assembled rectangle designated "Bottom" over the four Legs (C), 12 inches below the Top, as shown in *figure 3* on page 54. Again, apply glue to the meeting surfaces, and screw through the Short and Long Sides (A and B) into both sides of each Leg (C), using two 2-inch wood screws on each joint.

## Adding the Bottom Shelf

1 Cut two Support Trims (D) from lxl pine, each measuring $32^{3}/_{4}$ inches.

2 Cut eight Shelf Boards (E) from 1x4 pine, each measuring $13^{1}/_{2}$ inches.

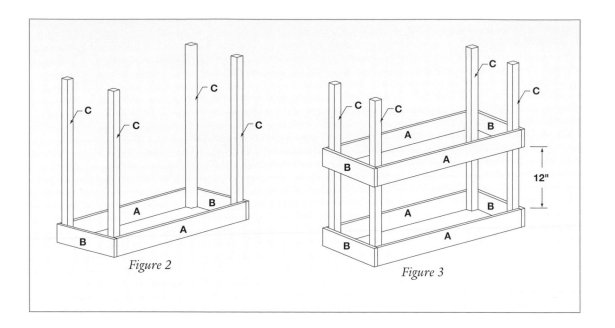

Figure 2

Figure 3

12"

**3** Place the Support Trims (D) inside the Long Sides (A) of the Bottom rectangle, $^{3}/_{4}$ inch from the top edge of the Long Sides (A), as shown in *figure 4*. Apply glue to the meeting surfaces, and nail through the Support Trims (D) into the Long Sides (A), using l$^{1}/_{4}$-inch finish nails evenly spaced about 3 inches apart.

**4** Place the eight Shelf Boards (E) between the Long Sides (A) over the Support Trims (D), as shown in *figure 5*. Space the Shelf Boards (E) approximately $^{1}/_{2}$ inch apart. Apply glue to the meeting surfaces, and nail through the Shelf Boards (E) into the Support Trims (D), using two 1$^{1}/_{4}$-inch finish nails on each joint.

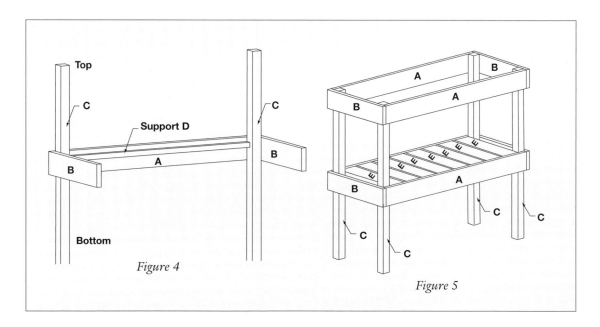

Figure 4

Figure 5

## Adding the Top

1 Cut one Top Support (F) from 1x4 pine, measuring 13½ inches.

2 Place the Top Support (F) between the two Long Sides (A) on the Top, centered between the two Short Sides (B), as shown in *figure 6*. Apply glue to the meeting surfaces, and screw through the Long Sides (A), using two 1⅝-inch wood screws on each joint.

3 Cut three Top Boards (G) from ⁵⁄₄x6 deck boards, each measuring 38 inches.

4 Place the three Top Boards (G) over the Top, as shown in *figure 7*. The Top Boards (G) will overhang the Top by 1 inch on all four sides. Apply glue to the meeting surfaces, and nail through the Top Boards (G) into the Long Sides (A), Short Sides (B), and Top Support (F), using two 2-inch wood screws on each joint.

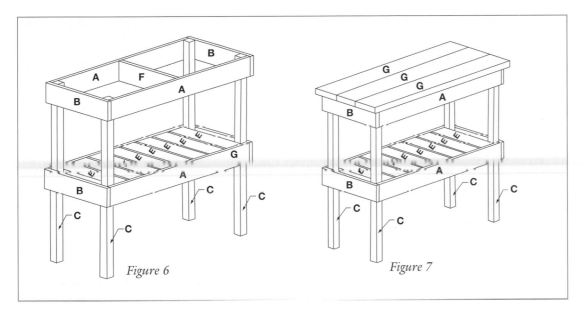

Figure 6

Figure 7

## Finishing

1 Fill any cracks or crevices with wood filler and sand the table thoroughly.

2 Paint or stain the table the color of your choice, or leave the wood natural. The bottom of this table has been stained a natural color, and the top was painted red. We have lettered "Let's Get Cookin'" on the bottom side of the finished tabletop.

3 Screw three cup hooks to one end of the tabletop for hanging barbecue tools.

# Picnic Table & Benches

*Who doesn't need a sturdy picnic table? We use ours just about every weekend when friends come to visit. This one has a checkerboard painted on it—our young friends love to play "shell" checkers on it with shells they collected on the beach. The benches stand alone as super garden seating.*

## Special Tools & Techniques

- Miter

## Materials for Picnic Table

- 28 linear feet of 2x4 pine
- 27 linear feet, of lx6 pine

## Materials for One Bench

- 15 linear feet of 2x10 pine

## Hardware

- 8 3½" carriage bolts with matching washers and nuts
- 30 2" wood screws
- 25 2½" wood screws

## Cutting List

| Code | Description | Qty. | Materials | Dimensions |
|------|-------------|------|-----------|------------|
| A | Leg | 4 | 2x4 pine | 37" long |
| B | Leg Support | 2 | 2x4 pine | 17¾" long |
| C | Top | 5 | 1x6 pine | 60" long |
| D | Top Support | 3 | 2x4 pine | 27½" long |
| E | Brace | 2 | 2x4 pine | 25" long |
| F | Bench Leg | 2 | 2x10 pine | 16" long |
| G | Bench Top | 1 | 2x10 pine | 60" long |
| H | Bench Brace | 2 | 2x10 pine | 7" long |

## Making the Legs

1 Cut four Legs (A) from 2x4 pine, each measuring 37 inches long.

2 Using *figure 1* as a guide, trim the ends of each Leg (A), and drill a ½-inch-diameter hole in the center.

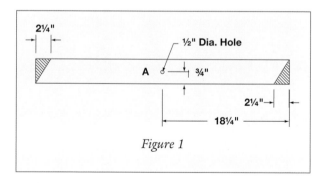

*Figure 1*

3 Position two Legs (A), one on top of the other, to form an X, aligning the two center holes. Insert a 3½-inch carriage bolt through the center holes and add a matching washer and nut. Adjust the Legs (A) so that the upper and lower outer measurement of the Legs (A) is 22½ inches, as shown in *figure 2* on page 57.

4 Repeat step 3 to form another X-shaped assembly with the remaining two Legs (A).

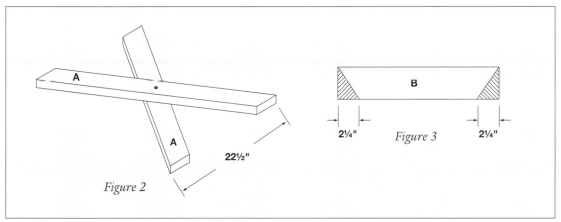

Figure 2

Figure 3

2¼"                    2¼"

5  Cut two Leg Supports (B) from 2x4 pine, each measuring 17³/₄ inches.

6  Using *figure 3* as a guide, trim both ends of each Leg Support (B).

7 Position one X-shaped assembly flat on a work surface, with the carriage bolt head on the underside. Place one Leg Support (B) flush with the top ends of the X-shaped assembly, as shown in *figure 4*. Note that the Leg Support (B) overlaps the lower Leg (A), and butts against the upper Leg (A).

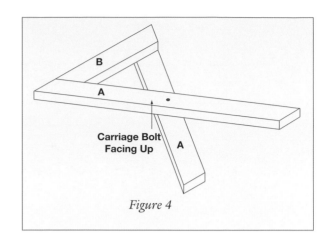

*Figure 4*

8 Repeat step 7 to attach the remaining Leg Support (B) to the remaining X-shaped assembly.

## Making the Top

1 Cut five Tops (C) from 1x6 pine, each measuring 60 inches.

2 Cut three Top Supports (D) from 2x4 pine, each measuring $27\frac{1}{2}$ inches.

3 Using *figure 3* as a guide, trim the corners on each of the three Top Supports (D).

4 Position three Top Supports (D) on a level surface (trimmed edges down), parallel to each other and $22\frac{1}{4}$ inches apart. Place the five Tops (C) over the three Top Supports (D), as shown in *figure 5*. Make certain that the assembly is square. Screw through the Tops (C) into each of the three Top Supports (D), using two 2-inch wood screws on each joint.

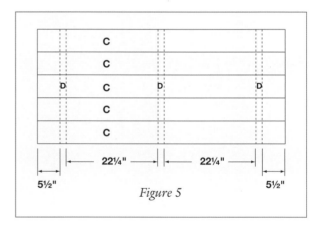

*Figure 5*

## Final Table Assembly

1 Turn the top assembly (Tops [C] and Top Supports [D]) upside down on a level surface. Position one X-shaped assembly so that the Leg Support (B) is flush against the inner surface of the Top Support (D), as shown in *figure 6* on page 59. Apply glue to the meeting surfaces, and screw through the Top Support (D) into the Leg Support (B), using two $2\frac{1}{2}$-inch wood screws. This will hold the assembly together temporarily.

2 Drill two $\frac{1}{2}$-inch-diameter holes through the Leg Support (B) and the Top Support (D), using *figure 7* on page 59 as a guide for exact placement.

**3** Drill one ¹/₂-inch-diameter hole through the Leg (A) and the Top Support (D). Again, refer to *figure 7* for exact placement.

**4** Insert a 3¹/₂-inch carriage bolt through each of the three drilled holes, add the nut, and tighten.

**5** Repeat steps 1 through 4 to attach the remaining X-shaped assembly and Leg Support (A) to the top assembly.

**6** Cut two Braces (E) from 2x4 pine, each measuring 25 inches.

**7** Miter the ends of each Brace (E) at opposing 45° angles, as shown in *figure 8*.

**8** Position the brace (short edge down) so that one mitered end is against the center of the X-shaped assembly and the opposite end is against the Tops (C), as shown in *figure 9*. Screw at an angle through the Brace (E) into the X-shaped assembly, using one 2¹/₂-inch wood screw.

**9** Repeat step 8 to attach the remaining Brace (E) to the opposite side of the table.

**10** Carefully turn the entire assembly right side up, and screw through the center Top (C) into the unattached end of the Brace (E), using two 2¹/₂-inch wood screws.

**11** Repeat step 10 to secure the remaining unattached Brace (E) to the center Top (C) on the opposite side of the table.

## Making the Bench

**1** Cut two Bench Legs (A) from 2x10 pine, each measuring 16 inches.

**2** Referring to the placement measurements given in *figure 10* on page 60, drill a 1¹/₄-inch-diameter hole centered horizontally and 7³/₈ inches from one end of a Bench Leg (F).

**3** Again referring to *figure 10* on page 60, cut away the center portion of the Bench Leg (F) to form an inverted V shape.

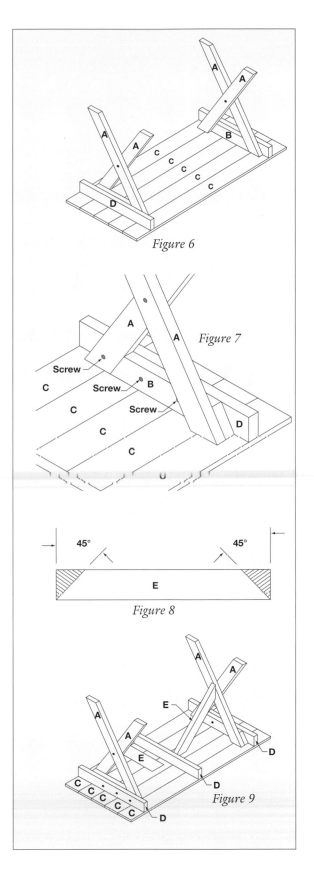

Figure 6

Figure 7

Figure 8

Figure 9

4 Repeat steps 2 and 3 to cut out the remaining Bench Leg (F).

5 Cut one Bench Top (G) from 2x10 pine, measuring 60 inches.

6 Position the two Bench Legs (F) on edge with the cutout against the work surface, parallel to each other and 45 inches apart. Place the Bench Top (G) over the Bench Legs (F). The Bench Top (G) should overhang each of the Bench Legs (F) by 6 inches. Screw through the Bench Top (G) into each of the Bench Legs (F), using three 2½-inch wood screws.

7 Cut two Bench Braces (H) from 2x10 pine, each measuring 7 inches.

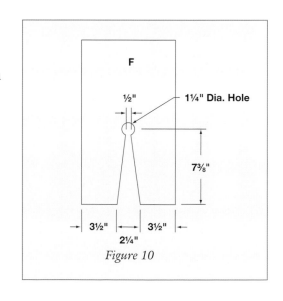

F

½"    1¼" Dia. Hole

7⅜"

3½"    3½"

2¼"

*Figure 10*

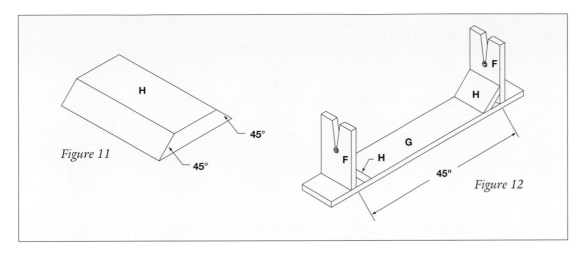

*Figure 11*

*Figure 12*

8 Miter the ends of the Bench Braces (H) at opposing 45° angles, as shown in *figure 11*.

9 Turn the bench assembly upside down. Fit the mitered Bench Braces (H) between the Bench Legs (F) and Bench Top (G), as shown in *figure 12*. Apply glue to the meeting surfaces, and screw at an angle through the Bench Braces (H) into both the Bench Top (G) and Bench Legs (F), using three 2¹/₂-inch wood screws on each joint.

10 If you want two benches, you will need to repeat the entire procedure.

## Finishing

1 Sand the entire picnic table and bench.

2 Painting a checkerboard pattern on the top of the picnic table will double its use. A checkerboard is easy to do—we simply drew eight rows of eight 2-inch squares in the center of the table and painted the squares alternating colors. We left the remainder of the table its natural color.

# Outdoor Bar

*You are sure to be the "hostess with the mostest" at your next party when, you outfit this outdoor bar with a choice of beverages. The bar is great for outdoor entertaining, since it keeps the beverage service out of the kitchen.*

## Special Tools & Techniques
- Bar clamps
- Miter
- $1/8$" V trowel
- Rubber tile float

## Materials
- 4'x8' sheet of $3/4$" plywood
- 16 linear feet of 2x2 pine
- 4 decorative 4x4 posts, at least 45" long
- 21 linear feet of 2x4 pine
- 10 linear feet of 1x2 pine
- 4'x 4' sheet of lattice
- 4"-wide top rail, 5' long
- 16 square feet of tile
- 1 qt. ceramic tile adhesive
- 7 lb. sanded grout, in color of your choice
- Small bottle of silicone grout sealer

## Hardware
- 25 $1^5/8$" wood screws
- 40 $2^1/2$" wood screws
- 35 2" wood screws
- 10 2" (6d) finish nails
- 20 $1^1/4$" (3d) finish nails
- 30 1" (2d) finish nails

## Cutting List

| Code | Description | Qty. | Materials | Dimensions |
|---|---|---|---|---|
| A | Side | 2 | $3/4$" plywood | 16"x17" |
| B | Front | 1 | $3/4$" plywood | 16"x41" |
| C | Support | 8 | 2x2 pine | 16" long |
| D | Leg | 4 | 4x4 pine | 44" long |
| E | Shelf Trim | 2 | 2x4 pine | 41" long |
| F | Short Brace | 2 | 1x2 pine | $15^1/2$" |
| G | Long Brace | 2 | 1x2 pine | 41" long |
| H | Shelf | 1 | $3/4$" plywood | 44"x20" |
| I | Top | 1 | $3/4$" plywood | 24"x48" |
| J | Front Trim | 1 | 2x4 pine | $51^1/8$" |
| K | Side Trim | 2 | 2x4 pine | $25^1/4$" long |
| L | Front Lattice | 1 | Lattice | 16"x41" |
| M | Side Lattice | 2 | Lattice | 16"x17" |
| N | Rail Support | 1 | 2x4 pine | 52" long |
| O | Foot Rail | 1 | 4"-wide top rail | 52" long |

## Building the Frame

1 Cut two Sides (A) from $3/4$-inch-thick plywood, each measuring 16x17 inches.

2 Cut one Front (B) from $3/4$-inch-thick plywood, measuring 16x41 inches.

3 Cut eight Supports (C) from 2x2 pine, each measuring 16 inches long.

4 Place two Supports (C) on a level surface parallel to each other and 14 inches apart. Place the short end of one Side (A) over the Supports (C), as shown in *figure 1*. Apply glue to the meeting surfaces, and screw through the Side (A) into the Supports (C), using four 1⅝-inch wood screws in each Support (C).

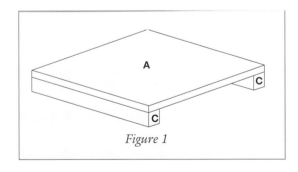

Figure 1

5 Repeat step 4 to assemble the remaining Side (A) and two Supports (C).

6 Place two Supports (C) parallel to each other on a level surface and 38 inches apart. In the same way that the Sides (A) were assembled, place the short end of the Front (B) over the two Supports (C). Apply glue to the meeting surfaces, and screw through the Front (B) into the 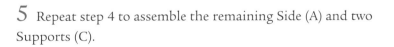 Supports (C), using four 1⅜-inch screws in each Support (C).

## Attaching the Posts

1 Cut four Legs (D) from 4x4 pine, each measuring 44 inches.

2 Place the assembled Front (B) and Supports (C) on edge and place one Leg (D) over the end of the Front (B) and Support (C) assembly, as shown in *figure 2*. Apply glue to the meeting surface, and clamp in place while you screw through the Support (C) into the Leg (D), using four 2½-inch wood screws.

3 Repeat step 1 to attach a Leg (D) to the other end of the assembled Front (B).

4 Place one of the assembled Sides (A) on edge, place one Leg (D) over one end of the Front (B) and Support (C) assembly, as shown in *figure 2*. Apply glue to the meeting surface, and clamp in place while you screw through the Support (C) into the Leg (D), using four 2½-inch wood screws.

5 Repeat step 3 to attach another Leg (D) to the other end of the assembled Side (A).

6 Repeat steps 3 and 4 to attach the Legs (D) to the remaining Side (A).

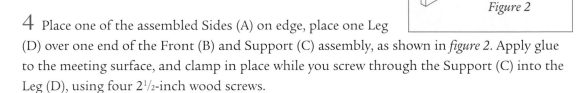

*Figure 2*

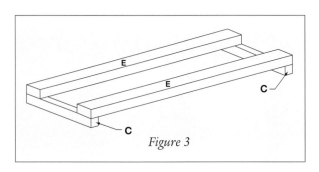

*Figure 3*

7 Cut two Shelf Trims (E) from 2x4 pine, each measuring 41 inches.

8 Place the remaining two Supports (C) flat on a level surface parallel to each other and 41 inches apart. Place the two Shelf Trims (E) over the Supports (C), as shown in *figure 3*. Screw through the Shelf Trims (E) into the Supports (C), using two 2-inch wood screws per joint.

9 Place the assembled Shelf Trims (E) and Supports (C) between the Legs (D) of the assembled Sides (A) and parallel to the Front (A). Apply glue to the meeting surfaces, and screw through the Supports (C) into the Legs (D), using four 2-inch wood screws. Note: Make sure that the Shelf Trims (E) are facing away from the inside of the frame.

## Adding the Shelf

1 Cut two Short Braces (F) from 1x2 pine, each measuring 15½ inches.

2 Cut two Long Braces (G) from 1x2 pine, each measuring 41 inches.

**3** Position the two Short Braces (F) on edge, parallel to each other and 39½ inches apart.

**4** Position the two Long Braces (G) over the ends of the Short Braces (F), as shown in *figure 4*. Apply glue to the meeting surfaces, and nail through the Long Braces (G) into the ends of the Short Braces (F), using two 2-inch finish nails in each joint.

**5** Cut one Shelf (H) from ¾-inch-thick plywood, measuring 44x20 inches. Refer to *figure 5* to cut out the corners.

**6** Place the Shelf (H) over the Long and Short Braces (F and G). Apply glue to the meeting surfaces, and nail through the Shelf (H) into the Short and Long Braces (F and G), using 1¼-inch finish nails spaced about every 5 inches.

**7** The assembled shelf will be installed with the bar frame lying down and the Front (B) facing the work surface. Place the assembled shelf inside the four corners formed by the Supports (C), as shown in *figure 6*. (Shelf not included in figure to better show braces.) Screw through the face of the Long and Short Braces (F and G) into the two Supports (C) in each corner, using 2-inch wood screws.

## Adding the Top

**1** Cut one Top (I) from ¾-inch-thick plywood, measuring 24x48 inches.

**2** Turn the assembled bar over onto its legs. Place the Top (I) over the ends of the legs (D), as shown in *figure 7*. Screw through the Top (I) into the ends of the Legs (D), using two 2-inch wood screws in each corner.

**3** Cut one Front Trim (J) from 2x4 pine, measuring 51⅛ inches. An optional step at this point is to bevel the edge of the trim at a 30° angle. The corners are also mitered at opposing 45° angles, as shown in *figure 8* on page 66.

**4** Cut two Side Trims (K) from 2x4 pine, each measuring 25¼ inches. We beveled one edge as we did for the front trim

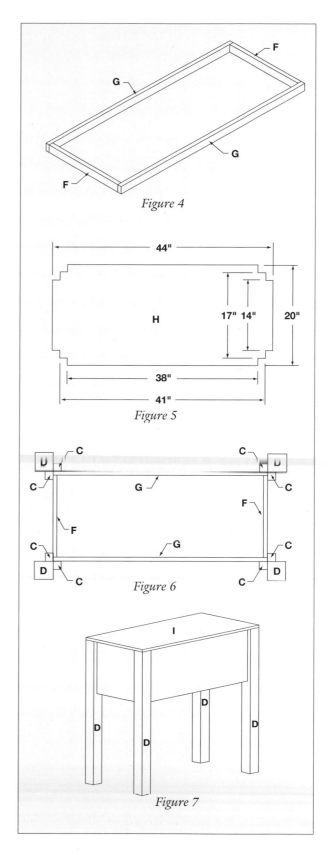

Figure 4

Figure 5

Figure 6

Figure 7

pieces and mitered one end of each board. Note: The miters on each board are opposites of each other.

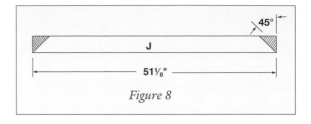

Figure 8

5 Attach the Front Trim (J) to the Legs (D) and Top (I) keeping the beveled edge of the Front Trim (J) up and ¼ inch above the Top (I) to leave room for the tile to be, installed. Screw through the Front Trim (J) into the Legs (D), using two 2½-inch wood screws in each Leg (D).

6 Attach one Side Trim (K) to one side of the bar so that the 45° miters meet. Screw through the Side Trim (K) into the Legs (D), using two 2½-inch screws in each leg.

7 Repeat step 6 to attach the remaining Side Trim (K).

## Adding the Lattice & Foot Rail

1 Cut one Front Lattice (L) from lattice, measuring 16x41 inches.

2 Place the Front Lattice (L) over the Front (B). Apply glue to the meeting surfaces, and nail through the Front Lattice (L), using 1-inch finish nails.

3 Cut two Side Lattices (M) from lattice, each measuring 16x17 inches.

4 Place one Side Lattice (M) over one Side (A). Apply glue to the meeting surfaces, and nail through the Side Lattice (M), using 1-inch finish nails.

5 Repeat step 4 to attach the remaining Side Lattice (M) to the opposite Side (A).

6 Cut one Rail Support (N) from 2x4 pine, measuring 52 inches.

7 Bevel one edge of the Rail Support (N) at a 45° angle along its length.

8 Center the Rail Support (N) over the two front Legs (D), 8 inches from the ground. Note that the Rail Support (N) will extend past the Legs (D) about 2 inches on each side. Apply glue to the meeting surfaces, and screw through the Rail Support (N) into the Legs (D), using two 2-inch wood screws on each joint.

9 Cut one Foot Rail (O) from 4-inch-wide top rail, measuring 52 inches.

10 Place the Foot Rail (O) over the Rail Support (N). Apply glue to the meeting surfaces, and screw through the Foot Rail (O) into the Rail Support (N), using 2-inch wood screws spaced every 6 inches.

## Adding the Tile

1 Following the manufacturer's directions, carefully spread an even coat of the tile adhesive over the surface of the Top (I) with an $\frac{1}{8}$-inch V trowel.

2 Place the tiles on the adhesive one at a time, making sure that they are positioned correctly. Do not slide the tiles, or the adhesive will be forced up on the sides of the tile. Let the adhesive dry overnight.

3 Mix the tile grout according to the manufacturer's directions.

4 Spread the grout over the tile, using a rubber-surfaced float held at a 45° angle so that the grout is forced evenly into the spaces between the tiles.

5 Use a wet sponge to wipe the excess grout off the tiles and joints; if you let it dry, the hardened grout will be very difficult to remove. Try to use as little water as possible when removing the excess, so that you do not thin the grout that remains. Let the grout dry overnight.

6 Rinse the remaining film from the tile and wipe it dry with an old towel.

7 Apply grout sealer, following the manufacturer's directions.

## Finishing

1 Sand the entire bar thoroughly.

2 Finish with a stain (we used cherry stain and green paint for the trim on this one), or leave natural.

# Cocktail Table with Tray

*This cocktail table does double duty—as a handy side table as well as a removable tabletop serving tray. It is the perfect size for carrying plates, pitchers, glasses, and many other items from the kitchen.*

## Special Tools & Techniques

- Miter

## Materials

- 33 linear feet of 1x4 pine
- 6 linear feet of 1x1 pine
- 7 linear feet of 1x6 pine
- Scrap wood

## Hardware

- 120 $1^{1}/_{4}$" wood screws
- 10 $2^{1}/_{2}$" wood screws
- 20 $1^{5}/_{8}$" wood screws

## Cutting List

| Code | Description | Qty. | Materials | Dimensions |
|------|-------------|------|-----------|------------|
| A | Side Connector | 2 | 1x4 pine | $15^{1}/_{2}$" long |
| B | Leg | 8 | 1x4 pine | 16" long |
| C | Side Spacer | 2 | 1x4 pine | $15^{1}/_{2}$" long |
| D | Front/Back Connector | 2 | 1x4 pine | 14" long |
| E | Front/Back Spacer | 2 | 1x4 pine | $8^{1}/_{2}$" long |
| F | Leg Support | 4 | 1x1 pine | 16" long |
| G | Corner Support | 4 | 1x4 pine | $8^{1}/_{2}$" long |
| H | Top Slat | 3 | 1x6 pine | 20" long |
| I | Long Tray Side | 2 | 1x4 pine | 22" long |
| J | Short Tray Side | 2 | 1x4 pine | $17^{1}/_{2}$" long |
| K | Narrow Tray Slat | 3 | 1x4 pine | $20^{1}/_{2}$" long |
| L | Wide Tray Slat | 1 | 1x6 pine | $20^{1}/_{2}$" long |

## Constructing the Side Assemblies

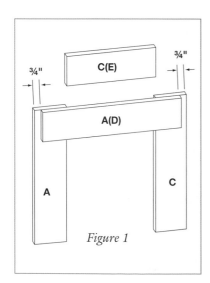

*Figure 1*

1 The table consists of two side assemblies: a front assembly and a back assembly. The construction of these assemblies is shown in *figure 2* on page 69.

2 To make the side assemblies, cut two Side Connectors (A) from 1x4 pine, each measuring $15^{1}/_{2}$ inches.

3 Cut four Legs (B) from 1x4 pine, each measuring l6 inches.

4 Position one Side Connector (A) over two Legs (B), spacing the pieces as shown in *figure 1*. The upper end of the Side Connector (A) should be flush with the ends of the Legs (B), and there should be a $^{3}/_{4}$-inch offset at each end of the Side Connector (A). Apply glue to the meeting surfaces, and screw through the Side Connector (A) into the Legs (B), using two $1^{1}/_{4}$-inch wood screws on each joint.

5  Cut two Side Spacers (C) from 1x4 pine, each measuring 15¹⁄₂ inches.

6  Place one Side Spacer (C) between the two legs (B), as shown in *figure 1* on page 68 Apply glue to the meeting surfaces, and screw through the Side Connector (A) into the Side Spacer (C), using three evenly spaced 1¹⁄₄-inch wood screws.

7  Repeat steps 1 through 6 to construct a second side assembly, using the remaining two Legs (B) and the remaining Side Connector (A) and Side Spacer (C).

## Constructing the Front & Back Assemblies

1  The front and back assemblies are constructed in the same fashion as the side assemblies (see *figure 1*). Cut four Legs (B) from 1x4 pine, each measuring 16 inches.

2  Cut two Front/Back Connectors (D) from 1x4 pine, each measuring 14 inches.

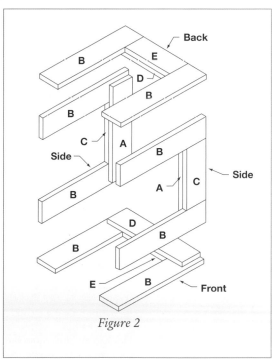

*Figure 2*

3 Assemble two Legs (B) and one Front/Back Connector (D), spacing the parts as shown in *figure 1*. Again, the pieces should be flush at the top, and there should be a $^{3}/_{4}$-inch offset at the ends of the Front/Back Connector (D). Secure the joints with glue and two $1^{1}/_{4}$- inch wood screws.

4 Cut two Front/Back Spacers (E) from 1x4 pine, each measuring $8^{1}/_{2}$ inches.

5 Insert one Front/Back Spacer (E) between the two Legs (B). Apply glue to the meeting surfaces, and screw through the Front/Back Connector (D) into the Front/Back Spacer (E), using three evenly spaced $1^{1}/_{4}$-inch wood screws.

6 Repeat steps 1 through 5 to construct a back assembly identical to the front assembly, using the remaining two Legs (B), as well as the remaining Front/Back Connector (D) and Front/Back Spacer (E).

## Joining the Assemblies

1 Attach the two side assemblies to the front and back assemblies as shown in *figure 2* on page 69 making certain that the Legs (B) are flush at both the top and the bottom. Note that the front and back assemblies overlap the exposed ends of the side assemblies. When properly assembled, the outside of the table should measure $15^{1}/_{2}$x$18^{1}/_{2}$ inches. Apply glue to the meeting surfaces, and screw through the overlapping Legs (B) into the adjoining Legs (B), using $1^{1}/_{4}$-inch wood screws spaced about every 5 inches.

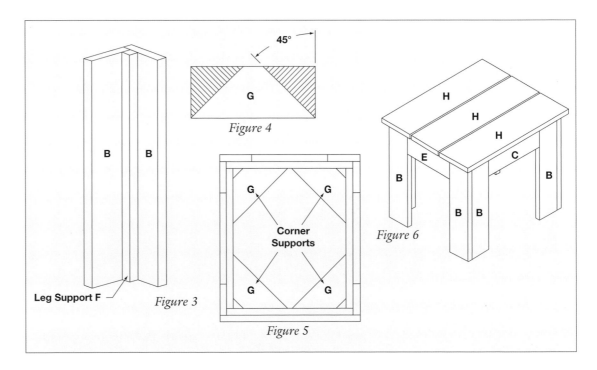

Figure 3

Leg Support F

B    B

45°

G

*Figure 4*

G    G

Corner
Supports

G    G

*Figure 5*

H

H

H

E

C

B    B

B    B

*Figure 6*

2 Cut four Leg Supports (F) from 1x1 pine, each measuring 16 inches.

3 Apply glue to the meeting surfaces, and attach one Leg Support (F) to the inside corner of each of the four leg assemblies, as shown in *figure 3* on page 70. Screw through the Leg Supports (F) into each of the Legs (B), using four evenly spaced 1¼-inch wood screws.

4 Cut four Corner Supports (G) from 1x4 pine, each measuring 8½ inches.

5 Set each Corner Support (G) on its face, and miter the ends at opposing 45° angles, as shown in *figure 4* on page 70.

6 Using *figure 5* on page 70 as a guide, position the mitered Corner Supports (G), making sure that their faces are flush with the top edges of the assembled frame. Apply glue to the meeting surfaces, and screw at an angle through the edges of each of the Corner Supports (G) into the frame assembly, using a 2½-inch wood screw on each joint.

## Adding the Top

1 Cut three Top Slats (H) from 1x6 pine, each measuring 20 inches.

2 Place the three Top Slats (H) over the top of the assembly, spacing them evenly so that the tabletop measures 17 inches wide and 20 inches long, and the tabletop extends ¾ inch over the sides, back, and front of the assembly, as shown in *figure 6* on page 70.

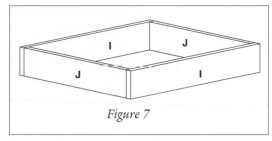

Figure 7

3 Apply glue to the meeting surfaces, and screw through the Top Slats (H) into the Corner Supports (G) and the frame assembly, using 1¼-inch wood screws.

## Making the Table Tray

1 Cut two Long Tray Sides (I) from 1x4 pine, each measuring 22 inches.

2 Cut two Short Tray Sides (J) from 1x4 pine, each measuring 17½ inches.

3 Position the two Long Tray Sides (I) on edge, parallel to each other and 17½ inches apart. Fit the two Short Tray Sides (J) between the ends of the Long Tray Sides (I), as shown in *figure 7*. Apply glue to the meeting surfaces, and screw through the Long Tray Sides (I) into the ends of the Short Tray Sides (J), using two 1⅝ inch wood screws on each joint.

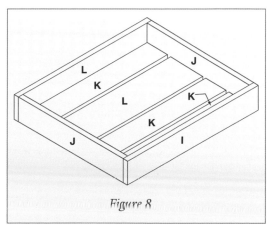

Figure 8

4 Cut three Narrow Tray Slats (K) from 1x4 pine, each measuring 20½ inches.

5 Cut one Wide Tray Slat (L) from 1x6 pine, measuring 20½ inches.

6 Place the assembled tray sides (I and J) on a flat surface. In order to elevate the Narrow and Wide Tray Slats (K and L), place several pieces of 1-inch-thick scrap wood inside the assembly. Then place the four Slats (K and L) inside the assembly, as shown in *figure 8* on page 71, spacing them evenly over the bottom. Apply glue to the meeting surfaces, and screw through the Short Tray Sides (J) into the Slats (K and L), using two 1⅝-inch screws on each joint.

## Finishing

1 Fill the cracks, crevices, and screw holes with wood filler.

2 Sand the completed tray and table thoroughly.

3 Stain or paint the table and tray the color(s) of your choice, or leave the natural color and seal with a waterproof sealer.

# Coffee Table

*Every outdoor living area needs a coffee table, and we are very proud of this one. It has a tiled center section, so it is easy to clean up and always looks nice. The table legs are adorned with fence-post finials, making the table seem a more complicated project than it actually is.*

## Special Tools & Techniques

- Framing or speed square
- Tile cutter (optional)
- $1/8''$ V trowel
- Rubber tile float

## Materials

- 16 linear feet of 1x4 pine
- 2'x4' sheet of $3/4''$ plywood*
- 6 linear feet of 4x4 pine
- 4 fence-post finials, approximately 3" high and $3^1/2''$ in diameter*
- 32 4"-square tiles, or your choice of any tile that covers an area measuring $3^1/2$ sq. feet
- Waterproof tile adhesive
- 5 lbs. tile grout
- Small bottle of grout sealer

## Hardware

- 25 $1^1/4''$ (3d) finish nails
- 35 $1^5/8$-inch wood screws
- 10 $2^1/2$-inch wood screws

## *Notes on Materials

The wooden finials we used for the table "feet" are designed to be used on a fence post. They can be purchased at most building-supply stores and have a large screw already attached in the center. The ones we used are 3 inches tall. You can substitute any exterior-rated finial you like, but if it is taller than 3 inches, be sure to adjust the length of your table legs accordingly, or your completed coffee table will not be the correct height.

When choosing tile for this table, consider that you must cover an area measuring $3^1/2$ square feet. We used standard 4-inch-square tiles. If the tile you purchased does not fit within these dimensions, you can either alter the dimensions of the table or cut some of the tiles to fit, using a tile cutter. Tile cutters can be rented at home centers and hardware stores, or some home centers will cut them for you.

## Cutting List

| Code | Description | Qty. | Materials | Dimensions |
|------|-------------|------|-----------|------------|
| A | Long Trim | 2 | 1x4 pine | $39^1/2''$ long |
| B | Short Trim | 2 | 1x4 pine | $16^1/2''$ long |
| C | Top | 1 | $3/4''$ plywood | $19^1/2''$x$35^1/2''$ |
| D | Long Side | 2 | 1x4 pine | $35^1/2''$ long |
| E | Short Side | 2 | 1x4 pine | 21" long |
| F | Leg | 4 | 1x4 pine | 13" long |

## Making the Tabletop

1 Cut two Long Trims (A) from 1x4 pine, each measuring $39^1/2$ inches.

2 Cut two Short Trims (B) from 1x4 pine, each measuring $16^1/2$ inches

3 Cut one Top (C) from $^3/_4$-inch plywood, measuring $19^1/_2$x$35^1/_2$ inches.

4 Place the Long Trims (A) flat on the work surface, parallel to each other and $16^1/_4$ inches apart.

5 Position the Short Trims (B) between the Long Trims (A), then place the Top (C) over the Short and Long Trims (A and B), as shown in *figure l*. When the

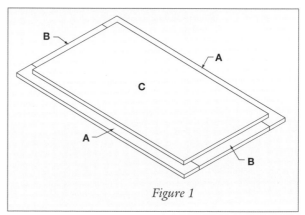

*Figure 1*

Top (C) is perfectly centered, the Short and Long Trims (A and B) should extend beyond the Top (C) by 2 inches on all sides. Apply glue to the meeting surfaces, and nail through the Top (C) into the Long and Short Trims (A and B), using $1^1/_4$-inch finish nails every 6 inches.

## Making the Base

1 Cut two Long Sides (D) from 1x4 pine, each measuring 35½ inches.

2 Cut two Short Sides (E) from 1x4 pine, each measuring 21 inches.

3 Place the two Long Sides (D) on edge, parallel to each other and 19½ inches apart. Fit the two Short Sides (E) over the ends of the two Long Sides (D) to form a rectangle measuring 21x37 inches (see *figure 2*). Apply glue to the meeting surfaces, and screw through the Short Sides (E) into the ends of the Long Sides (D), using two 1⅝-inch wood screws on each joint.

4 Place the assembled Long and Short Sides (D and E) over the Top (C) so that the assembled Long and Short Sides (D and E) fit around the plywood as shown in *figure 3*. Apply glue to the meeting surfaces, and screw through the Long and Short Sides (D and E) into the plywood Top (C) every 6 inches, using 1⅝-inch wood screws.

## Attaching the Legs

1 Cut four Legs (F) from 4x4 pine, each measuring 13 inches.

2 Place the four Legs (F) at the four corners of the assembled Top (C), as shown in *figure 4*. Use a square to make sure the Legs (F) are straight so that the table is not crooked when turned right side up. Apply glue to the meeting surfaces, and screw through the Long and Short Sides (D and E) into the Legs (F), using 2½-inch wood screws (4 screws in each leg, and 2 screws in each side).

3 To attach the fence-post finials to the exposed ends of the four Legs (F), predrill a starter hole in the center of each Leg (F). Screw a fence-post finial into each Leg (F).

## Adding the Tile

1 Following the manufacturer's directions, carefully spread an even coat of the tile adhesive over the surface of the Top (C) with an ⅛-inch V trowel.

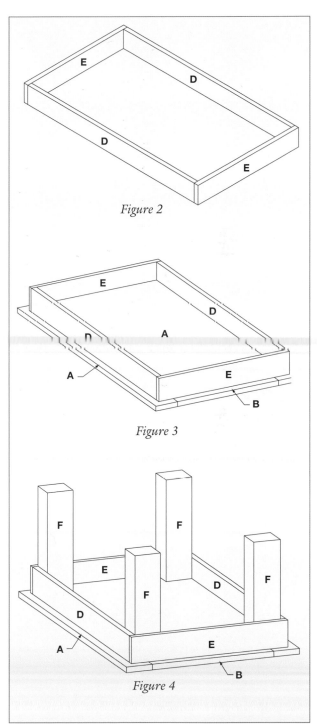

Figure 2

Figure 3

Figure 4

**2** Place the tiles on the adhesive one at a time, making sure that they are positioned correctly. Do not slide the tiles, or the adhesive will be forced up on the sides of the tile. Let the adhesive dry overnight.

**3** Mix the tile grout according to the manufacturer's directions.

**4** Spread the grout over the tile using a rubber-surfaced float held at a 45° angle so that the grout is forced evenly into the spaces between the tiles.

**5** Use a wet sponge to wipe the excess grout off the tiles and joints; if you let this excess grout dry, the hardened grout will be very difficult to remove. Try to use as little water as possible when removing the excess, so that you do not thin the grout that remains. Let the grout dry overnight.

**6** Rinse the remaining film from the tile and wipe it with an old towel.

**7** Apply grout sealer, following the manufacturer's directions.

## Finishing

**1** Fill any cracks or crevices with wood filler, and thoroughly sand all surfaces of the completed table.

**2** Either paint or stain the wood portions of the coffee table the color of your choice, or simply leave it natural.

# Seating

# Adirondack Chair

*Our own version of this furniture classic retains its essential characteristics: it's a perfect place to sit and enjoy a summer evening. The chair is equally at home in a garden, on a front porch, or on a boat dock. We originally planned to build just one chair, but quickly decided that one was just not enough. The chairs have become our family favorites.*

## Special Tools & Techniques

- C-clamp
- Bar clamp (optional)

## Materials
### (for one chair)

- 17 linear feet of 1x6 pine
- 28 linear feet of 1x4 pine
- 4 linear feet of 1x2 pine
- 3 linear feet of 2x4 pine

## Hardware

- 50 3dx1-$\frac{1}{4}$" nails
- 60 1$\frac{1}{4}$" screws
- 4 carriage bolts, $\frac{3}{8}$"x2" with washer and nut
- 2 carriage bolts, $\frac{3}{8}$"x3" with washer and nut

## Cutting List

| Code | Description | Qty. | Materials | Dimensions |
| --- | --- | --- | --- | --- |
| A | Seat Brace | 2 | 1x6 pine | 39" long |
| B | Front Seat Trim | 1 | 1x6 pine | 22" long |
| C | Seat Side | 2 | 1x4 pine | 24" long |
| D | Seat Slat | 6 | 1x4 pine | 22" long |
| E | Short Back Slat | 2 | 1x4 pine | 28" long |
| F | Medium Back Slat | 2 | 1x4 pine | 30" long |
| G | Long Back Slat | 1 | 1x6 pine | 32" long |
| H | Back Support | 2 | 1x2 pine | 22" long |
| I | Arm | 2 | 1x6 pine | 27" long |
| J | Arm Connector | 1 | 2x4 pine | 28$\frac{1}{2}$" long |
| K | Arm Brace | 2 | 1x4 pine | 9" long |

## Making the Seat

1 The trademark of the Adirondack chair is the angled seat. The braces that support the seat are simple to construct, but require exact dimensions to work. Cut two seat braces (A) from 1x6 pine, each measuring 39 inches long.

To achieve the necessary angles for the seat braces (A), refer to *figure 1*. Portions of the seat braces must be cut away. This is as simple as "connect the letters." Following the measurements in *figure 1*, label each point, and

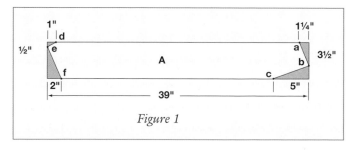

*Figure 1*

draw a straight line from "a" to "b," "b" to "c," "d" to "e," and "e" to "f." Cut along the lines you have just drawn to eliminate the shaded portions of one seat brace (A), as shown in *figure 1* on page 78. Use the resulting seat brace (A) as a pattern to cut the other seat brace (A).

2 Cut one front seat trim (B) from 1x6 pine, measuring 22 inches long.

3 The front seat trim (B) will be used to connect the two seat braces (A). Position the two seat braces parallel to each other and on edge, with the "e-f" edge facing up, 20½ inches apart.

Fit the seat trim (B) over the "e-f" edges, as shown in *figure 2*. Nail through the front seat trim (B) into the ends of the seat braces (A) using three 1¼ inch long nails on each joint.

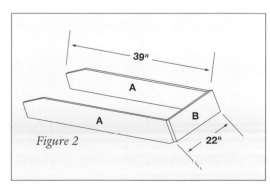

*Figure 2*

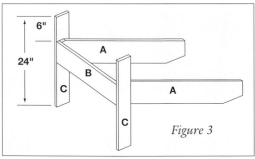

**24"**

**6"**

A

B

C

A

C

*Figure 3*

4 Cut two seat sides (C) from 1x4 pine, each measuring 24 inches long.

5 Turn the assembly right side up. Follow *figure 3* to connect the seat sides (C) to the seat braces (A), attaching them 6 inches from the top edge of the seat sides (C) and flush with the seat trim (B) on the front. Use two 2-inch-long carriage bolts to secure each of the joints, spacing them about 3 inches apart.

## Adding the Seat Slats

1 Cut six seat slats (D) from 1x4 pine, each measuring 22 inches long.

2 For comfort, round off the long edge of the slat (D) that will be attached to the front of the chair. Attach this slat to the "d-e" edges of the seat braces (A) so that it extends $1^3/_8$ inches over the seat trim (B), as shown in *figure 4*. Use two $1^1/_4$-inch-long nails on each side, and four nails spaced evenly across the front.

3 Attach the next four seat slats (D) to the seat braces (A), as shown in *figure 4*, spacing them approximately $^3/_8$ inch apart. Use two $1^1/_4$- inch-long nails on each joint. Attach the sixth slat (D) 2 inches from the fifth seat slat (D). This space will be needed later to accommodate the back of the chair.

## Constructing the Back

1 Cut two short back slats (E) from 1x4 pine, each measuring 28 inches long.

2 Cut two medium back slats (F) from 1x4 pine, each measuring 30 inches long.

3 Cut one long back slat (G) from 1x6 pine, measuring 32 inches long.

4 Cut two back supports (H) from 1x2 pine, each measuring 22 inches long.

5 Place the two back supports (H) on a level surface, parallel to each other and $22^1/_2$ inches apart.

6 Place the five back slats (E, F, and G) on top of the two back supports (H), spaced evenly, approximately $^1/_2$ inch apart, as shown in *figure 5*. Place the two short back slats (E) on the outside, the two medium back slats (F) in the middle, and the long back slat (G) in the center. Make sure that the back slats are square to the back supports (H). Note that the ends of all of the back slats (E, F, and G) are even with one back support (H) at what will be the lower chair back, and the opposite ends of the back slats are at various lengths at what will be the top of the chair back. Screw through each of the back slats (E, F, and G) into each of the back supports (H). Use two $1^1/_4$-inch-long screws at each joint.

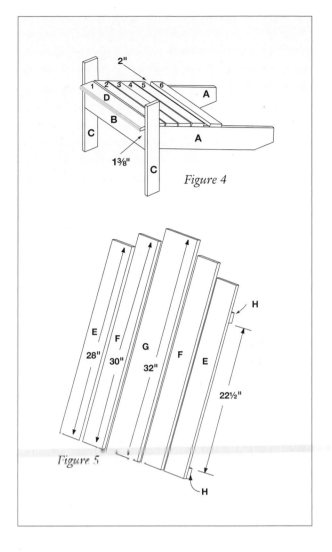

Figure 4

Figure 5

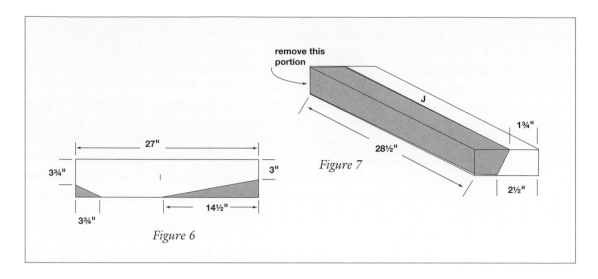

remove this portion

27"

3¾"

3"

3¾"

14½"

3¾"

*Figure 6*

J

28½"

1¾"

2½"

*Figure 7*

## Constructing the Arm Assembly

1 Cut two arms (I) from 1x6 pine, each measuring 27 inches long.

2 Follow the diagram shown in *figure 6* to remove the shaded portions from one arm (I) in the same manner you used to cut the seat braces (step 1, page 78). Use this cut arm as a pattern to cut the other arm (I).

3 Cut one arm connector (J) from 2x4 pine, measuring 28½ inches long.

4 In order to accommodate the back of the chair, one edge of the arm connector (J) must be angled. Rip the arm connector (J) 20 degrees along its length, as shown in *figure 7*.

5 Place the two arms (I) over the ends of the arm connector (J). Make certain that the space between the two arms (J) is just slightly over 22 inches in order to accommodate the back assembly. Clamp the two arms (I) to the ends of the arm connector (J).

## Final Assembly

1 Although you can perform this assembly with the assistance of bar clamps, it's easier to enlist the aid of a helper. First, fit the back

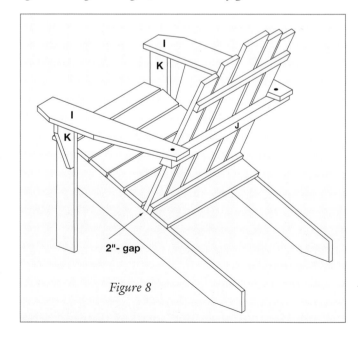

I

K

I

K

J

2"- gap

*Figure 8*

assembly into the 2-inch-wide gap in the seat slats, with the back slats facing the front of the chair, as shown in *figure 8*. Then wrap the clamped arm assembly around the back of the chair so that the front of the arm rests on the chair sides. Have the helper sit in the chair; then adjust the clamped arm assembly so that the arms are level to the floor and the back of the chair is at the most comfortable angle. Screw through the arms (I) to secure them to the chair sides, using two 114-inch-long screws on each joint. Mark the placement of the arm connector on the back assembly. (Remove the helper!)

2 Screw through each of the back slats (E, F, and G) into the arm connector (J). Use two $1^1/_4$-inch-long screws on each of the joints.

3 Drill a $^3/_8$"-wide hole in each arm (I) through the arm connector (J), and secure the joint by inserting a 3-inch-long carriage bolt through the drilled holes. Add a washer and a nut, and tighten the bolt securely.

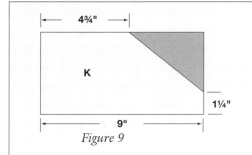

4 Cut two arm braces (K) from 1x4 pine, each measuring 9 inches long. Follow the diagram in *figure 9* to remove the shaded portion of one of the arm braces. Use the resulting piece as a pattern to mark and cut the second arm brace.

*Figure 9*

5 Fit the arm braces (K) onto the seat sides (C), under the arms, with the 9-inch-long edge facing the seat sides (C), as shown in *figure 8* on page 82. Screw through the seat sides (C) and arms (I) into the arm braces (K) using two or three $1^1/_2$-inch-long screws on each joint.

## Finishing

1 Fill any screw holes with wood filler. Sand all surfaces thoroughly. Remember that people will be sitting on this project, so don't spare the sandpaper! No one likes splinters in the derriere!

2 We primed and painted our Adirondack chair, but you can let it weather naturally, or stain it the color of your choice.

# Adirondack Sofa

*We have made many Adirondack chairs over the years and thought it would be neat to have one that was just a bit larger. So this time we built a good-sized bench. Whether you share the bench with a friend or stretch out on it all by yourself, you will enjoy the traditional Adirondack shape.*

---

### Special Tools & Techniques

- C clamp
- Bar clamp (optional)

### Materials

- 30 linear feet of 1x6 pine
- 56 linear feet of 1x4 pine
- 5 linear feet of 1x2 pine
- 5 linear feet of 2x4 pine

### Hardware

- 50 1⅝" wood screws
- 15 1¼" (3d) finish nails
- 60 1¼" wood screws

---

### Cutting List

| Code | Description | Qty. | Materials | Dimensions |
|------|-------------|------|-----------|------------|
| A | Seat Brace | 3 | 1x6 pine | 39" long |
| B | Front Seat Trim | 1 | 1x6 pine | 46" long |
| C | Seat Side | 2 | 1x4 pine | 24" long |
| D | Seat Slat | 6 | 1x4 pine | 46" long |
| E | Back Slat | 12 | 1x4 pine | 32" long |
| F | Back Support | 2 | 1x2 pine | 46" long |
| G | Arm | 2 | 1x6 pine | 27" long |
| H | Arm Connector | 1 | 2x4 pine | 52" long |
| I | Arm Brace | 2 | 1x4 pine | 9" long |

## Making the Seat

1 The trademark of the Adirondack sofa is the angled seat. The braces that support the seat are simple to construct but must be cut to the exact dimensions to work. Cut three Seat Braces (A) from 1x6 pine, each measuring 39 inches. To achieve the necessary angles for the Seat Braces (A), refer to *figure 1*. Portions of the Seat Braces (A) must be cut away. This is as simple as "connect the letters." Following the measurements in *figure 1*, label each point, then draw a straight line from "a" to "b," "b" to "c," "d" to "e," and "e" to "f." Cut along the lines you have just drawn to eliminate the shaded portions of one Seat Brace (A), as shown in *figure 1*. Use the resulting Seat Brace (A) as a pattern to cut the other two Seat Braces (A).

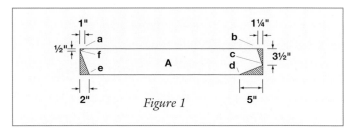

*Figure 1*

2 Cut one Front Seat Trim (B) from 1x6 pine, measuring 46 inches.

3 The Front Seat Trim (B) will be used to connect the three Seat Braces (A). Position two Seat Braces (A) parallel to each other and on edge, with the e-f edge facing up, 44$^{1}/_{2}$ inches apart. Fit the Front Seat Trim (B) over the e-f edge, as shown in figure 2. Screw through the Front Seat Trim (B) into the ends of the Seat Braces (A), using two 1$^{5}/_{8}$-inch wood screws on each joint. Center the third Seat Brace (A) between the two far Seat Braces (A), and screw through the Front Seat Trim (B) into the center Seat Brace (A), using 1$^{5}/_{8}$-inch wood screws (see *figure 2* on page 86).

4 Cut two Seat Sides (C) from 1x4 pine, each measuring 24 inches.

5 Turn the assembly right side up. Using *figure 3* as a guide, attach the Seat Sides (C) to the Seat Braces (A), 6 inches from the top edge of the Seat Sides (C) and flush with the Seat Trim (B) on the front. Drill a $^3/_8$-inch-diameter hole through each seat side (c) and seat brace (a), spacing the bolts about 3 inches apart. Secure the joint by slipping a 2-inch carriage bolt through the holes, and tighten the bolts with washers and nuts.

## Adding the Seat Slats

1 Cut six Seat Slats (D) from 1x4 pine, each measuring 46 inches.

2 For comfort, round off the long edge of one of the Seat Slats (D), which will be attached to the front of the bench. Attach this Seat Slat (D) to the f-a edge of the Seat Braces (A) so that it extends $1^3/_8$ inches over the Seat Trim (B), as shown in *figure 4* on page 87. Use two $1^1/_4$-inch finish nails on each side, and four $1^1/_4$-inch finish nails spaced evenly across the front.

3 Attach the next four Seat Slats (D) to the Seat Braces (A), as shown in *figure 4* on page 87, spacing them approximately $^3/_8$ inch apart. Use two $1^5/_8$-inch wood screws on each joint.

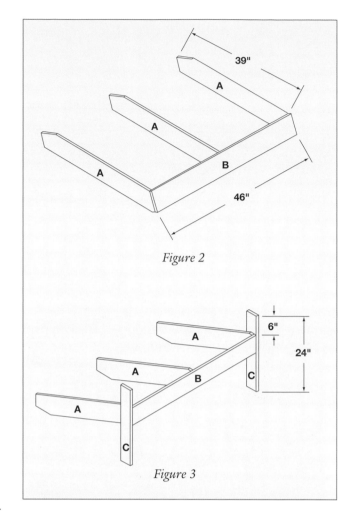

Figure 2

Figure 3

Attach the sixth Seat Slat (D) 2 inches from the fifth Seat Slat (D). (This extra space will be needed later to accommodate the back of the bench.)

## Constructing the Back

1 Cut 12 Back Slats (E) from 1x4 pine, measuring 32 inches.

2 Cut two Back Supports (F) from 1x2 pine, each measuring 46 inches.

3 Place the two Back Supports (F) on a level surface, parallel to each other and 24 inches apart.

4 Place the 12 Back Slats (E) on top of the two Back Supports (F), spaced evenly approximately ³/₈ inch apart, as shown in *figure 5*. Make sure that the Back Slats (E) are square to the Back Supports (F). Note that the ends of all of the Back Slats (E) are even with one Back Support (F) at what will be the lower bench back. Screw through each of the Back Slats (E) into each of the Back Supports (F). Use two 1¹/₄-inch wood screws at each joint.

5 Using *figure 6* on page 88 as a guide, cut off the two outer corners of the assembled back.

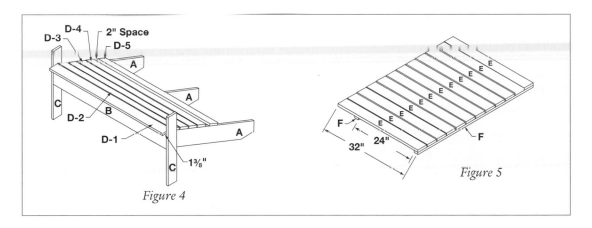

Figure 4

Figure 5

## Constructing the Arm Assembly

1 Cut two Arms (G) from 1x6 pine, each measuring 27 inches.

2 Using *figure 7* on page 88 as a guide, remove the shaded portions from one Arm (G) in the same manner as you cut the Seat Braces (A) (see *figure 1* on page 84). Use this Arm (G) as a pattern to cut the other Arm (G).

3 Cut one Arm Connector (H) from 2x4 pine, measuring 52 inches.

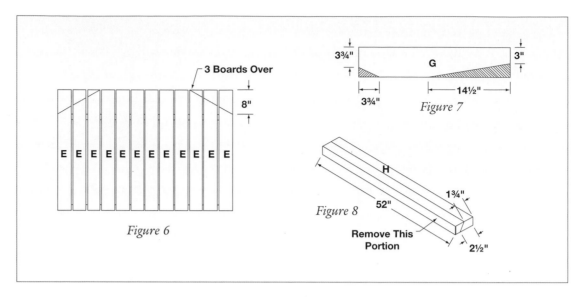

3 Boards Over

8"

E E E E E E E E E E E

*Figure 6*

3¾"    G    3"

14½"
3¾"
*Figure 7*

H
1¾"
52"
*Figure 8*
Remove This
Portion
2½"

4 In order to accommodate the back of the bench, one edge of the Arm Connector (H) must be angled. Rip the arm connector (H), roughly 33° along its length, as shown in *figure 8*.

5 Place the two Arms (G) over the ends of the Arm Connector (H). Make certain that the space between the two Arms (G) is just slightly more than 46 inches in order to accommodate the back assembly. Clamp the two Arms (G) to the ends of the Arm Connector (H), using C clamps.

## Final Assembly

1 Although you can perform this assembly with the assistance of bar clamps, it is easier to enlist the aid of a helper. First, fit the back assembly into the 2-inch-wide gap in the seat slats, with the back slats facing the front of the bench, as shown in *figure 9*. Then wrap the clamped arm assembly around the back of the bench so that the front of the Arm (G) rests on the bench sides. Have the helper sit in the bench, then adjust the clamped arm assembly so that the Arms (G) are level to the

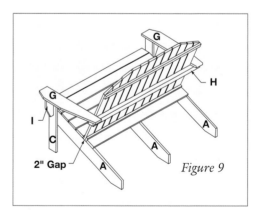

*Figure 9*

floor and the back of the bench is at the most comfortable angle. Screw through the Arms (G) to secure them to the bench sides, using two 1¼-inch wood screws on each joint. Mark the placement of the Arm Connector (H) on the back assembly.

2 Screw through each of the Back Slats (E) into the Arm Connector (H). Use two 1¼-inch wood screws on each joint.

3 Drill a ⅜-inch-diameter hole in each Arm (G) through the Arm Connector (H), and secure the joint by inserting a 3-inch carriage bolt through the drilled holes. Add a washer and a nut, and tighten the bolt securely.

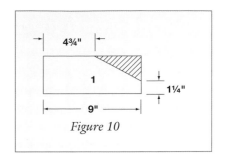

*Figure 10*

4 Cut two Arm Braces (I) from 1x4 pine, each measuring 9 inches. Using *figure 10* as a guide, remove the shaded portion of one of the Arm Braces (I). Use this Arm Brace (I) as a pattern to mark and cut the second Arm Brace (I).

5 Fit the Arm Braces (I) onto the Seat Sides (C), under the arms, with the 9-inch edge facing the Seat Sides (C), as shown in *figure 9*. Screw through the Seat Sides (C) and Arms (G) into the Arm Braces (I), using two or three 1⅝-inch wood screws on each joint.

## Finishing

1 Fill any screw holes with wood filler. Sand all surfaces thoroughly. (Remember that people will be sitting on this project, so you will want a very smooth surface.)

2 Let the sofa weather naturally or stain it the color of your choice.

# Garden Chair

*Build two of these chairs and group them with our Garden Sofa (page 95), and you'll have a pleasant area for backyard conversation. Or build a single chair, set our Occasional Table (page 48) next to it, and create a great place for drinking iced tea and reading a good book. This comfortable chair is sturdy enough to withstand summer winds, too!*

## Materials

- 30 linear feet of 2x4 pine
- 8 linear feet of 1x4 pine
- 12 linear feet of 1x2 pine

## Hardware

- 50 3dx1¼" nails
- 25 2½" screws
- 30 3½" screws

## Cutting List

| Code | Description | Qty. | Materials | Dimensions |
|------|-------------|------|-----------|------------|
| A | Horizontal Side | 4 | 2x4 pine | 15½" long |
| B | Long Vertical Side | 2 | 2x4 pine | 35" long |
| C | Short Vertical Side | 2 | 2x4 pine | 29" long |
| D | Outer Seat Support | 2 | 2x4 pine | 20" long |
| E | Inner Seat Support | 2 | 2x4 pine | 19½" long |
| F | Wide Slat | 4 | 1x4 pine | 20" long |
| G | Narrow Slat | 2 | 1x2 pine | 20" long |
| H | Horizontal Back | 2 | 2x4 pine | 20" long |
| I | Back Slat | 7 | 1x2 pine | 10" long |

## Constructing the Chair Sides

1 Cut four horizontal sides (A) from 2x4 pine, each measuring 15½ inches long.

2 Cut two long vertical sides (B) from 2x4 pine, each measuring 35 inches long.

3 Cut two short vertical sides (C) from 2x4 pine, each measuring 29 inches long.

4 Place two horizontal sides (A) parallel to each other, and between one long vertical side (B) and one short vertical side (C), as shown in *figure 1* on page 92. The top horizontal side (A) is exactly even with the end of the short vertical side (C), and the bottom horizontal side is 14 inches from the other end of that same vertical side (C), as shown in *figure 1* on page 92. Apply glue to the meeting surfaces, and screw at an angle through the edges of the horizontal sides (A) into both the long and short vertical sides (B and C), using two 3½-inch-long screws on each joint.

5 Repeat step 4 to assemble the other side.

## Adding the Seat

1 Cut two outer seat supports (D) from 2x4 pine, each measuring 20 inches long.

2 For the next step you may want to ask a willing helper to assist. If no one is available, use a bar clamp to hold the assembly while you screw it together. Place the side assemblies on one 35-inch-long edge, parallel to each other and 20 inches apart. Fit one outer seat support (D) between the two side assemblies, 14 inches from the upper edge of the two side assemblies. The top edge of the outer seat support (D) should be exactly even with the top edge of the

lower horizontal side (A), as shown in *figure 2*. Screw through the side assemblies into the ends of the outer seat supports (D), using two 2¹/₂-inch-long screws on each joint.

3 Turn the assembly upside down and attach the remaining outer seat support (D) to the opposite side of the side assemblies, in the same manner that you used in step 2.

4 Cut two inner seat supports (E) from 2x4 pine, each measuring 19 ¹/₂ inches long.

5 Fit one inner seat support (E)—wide surface up—between the two outer seat supports (D), ¹/₂ inch below the top edge of the lower horizontal side (A), as shown in *figure 3*. Screw through both of the outer seat supports (D) into the ends of the inner seat support (E), using two 2¹/₂-inch-long screws. Also screw through the lower horizontal side (A) into the edge of the inner seat support (E), using three 2¹/₂-inch-long screws spaced evenly along the joint.

6 Repeat step 5 to attach the remaining inner seat support (E) on the opposite side of the chair.

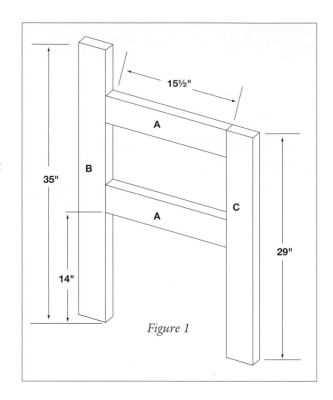

*Figure 1*

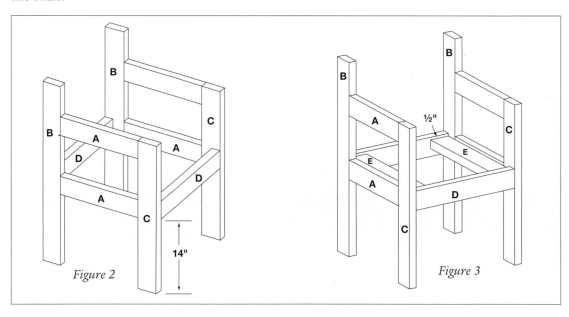

*Figure 2*

*Figure 3*

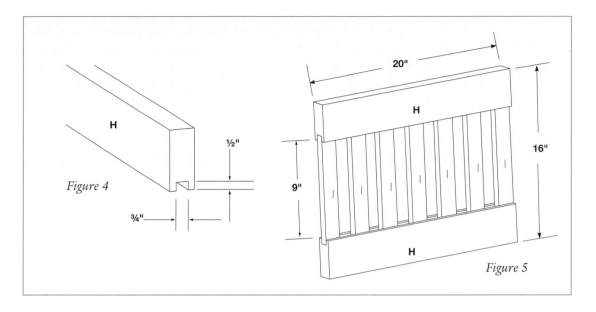

*Figure 4*

*Figure 5*

## Adding the Seat Slats

1 The chair seat is comprised of two different widths of wood that are alternated. Cut four wide slats (F) from 1x4 pine, each measuring 20 inches long.

2 Cut two narrow slats (G) from 1x2 pine, each measuring 20 inches long.

3 Begin by placing a wide slat (F) over the seat support (E) on the front of the chair. Then place a narrow slat (G) next to it. Continue alternating the wide and narrow slats, ending with two wide slats (F) at the back of the chair, as shown in *figure 6*. Adjust the spacing so that the slats are approximately ³/₈ inch apart. Nail through each of the slats (F and G) into the seat supports (E). Use two 1¹/₄-inch-long nails on each end of the wide slats (F), and one 1¹/₄-inch-long nail on each end of the narrow slats (G).

## Constructing the Chair Back

1 Cut two horizontal backs (H) from 2x4 pine, each measuring 20 inches long.

2 Cut a ³/₄-inch-wide dado, ¹/₂ inch deep down the length of one 20-inch-long edge of each of the horizontal backs (H), as shown in *figure 4*.

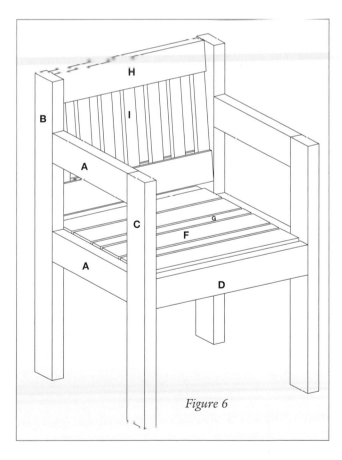

*Figure 6*

3 Cut seven back slats (I) from 1x2 pine, each measuring 10 inches long.

4 Working on a level surface, place the horizontal backs (H) parallel to each other, with the dadoes to the inside, as shown in *figure 5* on page 93. Fit the ends of the seven back slats (I) into the dadoes in each of the two horizontal backs (H). The spacing between the slats should be a little over $1\frac{1}{2}$ inches; try using an extra slat as a spacer. When the back slats (I) are properly fitted into the dadoes, the distance between the two horizontal backs (H) should measure 9 inches. The two outer back slats (I) should be even with the ends of the horizontal backs. When the position is perfect, the overall measurements of the back assembly should be 16 inches high and 20 inches wide. Apply glue to the meeting surfaces, and secure the slats by nailing through the dadoed edge of the horizontal backs (H) into the ends of the back slats (I), using two $1\frac{1}{4}$-inch-long nails on each joint.

5 Now you are ready to fit the back assembly between the two sides. To make the chair more comfortable, the back assembly is tilted at an angle—out at the top and in at the bottom. The tilt angle is determined by the width of the 2x4 on the side assemblies. The lower edge of the back is fitted flush with the front edge of the long vertical sides (B), and the upper edge of the back is fitted flush with the back edge of the long vertical sides (B), as shown in *figure 6* on page 93. When you have the back fitted perfectly, secure the assembly with bar clamps. Screw through the long vertical sides (B) into the ends of the horizontal backs (H), using two $3\frac{1}{2}$-inch-long screws on each joint.

## Finishing

1 Fill any cracks, crevices, or screw holes with wood filler, and thoroughly sand all surfaces of the completed chair.

2 Seal and paint or stain your chair the color of your choice.

# Garden Sofa

*This sofa would be at home in a garden, on a patio, or on a boat dock. It is constructed of pressure-treated wood so it can withstand the weather. The slats on the seat make the sofa comfortable and assure that rain will not puddle on top of it.*

## Special Tools & Techniques

- Dadoes
- Bar Clamps

## Materials

- 62 linear feet of 2x4 pine
- 20 linear feet of 1x4 pine
- 30 linear feet of 1x2 pine

## Hardware

- 30 3-$\frac{1}{2}$" screws
- 30 2-$\frac{1}{2}$" screws
- 160 3dx1$\frac{1}{4}$" nails
- 60 4dx1$\frac{1}{4}$" nails

## Cutting List

| Code | Description | Qty. | Materials | Dimensions |
|------|-------------|------|-----------|------------|
| A | Horizontal Side | 4 | 2x4 pine | 15$\frac{1}{2}$" long |
| B | Long Vertical Side | 2 | 2x4 pine | 35" long |
| C | Short Vertical Side | 2 | 2x4 pine | 29" long |
| D | Outer Seat Support | 2 | 2x4 pine | 59" long |
| E | Inner Seat Support | 5 | 2x4 pine | 19$\frac{1}{2}$" long |
| F | Wide Slat | 4 | 1x4 pine | 59" long |
| G | Narrow Slat | 2 | 1x2 pine | 59" long |
| H | Horizontal Back | 2 | 2x4 pine | 59" Long |
| I | Back Slat | 20 | 1x2 pine | 10" long |

## Constructing the Sofa Sides

1 Cut four horizontal sides (A) from 2x4 pine, each measuring 15$\frac{1}{2}$ inches long.

2 Cut two long vertical sides (B) from 2x4 pine, each measuring 35 inches long.

3 Cut two short vertical sides (C) from 2x4 pine, each measuring 29 inches long.

4 Place two horizontal sides (A) parallel to each other, and between one long vertical side (B) and one short vertical side (C), as shown in *figure 1* on page 97. The top horizontal side (A) is exactly even with the end of the short vertical side (C), and the bottom horizontal side (A) is 14 inches from the other end of that same vertical side (C), as shown in *figure 1*. Toenail through the edges of the horizontal sides (A), into both the long and short vertical sides (B and C), using two 3$\frac{1}{2}$-inch-long screws on each joint.

5 Repeat step 4 to assemble the second side.

## Adding the Seat

1 Cut two outer seat supports (D) from 2x4 pine, each measuring 59 inches long.

2 For the next step, you may want to ask a willing helper to assist. If no one is available (or willing), use a bar clamp to hold the assembly while you screw it together. Place each side assembly on its long vertical edge (B), 59 inches away from the other side, as shown in *figure 2* on page 97. Fit the front outer seat support (D) between the two short vertical sides (C), 14 inches from the lower edge of the sides. The top edge of the front outer seat support (D) should be exactly even with the top edge of the lower horizontal side (A). Screw through the side assemblies into the ends of the outer seat support (D), using two $2^1/_2$-long screws on each joint.

3 Repeat step 2 to attach the other outer seat support (D) to the back of the sofa between the side assemblies, as shown in *figure 2*. The top edge of the outer seat support (D) should be

exactly even with the top edge of the lower horizontal sides (A). Using two 2½-inch-long screws on each joint, screw through the long vertical sides (B) into the ends of the outer seat supports.

4 Cut five inner seat supports (E) from 2x4 pine, measuring 19½ inches long.

5 Turn the assembly right side up. As shown in *figure 3* on page 98, position one inner seat support (E) wide side up, between the two outer seat supports (D) and against one horizontal side (A), ¾ inch below the top of the outer seat supports (D). Screw through the outer seat supports (D) into the end of the inner seat support (E), using two 2½-inch-long screws.

6 Repeat this step with another inner seat support (E), placed at the other end of the outer seat supports.

7 Fit the remaining three inner seat supports (E) between the outer seat supports (D). Center one inner seat support (E), and space the other two evenly, as shown in *figure 3* on page 98. Remember to place them ¾ inch below the top of the outer seat supports (D). Screw through the outer seat supports (D) into the ends of the inner seat supports (E), using two 2½-inch-long screws on each joint.

## Adding the Seat Slats

1 The sofa seat is comprised of two different widths of wood that are alternated. Cut four wide slats (F) from 1x4 pine, each measuring 59 inches long.

2 Cut two narrow slats (G) from 1x2 pine, each measuring 59 inches long.

3 Begin by placing a wide slat (F) over the seat supports (E) on the front of the sofa. Then place a narrow slat (G) next to it. Continue alternating the wide and narrow slats, ending with two wide slats (F) at the back of the sofa, as shown in *figure 6* on page 99. Adjust the spacing so that the slats are approximately ⅜ inch apart. Nail through each of the slats (F and G) into the seat supports (E), securing each of the slats to one of the seat supports (E). Use two 1½-inch-long nails on each joint.

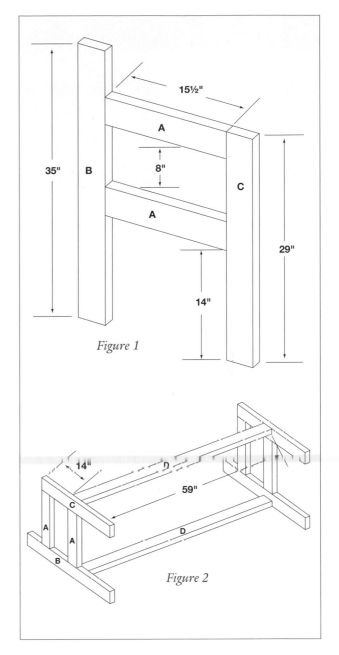

*Figure 1*

*Figure 2*

## Constructing the Sofa Back

1  Cut two horizontal backs (H) from 2x4 pine, each measuring 59 inches long.

2  Cut a ³/₄-inch-wide dado, ¹/₂-inch deep, down the length of one 59-inch edge of each of the horizontal backs (H), as shown in *figure 4*.

3  Cut 20 back slats (I) from 1x2 pine, each measuring 10 inches long.

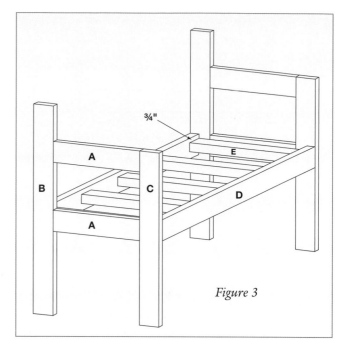

*Figure 3*

4  Working on a level surface, place the horizontal backs (H) parallel to each other, with the dadoes to the inside, as shown in *figure 5*. Fit the ends of the 20 back slats (I) into the dadoes in each of the two horizontal backs (H). The spacing between the slats should be approximately 1¹/₂ inches. In fact, we used an extra slat as a spacer. When the back slats (I) are properly fitted into the dadoes, the distance between the two horizontal backs (H) should be 9 inches. The two outer back slats (I) should be even with the ends of the horizontal backs (H). When the position is perfect, the overall measurements of the back assembly should be 16 inches high and 59 inches wide. Secure the slats by nailing through the dadoed edge of the horizontal back (H) into the ends of the back slats (I), using two 1¹/₄-inch-long nails on each joint.

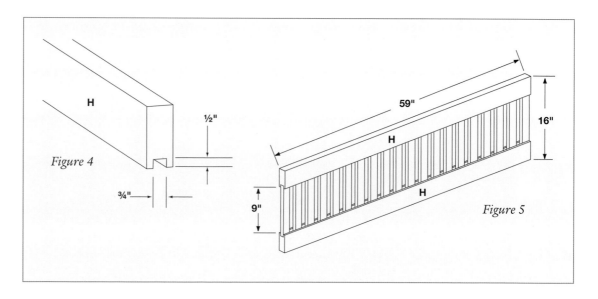

*Figure 4*

*Figure 5*

**5** Turn the assembly over and repeat the nailing procedure on the other side.

**6** It is now time to fit the back assembly between the two sides. To make the sofa more comfortable, the back assembly is tilted at an angle—out at the top and in at the bottom. The tilt angle is determined by the width of the 2x4 on the side assemblies. The lower edge of the back is fitted flush with the inside edge of the long vertical sides (B); the upper edge of the back is fitted flush with the outer edge of the long vertical sides (B), as shown in *figure 6*. When you have the back fitted perfectly, secure the assembly with bar clamps. Screw through the long vertical sides (B) into the ends of the horizontal backs (H), using two 3½-inch-long screws on each joint.

## Finishing the Sofa

**1** Fill any cracks, crevices, or screw holes with wood filler, and thoroughly sand all surfaces of the completed sofa.

**2** Seal and paint or stain your sofa the color of your choice.

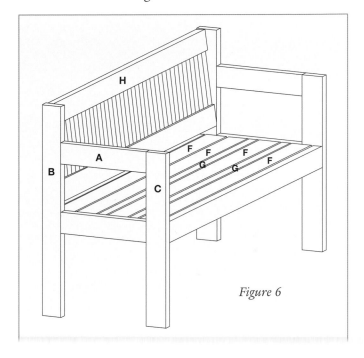

*Figure 6*

# Side Chair

*This handsome chair is comfortable, rugged enough for outdoor use, and very inexpensive to build. You might want to build four or more to go with the dining table shown on page 34, plus a few extra to keep in your garden, on the patio, or beside the jacuzzi.*

## Special Tools & Techniques

- Dadoes
- Miters

## Materials

- 10 linear feet of 2x4 pine
- 30 linear feet of 1"-thick pine, ripped to 2" in width (actual width after ripping will be $3/4$"x2")
- 6 linear feet of 2"-thick pine, ripped to 2" in width (actual width after ripping will be $1^1/2$"x2")

## Hardware

- 20 3dx$1^1/4$" nails
- 20 $1^1/4$" screws
- 6 3" screws

## Cutting List

| Code | Description | Qty. | Materials | Dimensions |
|------|-------------|------|-----------|------------|
| A | Back Leg | 2 | 2x4 pine | 37" long |
| B | Front Leg | 2 | 2x4 pine | 18" long |
| C | Front Rail | 1 | $3/4$"x2" ripped* | $15^1/2$" long |
| D | Side Rail | 2 | $3/4$"x2" ripped | 16" long |
| E | Back Rail | 1 | $3/4$"x2" ripped | $15^1/2$" long |
| F | Side Spacer | 2 | $3/4$"x2" ripped | $13^1/2$" long |
| G | Front Spacer | 1 | $3/4$"x2" ripped | 14" long |
| H | Side Brace | 2 | $1^1/2$"x2" ripped | $13^1/2$" long |
| I | Middle Brace | 1 | $1^1/2$"x2" ripped | 14" long |
| J | Short Slat | 1 | $3/4$"x2" ripped | 14" long |
| K | Long Slat | 12 | $3/4$"x2" ripped | 18" long |

*Note: All the ripped pieces are presented in actual dimensions.*

## Cutting the Legs

The back legs of the chair are cut from 2x4 pine. The chair legs are angled at the top to make the chair comfortable to sit in. Although it looks complicated, it's really simple to do. Just take your time and measure and cut correctly.

1 Cut two back legs (A) from 2x4 pine, each measuring 37 inches long.

2  Refer to *figure 1* to mark and cut the first chair leg. Measure and mark points "a," "b," "c," and "d." Draw a line connecting "a" to "b," "c" to "d," and "d" to "e." Then cut along the lines to remove the shaded areas of the pattern. Use the resulting back leg (A) to cut a second back leg (A).

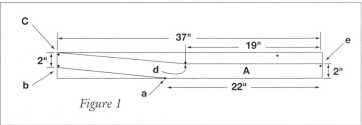

*Figure 1*

3  Measure 16 inches from what will be the bottom of the leg and cut a 2-inch-wide dado, ³/₄ inch deep in the leg (A), as shown in *figure 2* on page 102. Repeat this procedure to dado the remaining back leg (A). Because the dadoes will be on the inside of the chair back, the second dado must be a mirror image of the dado in the first back leg (A)

**4** Cut two front legs (B) from 2x4 pine, each measuring 18 inches long. Rip each leg to a width of 2 inches.

**5** The front legs (B) are dadoed to accept the seat rails. Follow *figure 3* to dado the first front leg (B). Repeat this procedure to dado the second front leg (B). As with the back legs, the second front leg (B) must be the mirror image of the first front leg (B).

## Adding the Chair Rails

**1** Cut one front rail (C) from ³/₄-inchx2-inch ripped pine, measuring 15¹/₂ inches long.

**2** Miter both ends of the front rail (C) at opposing 45-degree angles, as shown in *figure 4* on page 103.

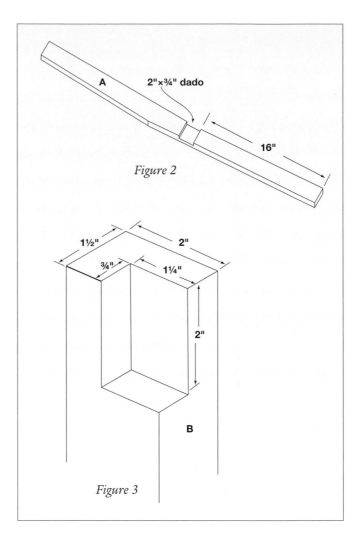

Figure 2

Figure 3

**3** Cut two side rails (D) from ³/₄-inchx2-inch ripped pine, each measuring 16 inches long. Miter one end of each of the side rails at opposing 45-degree angles, as shown in *figure 5*.

**4** Cut one back rail (E) from ³/₄-inchx2-inch ripped pine, measuring 15¹/₂ inches long.

**5** Refer to *figure 6* on page 103 to connect the chair rails to the chair legs. First fit the unmitered ends of the side rails (D) into the dado in the back legs (A), ³/₄ inch from the back edge of the dado. Be sure that the miters in the side rails (D) face each other. Apply glue to the meeting surfaces and screw through the side rails (D) into the dado in the back leg (A), using two 1¹/₄-inch-long screws on each joint.

**6** Fit the back rail (E) over the unmitered ends of the side rails (D) inside the dadoes in each of the back legs (A). Apply glue to the meeting surfaces and screw through the back rail (E) into the ends of the side rails (D). Use two 1¹/₄-inch-long screws on each joint.

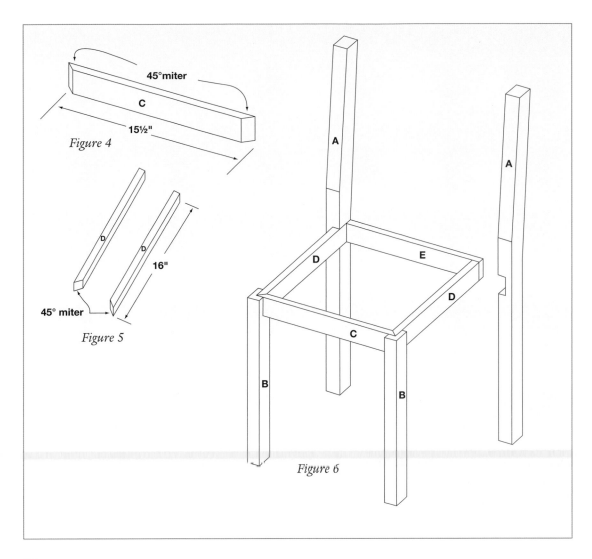

**45°miter**

C

15½"

*Figure 4*

D

D

16"

45° miter

*Figure 5*

A

A

D

E

D

B

B

C

*Figure 6*

7 Fit the front rail (C) between the two mitered ends of the side rails (D) inside the dadoes in the front legs (B). Apply glue to the meeting surfaces and screw through the front rail (C) into the front legs (B). Use two 1¼-inch-long screws on each joint.

## Adding the Spacers

1 Cut two side spacers (F) from ¾-inchx2-inch ripped pine, each measuring 13½ inches long.

2 Fit one side spacer (F) face-to-face on the outside of the side rail (D), between the back leg (A) and the front leg (B), as shown in *figure 7* on page 104. Apply glue to the meeting surfaces, and screw through the side rail (D) into the side spacer (F), using three 1¼-inch-long screws. Repeat this procedure to attach the remaining side spacer (F) to the opposite side rail (D).

3 Cut one front spacer (G) from ³/₄-inchx2-inch ripped pine, measuring 14 inches long.

4 Fit the front spacer (G) face-to-face on the outside of the front rail (C), as shown in *figure 7*. Apply glue to the meeting surfaces and screw through the front rail (C) into the front spacer (G), using three 1¹/₄-inch-long screws.

## Adding the Leg Braces

1 Cut two side braces (H) from ¹/₂-inchx2-inch ripped pine, each measuring 13¹/₂ inches long.

2 Fit one side brace (H) between a front leg (B) and back leg (A), 7 inches from the bottom of each of the legs, as shown in *figure 7*. Screw through the front and back legs (A and B) into the ends of the side braces (H), using a 3-inch-long screw on each joint. Repeat this procedure to attach the second side brace (H) between the remaining front and back legs (A and B).

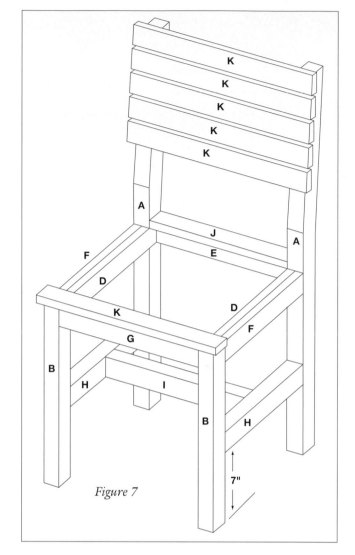

Figure 7

3 Cut one middle brace (I) from 1¹/₂-inchx2-inch ripped pine, measuring 14 inches long.

4 Center the middle brace (I) between the two side braces (H), as shown in *figure 7*. Screw through the side braces (H) into the ends of the middle brace (I), using a 3-inch-long screw.

## Adding the Slats

1 Cut one short slat (J) from ³/₄-inchx2-inch ripped pine, measuring 14 inches long.

2 Fit the short slat (J), wide surface up, on top of the back rail (E) between the two back legs (A), as shown in *figure 7*. Apply glue to the meeting surfaces and nail through the short slat (J) into the back rail (E), using three 1¹/₄-inch nails.

3  Cut 12 long slats (K) from ³/₄-inchx2-inch ripped pine, each measuring 18 inches long.

4  Seven long slats (K) will be used to complete the chair seat. Attach the first long slat (K) at the chair front, overhanging the front spacer (G) and each front leg (B) by ¹/₂ inch, as shown in *figure 7*. Apply glue to the meeting surfaces and nail through the long slat (K) into the front legs (B) and the front rail (C). Use two 1¹/₄-inch-long nails on each front legs, and four 1¹/₄-inch long nails on the front rail (C).

5  Attach the second long slat (K) at the back of the seat, ³/₈ inch from the back legs (A) and overhanging the side spacers (F) by ¹/₂ inch. Apply glue to the meeting surfaces and nail through the long slat (K) into the side rails (D). Use two 1¹/₄-inch-long nails on each joint.

6  Repeat the procedure in step 5 to attach five more long slats (K) to the chair seat, spacing them approximately ³/₈ inch apart.

7  The remaining five long slats (K) are used for the chair back. Attach the first long slat ¹/₂ inch higher than the top of the back legs (A), with equal overlap on both side, as shown in *figure 7*. Nail through each long slat (K) into the back legs (A), using two 1¹/₄-inch-long nails on each joint.

8  Attach the remaining four long slats (K) below the first one, about ³/₈ inch apart, as shown in *figure 7*.

## Finishing

1  Fill any cracks, crevices, or screw holes with wood filler, and thoroughly sand all surfaces of the completed chair.

2  Seal and paint or stain your chair the color of your choice.

# Victorian Loveseat

*Looks are deceiving in the case of this romantic loveseat. Although the piece looks difficult to make, the Victorian touches are gingerbread wooden brackets that can be purchased in most building-supply stores. By the time you sand and finish the loveseat, friends will assume it was built by a master woodworker!*

## Special Tools & Techniques

- Dadoes
- Bar clamps

## Materials

- 40 linear feet of 2x4 pine
- 15 linear feet of 1x4 pine
- 12 linear feet of 1x2 pine
- 1 piece of $1/2$"-thick exterior plywood, measuring $20 1/4$"x46"
- 2 decorative gingerbread brackets, each measuring 8"x12" on the straight sides*
- 2 decorative gingerbread brackets, each measuring 6"x$8 1/2$" on the straight sides*

## Hardware

- 125 3dx$1 1/4$" nails
- 80 4dx$1 1/2$" nails
- 20 $3 1/2$" screws
- 15 $2 1/2$" screws

## *Notes on Materials

It's not a necessity to find the exact decorative brackets that we used. Any design will work, but the size of the large brackets should be approximately the same as specified. If they are slightly different, you will need to alter the length of the center trim piece (K) to match the measurement of your bracket.

## Cutting List

| Code | Description | Qty. | Materials | Dimensions |
|------|-------------|------|-----------|------------|
| A | Side Slat | 6 | 1x4 pine | 14" long |
| B | Horizontal Side | 4 | 2x4 pine | $15 1/2$" long |
| C | Vertical Sides | 4 | 2x4 pine | 34" long |
| D | Outer Seat Support | 2 | 2x4 pine | $45 1/2$" long |
| E | Center Seat Support | 1 | 2x4 pine | $19 1/2$" long |
| F | Short Inner Support | 2 | 1x2 pine | $19 1/2$" long |
| G | Long Inner Support | 4 | 1x2 pine | $20 1/4$" long |
| H | Seat | 1 | $1/2$" plywood | $19 1/2$x$45 1/2$" |
| I | Horizontal Back | 2 | 2x4 pine | $45 1/2$" long |
| J | Back Slat | 8 | 1x4 pine | $10 1/4$" long |
| K | Center Trim | 1 | 2x4 pine | 8" long* |
| L | Large Bracket | 2 | | 8"x12" |
| M | Small Bracket | 2 | | 6"x$8 1/2$" |

## Constructing the Bench Sides

1 Cut six side slats (A) from 1x4 pine, each measuring 14 inches long.

2 Cut four horizontal sides (B) from 2x4 pine, each measuring $15 1/2$ inches long.

3 Cut a ³/₄-inch-wide dado, ¹/₂ inch deep, down the length of one edge of each of the horizontal sides (B), as shown in *figure 1*.

4 Working on a level surface, place two horizontal sides (B) parallel to each other, with the dadoes to the inside, as shown in *figure 2* on page 108. Fit the ends of three side slats (A) into the dadoes in each of the two horizontal sides (B). When the side slats (A) are properly fitted into the dadoes, the distance between the two horizontal sides (B) should measure 13 inches, as shown in *figure 2*. The two outer side slats (A) should be even with the ends of the horizontal sides (B), and 2¹/₂ inches from the center side slat (A). When the position is perfect, the overall measurements of

B

¹/₂"

*Figure 1*

³⁄₄"

the slat assembly should be 20 inches high and 15½ inches wide. Secure the slats in place by nailing through the dadoed edge of the horizontal sides (B) into the ends of the side slats (A), using two 1¼-inch-long nails on each joint.

5 Cut four vertical sides (C) from 2x4 pine, each measuring 34 inches long.

6 Place the slat assembly between two vertical sides (C), so that the top edge of the slat assembly is even with one end of the vertical sides (C), and is 14 inches from the other end of that same vertical side (C), as shown in *figure 3*. Toenail through the edges of the horizontal sides (B) into the vertical sides (C), using a 3½-inch-long nail on each joint.

7 Repeat steps 3 through 6 to assemble the second side.

## Adding the Seat

1 Cut two outer seat supports (D) from 2x4 pine, each measuring 45½ inches long.

2 For the next step, you may want to ask a helper to assist. If you are working alone, use a bar clamp to hold the assembly while you screw it together. Place the side assemblies (C) on one 34-inch-long edge, parallel to each other, 45½ inches apart, as shown in *figure 4*. Fit one

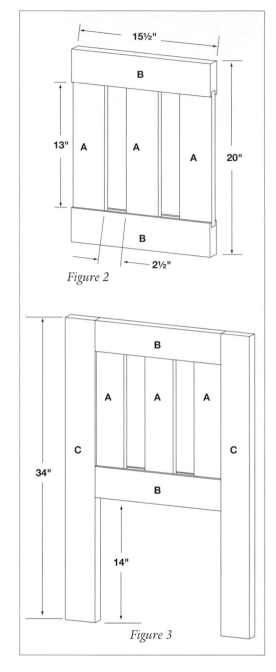

*Figure 2*

*Figure 3*

outer seat support (D) between the two side assemblies, 16½ inches down from the upper edge of the two side assemblies. The top edge of the outer seat support (D) should be exactly even with the top edge of the lower horizontal side (B). Screw through the side assemblies into the ends of the outer seat support (D), using two 2½-inch-long screws on each joint.

3 Turn the assembly upside down, and attach the remaining outer seat support (D) to the opposite side of the side assemblies in the same manner you used in step 2.

**4** Cut one center seat support (E) from 2x4 pine, measuring 19½ inches long.

**5** Fit the center seat support (E) in the center of the assembly (wide surface up), between the outer seat supports (D), as shown in *figure 5*. The center seat support (E) should be placed ½ inch below the top of the outer seat supports (D), centered between the side assemblies. Screw through the outer seat supports (D) into the ends of the center seat support (E). Use two 2½-inch-long screws on each of the joints.

## Adding the Inner Supports

**1** Cut two short inner supports (F) from 1x2 pine, each measuring 19½ inches long.

**2** Attach one short inner support (F) to the lower horizontal side (B), between the two outer seat supports (D), ½ inch below the top edge of the lower horizontal sides (B), as shown in *figure 6*. Apply glue to the meeting surfaces, and nail through the short inner support (F) into the lower horizontal side (A). Use three 1½-inch-long nails to secure it in place.

**3** Repeat step 2 to attach the remaining short inner support (F) to the opposite lower horizontal side (A).

**4** Cut four long inner supports (G) from 1x2 pine, each measuring 20¼ inches long.

**5** Attach one long inner support (G) to the inner surface of the outer seat supports (D), ½ inch below the top edge of the outer seat supports (D), between the one short inner support (F) and the center seat support (E), as shown in *figure 6*. Apply glue to the meeting surfaces, and use four 1½-inch-long nails spaced evenly along the length to secure it in place.

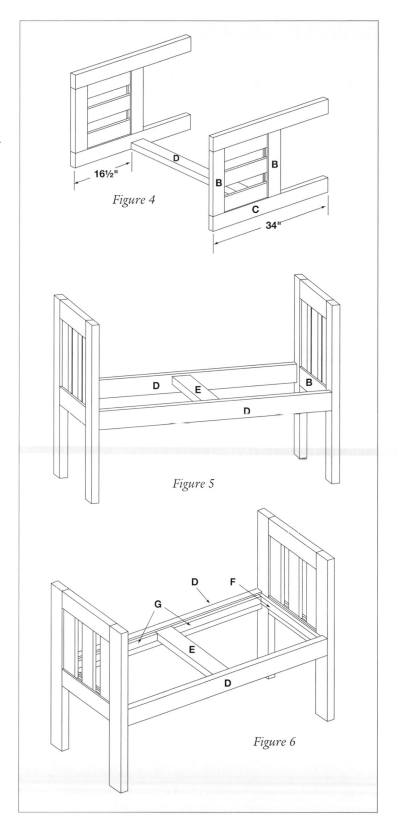

*Figure 4*

*Figure 5*

*Figure 6*

6 Repeat step 5 three more times to attach the remaining long inner supports (G) to the inside of the other outer seat supports (D).

7 Cut one seat (H) from $^1/_2$-inch plywood, measuring $19^1/_2$x$45^1/_2$ inches.

8 Place the seat (H) over the inner supports (F and G) and the center support (E). Apply glue to the meeting surfaces, and nail through the seat (H) into the center seat support (E) and into the inner seat supports (F and G). Use $1^1/_4$-inch-long nails spaced about every 4 or 5 inches.

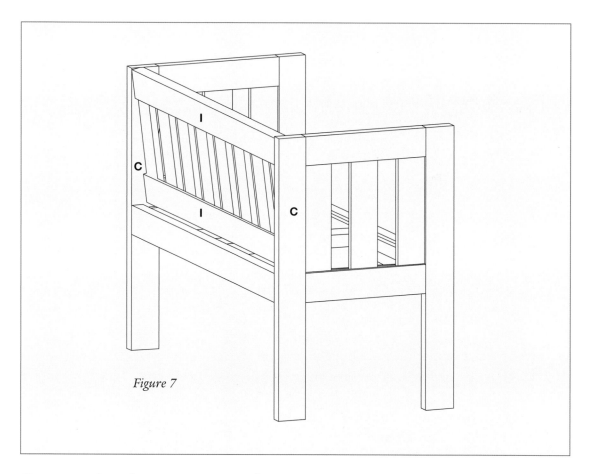

Figure 7

## Constructing the Loveseat Back

1 Cut two horizontal backs (I) from 2x4 pine, each measuring $45^1/_2$ inches long.

2 Cut a $^3/_4$-inch-wide dado, $^1/_2$ inch deep down the length of one edge of each of the horizontal backs (I), in the same manner as shown in *figure 1* on page 107.

3 Cut eight back slats (J) from 1x4 pine, each measuring $10^1/_4$ inches long.

4 Working on a level surface, place the horizontal backs (I) parallel to each other, with the dadoes to the inside, in the same manner as shown in *figure 2* on page 108. Fit the ends of the eight back slats (J) into the dadoes in each of the two horizontal backs (I). When the back slats (E) are properly fitted into the dadoes, the distance between the two horizontal backs (I) should measure 9$\frac{1}{4}$ inches. The two outer back slats (E) should be even with the ends of the horizontal backs (I) and 2$\frac{1}{2}$ inches from each other, in the same manner as shown in *figure 3* on page 108. When the position is perfect, the overall measurements of the back assembly should be 16$\frac{1}{4}$ inches high and 45$\frac{1}{2}$ inches wide. Secure the slats by nailing through the dadoed edge of the horizontal backs (I) into the ends of the back slats (J), using two 1$\frac{1}{4}$-inch-long nails on each joint.

5 Now you are ready to fit the back assembly between the two sides. To make the loveseat more comfortable, the back assembly is tilted at an angle—out at the top and in at the bottom. The tilt angle is determined by the width of the 2x4 on the side assemblies. The lower edge of the back is fitted flush with the inside edge of the vertical sides (C), and the upper edge of the back is fitted flush with the outer edge of the vertical sides (C), as shown in *figure 7*. When you have the back fitted perfectly, secure the assembly with bar clamps. Screw through the vertical sides (C) into the ends of the horizontal backs (I), using two 3$\frac{1}{2}$-inch-long screws on each joint.

## Adding the Decorative Trim

1 Cut one center trim (K) from 2x4 pine, measuring 8 inches long. (Note: You will need to adjust this measurement if the gingerbread corner pieces you purchased differ in height from those specified in the materials list.)

2 Attach one large wooden bracket (L) to the 8-inch edge of the center trim (K), using the photograph on page 112 as a guide. Apply glue to the meeting edges, and toenail though the sides and the ends of the large bracket (L) into the edge of the center trim (K). Use three 1$\frac{1}{2}$-inch-long nails on each side, and one nail on each end. Repeat this procedure to attach the other large bracket.

3 Measure carefully to find the center of the back assembly and the center of the trim assembly. Matching those two points, apply glue to the meeting surfaces, attach the trim assembly to the top back center of the bench. Toenail through the brackets into the top back of the bench, using 1$\frac{1}{2}$-inch-long nails.

4 Attach the smaller wooden brackets (M) to the loveseat in the same manner, flush with the inside corner formed by the front edges of the vertical sides (C) and the outer seat supports (D), using the photograph below as a guide. The 8$\frac{1}{2}$-inch-long side of the small bracket should be against the outer seat supports (D).

## Finishing

1 Fill any cracks, crevices, or screw holes with wood filler, and thoroughly sand all surfaces of the completed loveseat.

2 Seal and paint or stain your Victorian loveseat the color of your choice.

*A word of caution: Because the gingerbread trim pieces are fragile, never attempt to move the finished loveseat by holding onto the trim pieces, as they will most likely break.*

# Potting Bench

*This simple pine potting bench is a great help to any gardener. The bottom shelf can store large gardening items that take up space in the garage, and the top shelves can accommodate small pots, insecticides, and other necessaries. There is also a drawer for stowing gardening tools. The work surface features a drop-in container to hold potting soil. With this handy potting bench on your side, we bet your garden will be the prettiest in the neighborhood!*

## Special Tools & Techniques

- Bar clamps
- Mitering

## Materials

- 32 linear feet of 1x8 pine
- 12 linear feet of 1x6 pine
- 45 linear feet of 1x4 pine
- 10 linear feet of 1x2 pine
- 4 linear feet of 1x1 pine
- 25 linear feet of 2x4 pine
- 1 piece of $3/8$"-thick exterior plywood, measuring 2'x2'
- Heavy-duty plastic dishpan, approximately 11"x13"

## Hardware

- 20 $2^{1}/_{2}$" screws
- 50 $1^{5}/_{8}$" screws
- 50 $1^{1}/_{2}$" screws
- 35 $1^{1}/_{4}$" screws
- 10 4dx$1^{1}/_{2}$" nails
- 20 3dx$1^{1}/_{4}$" nails
- 35 2dx1" nails

## Cutting List

| Code | Description | Qty. | Materials | Dimensions |
|---|---|---|---|---|
| A | Horizontal Sides | 4 | 2x4 pine | $20^{1}/_{2}$" long |
| B | Vertical Sides | 4 | 2x4 pine | 33" long |
| C | Side Trim | 2 | 1x4 pine | $23^{1}/_{2}$" long |
| D | Long Trim | 1 | 1x4 pine | $52^{1}/_{2}$" long |
| E | Shelf Slat | 4 | 1x4 pine | 51" long |
| F | Wide Top | 2 | 1x8 pine | $60^{1}/_{2}$" long |
| G | Narrow Top | 2 | 1x6 pine | $60^{1}/_{2}$" long |
| H | Edge Support | 2 | 1x2 pine | 20" long |
| I | Reinforcements | 2 | 1x2 pine | 14" long |
| J | Shelf Sides | 2 | 1x8 pine | 34" long |
| K | Shelf Back | 2 | 1x4 pine | 59" long |
| L | Shelf | 2 | 1x8 pine | 59" long |
| M | Bottom Support | 1 | 2x4 pine | 59" long |
| N | Drawer Side | 2 | $3/8$" plywood | 5"x$6^{7}/_{8}$" |
| O | Drawer Glides | 2 | 1x1 pine | $7^{1}/_{4}$" long |
| P | Drawer Bottom | 1 | $3/8$" plywood | $14^{1}/_{2}$"x$6^{7}/_{8}$" |
| Q | Drawer Back | 1 | $3/8$" plywood | $15^{1}/_{2}$"x5" |
| R | Drawer Front | 1 | 1x8 pine | $18^{3}/_{4}$" long |
| S | Horizontal Drawer Support | 1 | 1x2 pine | 22" long |
| T | Vertical Drawer Support | 1 | 1x1 pine | 22" long |
| U | Top Support | 2 | 2x4 pine | 8" long |

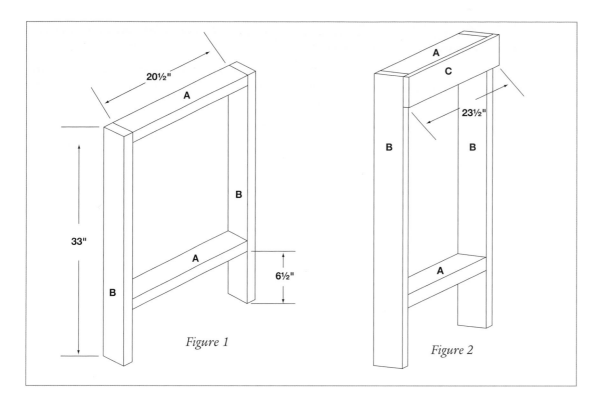

*Figure 1*

*Figure 2*

## Constructing the Side Supports

1 Cut four horizontal sides (A) from 2x4 pine, each measuring 20½ inches long.

2 Cut four vertical sides (B) from 2x4 pine, each measuring 33 inches long.

3 To form the side supports, place two vertical sides (B) parallel to each other and 20½ inches apart. Fit two horizontal sides (A) between the two vertical sides (B), as shown in *figure 1*. The uppermost horizontal side (A) should be even with the top ends of both vertical sides (B), and the lower horizontal side (A) should be 6½ inches from the lower ends of both vertical sides (B). Screw through the vertical sides (B) into the ends of the horizontal sides (A). Use two 2½-inch-long screws on each of the joints. Repeat this procedure to form a second side support, using the remaining two vertical sides (B) and horizontal sides (A).

## Adding the Trim

1 Cut two side trims (C) from 1x4 pine, each measuring 23½ inches long.

2 Apply glue to the meeting surfaces, and attach one side trim piece (C) to the top of one assembled side support, as shown in *figure 2*. Screw through the side trim (C) into the upper horizontal side (A) and the two vertical sides (B). Use two 1⅝-inch-long screws on each of the vertical sides (B) and three screws on the horizontal sides (A). Repeat this procedure to attach

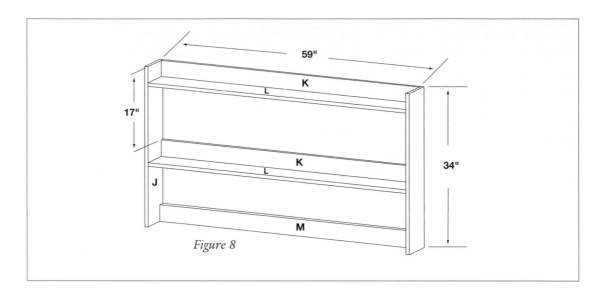

Figure 8

## Making the Upper Shelf Section

1 Cut two shelf sides (J) from 1x8 pine, each measuring 34 inches long.

2 Cut two shelf backs (K) from 1x4 pine, each measuring 59 inches long.

3 Cut two shelves (L) from 1x8 pine, each measuring 59 inches long.

4 Glue one shelf (L) to the edge of one shelf back (K), aligning the bottoms of the two pieces, as shown in *figure 7* on page 118. Reinforce the joint by driving $1^5/_8$-inch-long screws every 6 inches. Repeat this step to join the other shelf (L) and shelf back (K).

5 Place the two shelf sides (J) on a level surface, parallel to each other, and 59 inches apart. Fit one shelf/back assembly between the two shelf sides (J), flush with the ends of both shelf sides (J), as shown in *figure 8*. Screw through the shelf sides (J) in the ends of the shelf back (K) and the shelf (L). Use two $1^5/_8$-inch-long screws in each end of the shelf back (K) and three screws in each end of the shelf (L).

6 Repeat step 5 to attach the remaining shelf/back assembly between the two shelf sides (J), 17 inches from the top of the shelf sides (J), as shown in *figure 8*.

7 Cut one bottom support (M) from 2x4 pine, measuring 59 inches long.

8 Attach the bottom support (M) between the two shelf sides (J), flush with the lower ends of the shelf sides (J), as

Figure 9

shown in *figure 8*. Screw through the shelf sides (J) into the ends of the bottom support (M), using two 2½-inch-long screws on each of the joints.

## Adding the Drawer

1 Cut two drawer sides (N) from ⅜-inch exterior plywood, each measuring 5x6⅞ inches.

2 Cut two drawer glides (O) from 1x1 pine, each 7¼ inches long. To allow the drawers to slide without binding, plane or rip the drawer slides (O) on one side so they measure ¹¹⁄₁₆x¾ inch.

3 Apply glue to the meeting surfaces, and attach one drawer glide (O) to one 6⅞-inch edge of a drawer side (N), using three 1-inch-long finishing nails, as shown in *figure 9* on page 118. Note that the drawer glide (O) extends past the drawer side (N) by ⅜ inch on one end.

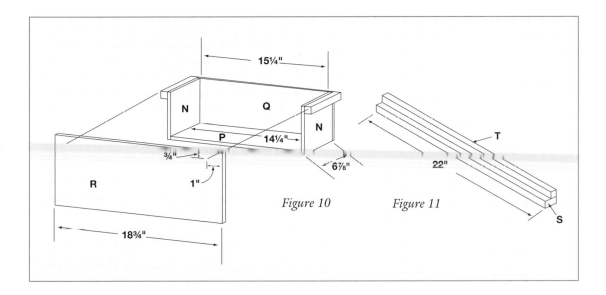

Figure 10    Figure 11

4 Repeat step 3 to attach the remaining drawer glide (O) to the other drawer side (N). The ⅜-inch extension should be a mirror image of the one in step 3.

5 Cut one drawer bottom (P) from ⅜-inch exterior plywood, measuring 14½x6⅞ inches.

6 Cut one drawer back (Q) from ⅜-inch exterior plywood, measuring 15¼x5 inches.

7 Assemble the drawer bottom (P), drawer sides (N), and drawer back (Q), as shown in *figure 10*, fitting the drawer back (Q) over the ends of the sides (N), and the drawer bottom (P) flush with the bottom edges of the drawer sides (N). Nail through the drawer sides (N) and drawer back (Q) into the edges of the drawer bottom (P). Use 1-inch-long finishing nails spaced about 3 inches apart.

8 Cut one drawer front (R) from 1x8 pine, measuring 18³/₄ inches long.

9 Rout the edges of the drawer front (R) with a round-over bit (optional) or simply sand the edges to slightly round them.

10 Attach the drawer front (R) to the drawer assembly. Center the drawer front (R) so that it is ³/₄ inch above the drawer assembly at the top and extends 1 inch beyond each of the drawer glides (O), as shown in *figure 10*. Nail through the drawer front into the ends of the drawer sides (N), drawer bottoms (P), and drawer glides (O), using 1¹/₂-inch long finishing nails. Use two nails on each joint.

## Adding the Drawer Supports

1 The drawer supports are comprised of two pieces of wood glued together. We will assemble the two pieces first, and cut the resulting assembly to form two supports. Cut one horizontal drawer support (S) from 1x2 pine, measuring 22 inches long.

2 Cut one vertical drawer support (T) from 1x1 pine, measuring 22 inches long.

3 Apply glue to the meeting surfaces, and attach the vertical drawer support (T) to one edge of the horizontal support (S), as shown in *figure 11*. Align the long edges accurately. Use 1¹/₄-inch finishing nails, spacing them every 3 or 4 inches. Allow the glue to set up.

4 Cut two drawer supports from the glued support assembly, each measuring 7¹/₄ inches long.

5 Mount one drawer support under the lower shelf (L), ¹/₂ inch from the right shelf s ide (J), as shown in *figure 12*. Screw through the top of the shelf (L) into the drawer support, using two 1¹/₄-inch- long screws.

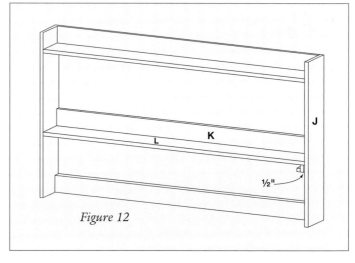

*Figure 12*

6 Slide the drawer in place, and mark the placement of the second drawer support. Be sure to leave a little play in your measurements—you don't want to have to force the drawer open and closed. Attach the second drawer support under the lower shelf following your placement marks.

## Attaching the Top Shelf Section

1 Cut two top supports (U) from 2x4 pine, each measuring 8 inches long.

2 Miter one end of each of the two top supports (U) at a 45-degree angle, as shown in *figure 13*.

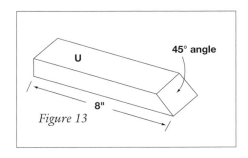

*Figure 13*

3 Apply glue to the meeting surfaces and attach the top supports to the back of the side supports on the lower section, against the rectangular top. Screw through the top supports (U) into the ends of the horizontal sides (A) and the edges of the vertical sides (B). Use two 2½-inch-long screws on each joint.

4 Place the top shelf assembly over the bottom assembly, matching the sides and backs. To make the potting bench portable, we skipped the glue; that way, the two sections can be separated for transporting. Screw through the bench top (from underneath) into the bottom ends of the shelf sides (J). Use three 1⅝-inch long screws on each joint.

## Finishing

1 We used a 6-inch-length of the remaining support assembly to fashion our drawer pull, and screwed it to the front of the drawer front using two 1⅝-inch-long screws. You can use the same technique, or purchase a different drawer pull at the hardware store.

2 Fill any cracks, crevices, or screw holes with wood filler, and thoroughly sand all surfaces of the completed potting bench.

3 It is a good idea to seal the completed bench with an exterior grade sealer.

# Lawn Bench

*This versatile lawn bench can serve a multitude of purposes. We've used it as a bench for seating, as an outdoor coffee table, and even to hold a collection of plants. It's easy to make, and very sturdy when completed.*

## Materials

- 30 linear feet of 1x4 pine
- 22 linear feet of 1x2
- 10 linear feet of 2x2 pine

## Hardware

- 60 3dx1$^{1}/_{4}$" nails
- 15 4dx1$^{1}/_{2}$" nails
- 30 1$^{1}/_{4}$" screws
- 30 1$^{5}/_{8}$" screws
- 20 2$^{1}/_{2}$" screws

## Cutting List

| Code | Description | Qty. | Materials | Dimensions |
|------|-------------|------|-----------|------------|
| A | Long Top | 2 | 1x4 | 53" long |
| B | Short Top | 2 | 1x4 | 14" long |
| C | Leg | 4 | 2x2 | 16$^{1}/_{4}$" long |
| D | Long Inner Support | 2 | 1x2 | 48$^{1}/_{2}$ "long |
| E | Slat | 14 | 1x4 | 14" long |
| F | Leg Brace | 2 | 2x2 | 11" long |
| G | Lower Support | 2 | 1x2 | 48$^{1}/_{2}$" long |
| H | Spacer | 3 | 1x2 | 2$^{1}/_{4}$" long |

## Constructing the Bench Top

1 Cut two long tops (A) from 1x4 pine, each measuring 53 inches long.

2 Cut two short tops (B) from 1x4 pine, each measuring 14 inches long.

3 Place the two short tops (B) between the ends of the long tops (A), as shown in *figure 1*. Screw through the long tops (A) into the ends of the short tops (B), using two 1$^{5}/_{8}$-inch-long screws on each joint.

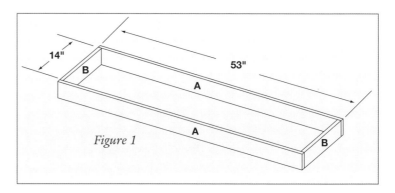

Figure 1

## Adding the Legs

1 Cut four legs (C) from 2x2 pine, each measuring 16$^{1}/_{4}$ inches long.

2 Attach each of the four legs to the four inner corners of the top assembly, ³/₄ inch from the top edges of the long and short tops (A and B), as shown in *figure 2* on page 124. Screw through the long and short tops (A and B) into the legs (C), using two 1⅝-inch-long screws in each side of the legs (C).

## Adding the Inner Supports

1 Cut two long inner supports (D) from 1x2 pine, each measuring 48¼ inches long.

2 Attach one long inner support (D) to the inside of the one long top (A), as shown in *figure 3* on page 124. It should be positioned flush with the top of the leg (C), ³/₄ inch from the top edge of the long top (A). Screw through the long inner support (D) into the long top (A), using 1⅝-inch- long screws, approximately every six inches.

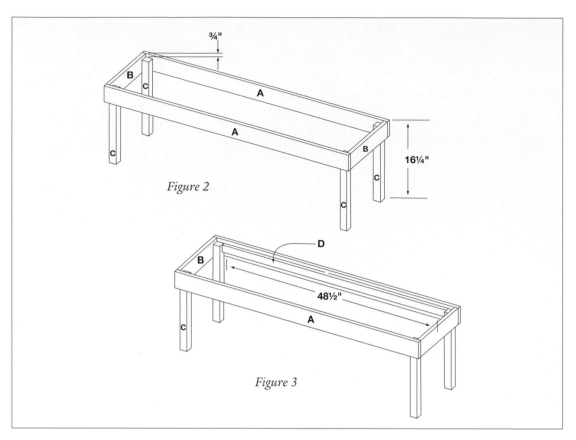

Figure 2

Figure 3

3 Repeat step 1 to attach the remaining long inner support (D) to the inside of the opposite long top (A).

## Adding the Slats

1 Cut 14 slats (E) from 1x4 pine, each measuring 14 inches long.

2 Place the 14 slats (E) over the assembled inner supports, as shown in *figure 4* on page 125. Space them evenly between the short tops (B), leaving a small space between slats. The exact measurement is not critical—just make certain that all the spaces are equal and that the slats are all straight. Nail through the ends of each of the slats into the long inner supports (D) and the legs (C), using two $1^{1}/_{4}$-inch-long nails on each end.

## Adding the Leg Supports

1 Cut two leg braces (F) from 2x2 pine, each measuring 11 inches long.

2 Attach a leg brace (F) between two of the legs (C), 8 inches from the bottom, as shown in *figure 4*. Screw through the legs (C) into the ends of the leg braces (F), using two $2^{1}/_{2}$ inch-long screws on each joint.

3 Repeat step 2 to attach the other leg brace (F) between the opposite legs (C).

## Adding the Lower Support

1 Cut two lower supports (G) from 1x2 pine, each measuring 48½ inches long.

2 Cut three spacers (H) from 1x2 pine, each measuring 2¼ inches long.

3 Place the two lower supports (G) on a level surface, parallel to each other, and 2½ inches apart. Fit the three spacers (H) evenly between the two lower supports, just over 11½ inches apart, as shown in *figure 5*.

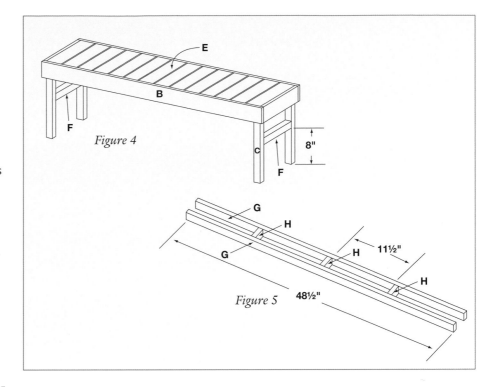

*Figure 4*

*Figure 5*

4 Nail through the two lower supports (G) into the ends of the spacers (H). Use two 1¼ inch long nails on each joint.

5 Fit the assembled lower support between the two leg braces (F), centering it on the braces. Screw through the leg braces (F) into the ends of the two lower supports (G). Use two 2½-inch-long screws on each joint.

## Finishing the Bench

1 Fill any cracks, crevices, or screw holes with wood filler and thoroughly sand all surfaces of the lawn bench.

2 Seal and paint, or stain the completed bench the color of your choice. We left our project the natural color of the pressure-treated pine.

# Chaise Lounge

*This easy-to-make chaise lounge will become a favorite place for napping in the sun or reading a good book underneath a shade tree. Because it's on wheels, you can move it to any location you wish—even to the beach!*

## Special Tools & Techniques

- Dadoes

## Materials

- 30 linear feet of 2x4 pine
- 45 linear feet of 1x4 pine
- 25 linear feet of 1x2 pine
- 2 linear feet of 1"-wide dowel rod

## Hardware

- 60 $1^1/_4$" screws
- 12 $1^1/_2$" screws
- 15 $2^1/_2$" screws
- 50 3dx$1^1/_4$" nails
- 50 4dx$1^1/_2$" nails
- 2 $^3/_8$"x2" carriage bolts with matching washers and nuts
- 2 $^3/_8$"x3" carriage bolts with matching washers and nuts
- 2 $^1/_2$"x4" machine bolts with matching washers and nuts
- 27"-diameter wheels (the type used for lawn mowers)

## Cutting List

| Code | Description | Qty. | Materials | Dimensions |
|------|-------------|------|-----------|------------|
| A | Side | 2 | 2x4 pine | 80" long |
| B | Front/Back | 2 | 2x4 pine | 24" long |
| C | Front Leg | 2 | 2x4 pine | 14" long |
| D | Back Leg | 2 | 2x4 pine | 12" long |
| E | Leg Support | 1 | 2x4 pine | 24" long |
| F | Inner Support | 2 | 1x2 pine | 44" long |
| G | Slat | 11 | 1x4 pine | 24" long |
| H | Inner Rack | 1 | 1x4 pine | 19" long |
| I | Short Back Support | 2 | 1x2 pine | $22^3/_8$" long |
| J | Long Back Support | 2 | 1x2 pine | $31^1/_2$" long |
| K | Back Slat | 8 | 1x4 pine | $23^7/_8$" long |
| L | Rod | 1 | 1" dowel rod | $23^7/_8$" long |
| M | Extender | 2 | 1x2 pine | 15" long |

## Making the Frame

1  Cut two sides (A) from 2x4 pine, each measuring 80 inches long.

2  Cut two dadoes across the width of side (A), as shown in *figure 1* on page 128. Each dado is $3^1/_2$ inches wide and $^3/_4$ inch deep.

3 Cut two front/backs (B) from 2x4 pine, each measuring 24 inches long.

4 Place the sides (A) on a level surface, parallel to each other and 24 inches apart. The dadoed surfaces should be facing each other. Place the two front/backs (B) between the two sides (A), as shown in *figure 2* on page 128. Screw through the sides (A) into the ends of the front/backs (B), using two 2¹/₂-inch-long screws on each joint.

## Adding the Legs

1 Cut two front legs (C) from 2x4 pine, each measuring 14 inches long.

2 Cut a lap dado on one end of a front leg (C), measuring 3¹/₂ inches wide and ³/₄ inches deep, as shown in *figure 3* on page 129. Repeat the procedure to cut a lap dado on the remaining front leg (C)

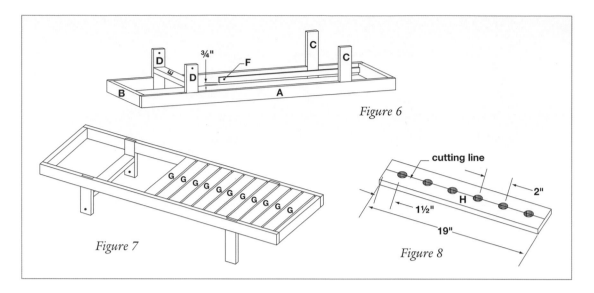

*Figure 6*

*Figure 7*

*Figure 8*

3 Repeat the same procedure to attach the remaining 10 slats (G) on top of the inner supports (F), spacing each slat ¹/₂ inch from the previous one.

## Making the Inner Rack

1 The angle of the chaise back is adjusted by placing a wooden rod into your choice of multiple slots in the inner rack. Cut one inner rack (H) from 1x4 pine, measuring 19 inches long.

2 Drill six 1-inch-diameter holes 2 inches apart along the length of the inner rack (H), beginning 1¹/₂ inches from the end, as shown in *figure 8*. These holes must be centered widthwise on the 1x4.

3 Cut the inner rack (H) in half lengthwise along the dotted lines shown in *figure 8*, cutting through the center of all six drilled holes. The resulting two half-pieces will now provide the slots for the chaise back adjustment.

4 Attach one half-piece (drilled half-circles up) 2¹/₄ inches from the top of the lower edge of side (A), 1¹/₂ inches from the front/back (B), as shown in *figure 9*. Note that the half-piece will extend below the lower edge of side (A). Apply glue to the meeting surfaces, and use four evenly spaced 1¹/₂-inch-long screws along the length to attach the inner rack (H) to the side (A). Repeat this procedure to attach the remaining half-piece (H) to the opposite side (A).

## Making the Chaise Back

1 Cut two short back supports (I) from 1x2 pine, each measuring 22³/₈ inches long.

2 Cut two long back supports (J) from 1x2 pine, each measuring 31¹/₂ inches long.

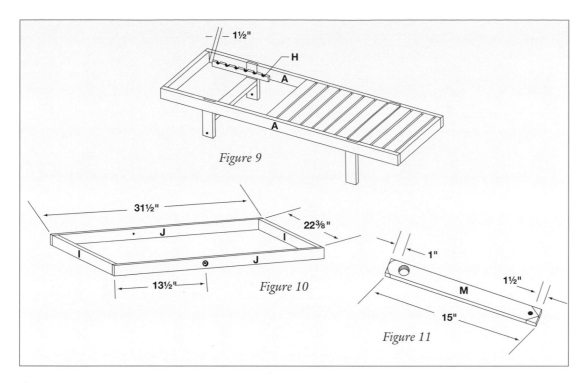

Figure 9

Figure 10

Figure 11

3 Measure 13¹/₂ inches from one end of each long back support (J) and center a mark on the wide face. Drill a ³/₄-inch countersink ¹/₄ inch deep. Then drill a ³/₈-inch hole through the back support (J), as shown in *figure 10*.

4 Place the two long back supports (J) on a flat surface, parallel to each other and 22³/₈ inches apart. Fit the two short back supports (I) between the two long back supports (K), as shown in *figure 10*. Nail through the long back supports (J) into the ends of the short back supports (I), using two 1 1¹/₂-inch-long nails on each joint.

5 Cut eight back slats (K) from 1x4 pine, each measuring 23⁷/₈ inches long.

6 Fit the back slats (K) over the assembled frame, spacing them ¹/₂ inch apart, in the same manner that you used to attach the 11 slats (G). Nail through the end of the back slats (K) into the edges of the two long inner supports. Use two 1¹/₂-inch-long nails on each joint.

## Making the Rod Assembly

1 Cut one rod (L) from 1-inch-diameter dowel rod to a length of 23⁷/₈ inches.

2 Cut two extenders (M) from 1x2 pine, each measuring 15 inches long.

3 Drill a 1-inch-diameter hole through one end of one extender (M), as shown in *figure 11* above. Then round off the end of the extender around the hole that you just drilled.

**4** Shape the opposite end of the extender (M) by cutting off both corners, and drill a ³/₈-inch hole in that same end, as shown in *figure 11* on page 131.

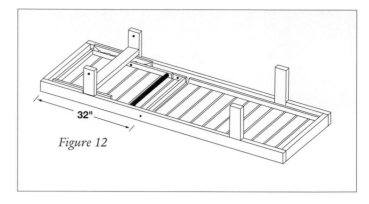

Figure 12

**5** Thread the rod (L) through the 1-inch holes you drilled in each of the extenders (M). Make certain that the rod length on each side of the extenders is equal. Then nail through each extender into the rod, using a 1¹/₂-inch-long nail.

**6** Place the extenders inside the chaise back, matching the drilled holes. Secure them by inserting a 2-inch-long bolt through the chaise back and then through the extender (M). Add a washer and nut, and tighten securely.

**7** The finished chaise consists of the assembled back portion, which can be raised or lowered, and the slats that accommodate the legs. A hole must be drilled through the chaise and the back assembly to accommodate a bolt that enables the back to be raised and lowered.

To add the back portion to the assembled chaise, place the assembled chaise upside down on a level surface. Holding the assembled chaise back upside down, fit it underneath the leg support (E), between the two sides (A), so that the back slats (K) rest against the work surface, as shown in *figure 12*. Clamp the long back supports (J) to the sides (A) to hold them securely while you drill a hole.

Measure down 32 inches from the rear of the chaise on side (A), and drill a hole through both sides (A) and through the long back support (J), large enough to accommodate a 3-inch-long bolt. Insert the bolt through the side (A) and through the long back support (J). Add a washer and nut, and tighten securely.

## Finishing

**1** Thread a washer over a 4-inch bolt. Then fit the bolt through one wheel and through the drilled hole in the back leg (D). Add a washer and nut, and tighten. Repeat this procedure to attach the remaining wheel to the opposite back leg (D).

**2** Thoroughly sand the completed chaise.

**3** We wanted a natural appearance for our chaise so we didn't even fill the holes. However, if you wish a more finished look, fill all of the screw holes and cracks with wood filler, and sand again. You can leave the chaise its natural color or stain or paint it whatever color you wish.

# Lawn Chair

*These simple-to-make chairs are a great addition to any backyard or deck—and even without a pillow, they are surprisingly comfortable. A great way to add seating to your backyard living space when you have very little time and money.*

**Special Tools & Techniques**

- Bar clamps

**Materials**

- 17 linear feet of 2x4 pine
- 30 linear feet of 1x4 pine

**Hardware**

- 95 2½" wood screws
- 4 3½" carriage bolts
- 4 3½" lag screws

**Cutting List**

| Code | Description | Qty. | Materials | Dimensions |
|---|---|---|---|---|
| A | Seat Front | 1 | 2x4 pine | 20" long |
| B | Seat Side | 2 | 2x4 pine | 19" long |
| C | Seat Slat | 5 | 1x4 pine | 20" long |
| D | Back Support | 2 | 2x4 pine | 14½" long |
| E | Back | 5 | 1x4 pine | 20" long |
| F | Arm | 2 | 1x4 pine | 21" long |
| G | Arm Support | 4 | 2x4 pine | 24" long |

## Building the Seat

1 Cut one Seat Front (A) from 1x4 pine, measuring 20 inches.

2 Cut two Seat Sides (B) from 2x4 pine, each measuring 19 inches.

3 Position the two Seat Sides (B) on edge, parallel to each other and 17 inches apart. Fit the Seat Front (A) over the ends of the Seat Sides (B), as shown in *figure 1*. Apply glue to the meeting surfaces, and screw through the Seat Front (A) into the ends of the Seat Sides (B), using two 2½-inch wood screws on each joint.

4 Cut five Seat Slats (C) from 1x4 pine, each measuring 20 inches.

5 Place the seat assembly [Seat Front (A) and Seat Sides (B)] on a flat surface. Position the five Seat Slats (C) over the assembly, as shown in *figure 2* on page 134. The first Seat Slat (C) should be set back ½ inch from the face of the Seat Front (A), and the Seat

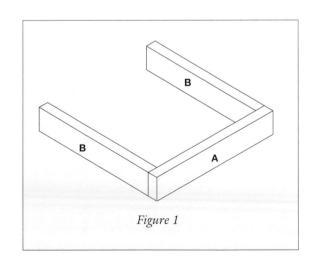

*Figure 1*

Sides (B) should remain exposed at the other end. Screw through the Seat Slats (C) into the Seat Sides (B), using two 2½-inch wood screws on each joint.

## Making the Back

1 Cut two Back Supports (D) from 2x4 pine, each measuring 14½ inches.

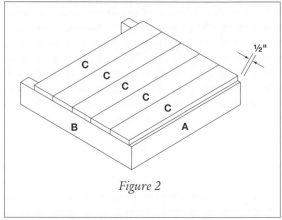

*Figure 2*

2 Cut five Backs (E) from 1x4 pine, each measuring 20 inches.

3 Position the two Back Supports (D) on a flat surface, parallel to each other and 13 inches apart. Position one Back (E) over the two Back Supports (D), as shown in *figure 3* on page 135. The first Back (E) should overhang the ends of the two Back Supports (D) by 1 inch. Apply glue to the meeting surfaces, and screw through the Back (E) into each of the Back Supports (D), using two 2½-inch wood screws on each joint.

**4** Repeat step 3 four times to attach the remaining four Backs (E) to the two Back Supports (D).

## Making the Sides

**1** Cut two Arms (F) from 1x4 pine, each measuring 21 inches.

**2** Using *figure 4* as a guide, shape the one Arm (F) by eliminating cutting off the shaded portions. Use the shaped Arm (F) as a pattern to cut the remaining Arm (F).

**3** Cut four Arm Supports (G) from 2x4 pine, each measuring 24 inches.

**4** Position two Arm Supports (G) face down on a level surface, parallel to each other and 12 inches apart. Place one Arm (F), uncut edge down, over the ends of the two Arm Supports (G), as shown in *figure 5*. The Arm (F) should overlap each of the Arm Supports (G) by 1 inch on each side. Apply glue to the meeting surfaces, and screw through the Arm (F) into the end of the Arm Supports (G), using two 2¹/₂-inch wood screws on each joint.

**5** Repeat step 4 to construct another side, using the remaining two Arm Supports (G) and the remaining Arm (F).

## Attracting the Arms

**1** Draw a line across the inside of each Arm Support (G), 18 inches from the unattached end. This will be the placement line for the next step.

**2** This step is easier with a helper. The object is to clamp the assembled seat between the two side assemblies (as shown in *figure 6* on page 136), then secure the seat with carriage bolts. The top of the seat should be positioned at the placement marks that you drew on the Arm Supports (G). The front Arm Supports (G) should be positioned 2 inches from the front of the seat assembly. When the sides are in position, clamp the two sides and seat assemblies tightly together, using bar clamps.

**3** Drill a hole slightly larger than the diameter of the 3¹/₂-inch carriage bolt through the center of each of the Arm Supports (G) and into the Seat Sides (B). Then insert a 3¹/₂-inch carriage bolt through each of the holes. Tighten the bolts securely.

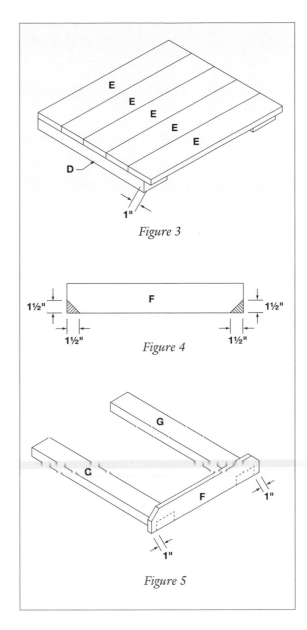

Figure 3

Figure 4

Figure 5

## Adding the Back

1 Insert the back assembly between the two assembled sides. The Backs (E) should face the front of the chair, and the recessed end of the two Back Supports (D) should be at the top of the chair. To make the chair more comfortable, tilt the back assembly at a slight angle—out at the top and in at the bottom. The tilt angle is determined by the width of the 2x4 on the Arm Supports (G) and the back of the Arm (F).

2 When you have the back fitted perfectly, secure the assembly with bar clamps. Screw through the Arm Supports (H) into the Back Supports (E), using two 2$^1$/$_2$-inch wood screws. Then insert a 3$^1$/$_2$-inch lag screw through the Arm Supports (H) and into the Back Supports (E).

## Finishing

1 Fill any cracks, crevices, or screw holes with wood filler.

2 Sand the completed chair thoroughly.

3 Paint or stain the chair the color of your choice—or simply leave it the natural color.

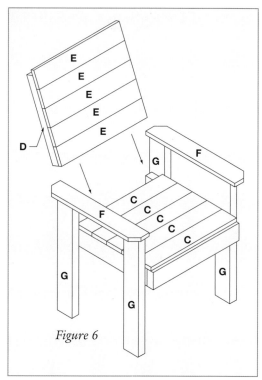

*Figure 6*

# Porch Swing

*Once a favorite of my grandmother's, this wonderful seat is now a favorite of ours. In fact, this wooden porch swing is just like the one my grandmother had on her front porch. It is a peaceful place for resting, and brings back memories of the neighbors coming to call.*

## Special Tools & Techniques

- Bar clamps

## Materials

- 20 linear feet of 2x4 pine
- 30 linear feet ⁵/₄ pine decking
- 5 linear feet of 1x4 pine

## Hardware

- 35 2¹/₂″ wood screws
- 12 2″ wood screws
- 4 3¹/₂″ lag screws
- 4 3¹/₂″ lag bolts
- 4 3″ eye bolts
- Chain and fittings for hanging swing*

## *Notes on Materials

Because each situation is unique, we have not specified the hardware necessary to hang the swing, though it is very important to make certain that the swing is hung securely. We suggest that it be hung only from an extremely solid structural member on your porch or deck. We used chain and eye bolts rated to hold 1,500 pounds. We do not really expect it to have to bear that kind of weight, but it is better to be safe than sorry. If you are in doubt about your particular situation, consult an expert at your local hardware or building supply store.

## Cutting List

| Code | Description | Qty. | Materials | Dimensions |
|------|-------------|------|-----------|------------|
| A | Seat Front/Back | 2 | 2x4 pine | 48″ long |
| B | Seat Side | 2 | 2x4 pine | 19″ long |
| C | Seat Support | 1 | 2x4 pine | 19″ long |
| D | Seat Slat | 4 | ⁵/₄ pine decking | 48″ long |
| E | Back Support | 2 | 2x4 pine | 16″ long |
| F | Back | 3 | ⁵/₄ pine decking | 48″ long |
| G | Arm | 2 | 1x4 | 26″ long |
| H | Arm Support | 4 | 2x4 | 11¹/₂″ long |

## Building the Seat

1 Cut two Seat Front/Backs (A) from 2x4 pine, each measuring 48 inches.

2 Cut two Seat Sides (B) from 2x4 pine, each measuring 19 inches.

3 Place the two Seat Front/Backs (A) on edge, parallel to each other and 19 inches apart. Fit the two Seat Sides (B) between the ends of the Seat Front/Backs (A) to form a rectangle measuring 22x48 inches, as shown in *figure 1* on page 138. Apply glue to the meeting surfaces, and screw through the Seat Front/Backs (A) into the ends of the Seat Sides (B), using two 2¹/₂-inch wood screws on each joint.

4 Cut one Seat Support (C) from 2x4 pine, measuring 19 inches.

5 Place the Seat Support (C) in the center of the rectangle, parallel to and centered between the two Seat Sides (B), as shown in *figure 1*.

6 Cut four Seat Slats (D) from $^5/_4$ pine decking, each measuring 48 inches.

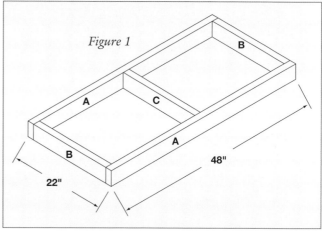

*Figure 1*

22"

48"

7 Place the rectangular seat assembly (Seat Front/Backs [A], two Seat Sides [B], and Seat Support [C]) on a flat surface. Position the four Seat Slats (D) over the assembly, as shown in *figure 2*. Screw through the Seat Slats (D) into the Seat Sides (B) and Seat Support (C), using two 2$^1/_2$-inch wood screws on each joint.

## Making the Back

1 Cut two Back Supports (E) from 2x4 pine, each measuring 16 inches

2 Cut three Backs (F) from $^5/_4$ pine decking, each measuring 48 inches.

3 Position the two Back Supports (E) on a flat surface, parallel to each other and 41 inches apart. Place one Back (F) over the two Back Supports (E), as shown in *figure 3* on page 140.

4 The first Back (F) should overhang the ends of the two Back Supports (E) by ¹/₂ inch. Apply glue to the meeting surfaces, and screw through the Back (F) into each of the Back Supports (E), using two 2-inch wood screws on each joint.

**5** Repeat step 4 twice (without the ½-inch overhang) to attach the remaining two Backs (F) to the two Back Supports (E).

## Making the Sides

**1** Cut two Arms (G) from 1x4 pine, each measuring 26 inches.

**2** Using *figure 4* as a guide, shape one Arm (G), eliminating the shaded portions. Use the resulting Arm (G) as a pattern to shape the remaining Arm (G).

**3** Cut four Arm Supports (H) from 2x4 pine, each measuring 11½ inches.

**4** Place the seat assembly (A, B, C, and D) on a level surface. Position the four Arm Supports (H) on end at each of the four corners of the seat assembly, as shown in *figure 5*. The Arm Supports (H) should be flush with the Seat Front/Backs (A) at the front and back of the assembly. Screw through the Arm Supports (H) into the Seat Front/Backs (A), using a 2½-inch wood screw. To reinforce the joint, insert a 3½-inch lag bolt through the Arm Support (H) and the Seat Sides (B). Tighten the bolt securely. Repeat the procedure to attach the remaining three Arm Supports (H).

**5** Using *figure 4* as a placement guide, place one Arm (G) over the ends of the two Arm Supports (H). The rear Arm Support (H) should be flush against the 3½ x ¾-inch cutout in the Arm (G), and the front Arm Support (H) should be ¾ inch from the same edge. Apply glue to the meeting surfaces, and screw through the Arm (G)

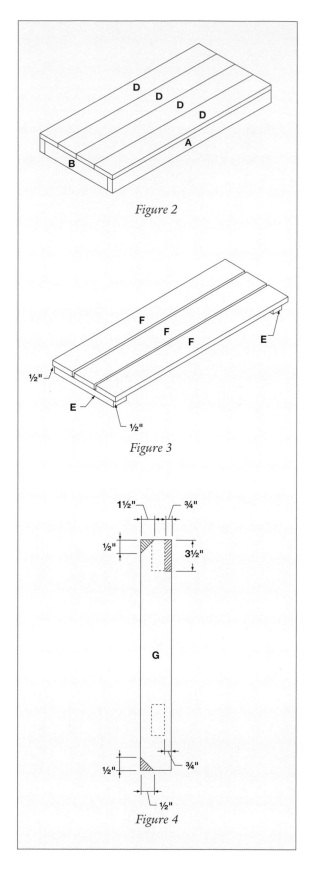

*Figure 2*

*Figure 3*

*Figure 4*

into the Arm Support (H), using one 2¹/₂-inch wood screw on each joint.

## Adding the Back

1 Insert the back assembly between the two assembled arms. The Backs (F) should face the front of the swing, and the exposed portion of the two Back Supports (E) should be against the seat. The back assembly will be secured to the rear Arm Supports (H). To make the swing more comfortable, tilt the back assembly at a slight angle—out at the top and in at the bottom. The tilt angle is determined by the width of the 2x4 on the Arm Supports (H).

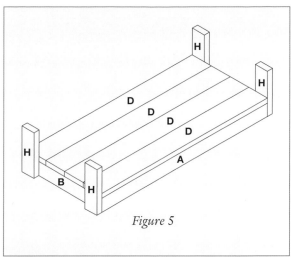

*Figure 5*

**2** When you have the back fitted perfectly, secure the assembly with bar clamps. Screw through the Arm Supports (H) into the Back Supports (E), using two 2½-inch wood screws. Then insert two 3½-inch lag screws through each of the Arm Supports (H) into the Back Supports (E).

### Finishing

**1** Fill any cracks, crevices, and screw holes with wood filler.

**2** Sand the completed swing thoroughly.

**3** Paint or stain the swing the color of your choice—or simply leave it the natural color.

**4** Screw a 3-inch eye bolt through the top of the Arm (G) into both the front and rear Arm Supports (H) on both sides of the swing.

**5** Hang the swing using heavy-duty chain. Make certain that the structure you hang it from can support the weight.

**6** Mix up a pitcher of lemonade, and enjoy!

# Hammock Stand

*If you've always wanted to have a hammock in your backyard, but couldn't because your trees weren't in the right place, here's the solution: No, you don't have to dig up two trees and replant them! Build this sturdy hammock stand instead, hang your favorite hammock on it, and place it anywhere you want—preferably where no one will disturb you!*

## Special Tools & Techniques

- Dadoes
- Miters

## Materials

- 44 linear feet of 4x4 pine
- 2 fencepost finals

## Hardware

- 40 3″ screws
- 40 2″ screws
- 2 $^5/_{16}$″x4″ bolts, with 4 washers and 2 nuts
- 2 T-shaped metal back plates, 4″ wide
- 2 metal screw hangers (sturdy enough to hold a hammock and two adults)

## Cutting List (for both stands)

| Code | Description | Qty. | Materials | Dimensions |
|------|-------------|------|-----------|------------|
| A | Cross Tie | 2 | 4x4 pine | 80″ long |
| B | Upright | 2 | 4x4 pine | 56½″ long |
| C | Front Brace | 2 | 4x4 pine | 33½″ long |
| D | Side Brace | 4 | 4x4 pine | 12″ long |
| E | Footing | 2 | 4x4 pine | 60″ long |

## Cutting the Pieces

Each stand consists of two identical pieces constructed of 4x4 pine. Its strength comes from the system of dadoes cut into the individual pieces. It's not difficult to do, but requires some patience and rechecking to make certain that each of the boards is properly shaped. Take your time and work carefully, and all the pieces will fit together perfectly. The following are instructions for making one stand. Two stands will be required; if you wish to make them both at the same time, simply repeat each step.

1 Cut one cross tie (A) from 4x4 pine, measuring 80 inches long.

2 Follow *figure 1* to measure and then cut a lap dado across the width of one end of the cross tie (A), 3 inches across and 1½ inches deep.

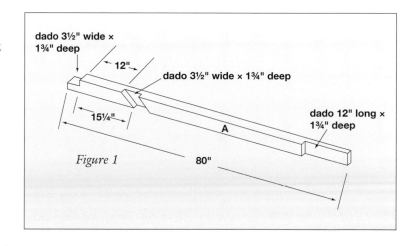

dado 3½″ wide × 1¾″ deep

12″

dado 3½″ wide × 1¾″ deep

15¼″

dado 12″ long × 1¾″ deep

A

*Figure 1*

80″

3 As shown in *figure 1* on page 143, cut a 45-degree diagonal dado in the cross tie (A), 12 inches from the lap dado, 3½ inches wide and 1¾ inches deep. *Figure 1* shows an additional 12-inch-long dado cut on the remaining end. This dado will be cut later.

4 Cut one upright (B) from 4x4 pine, measuring 56½ inches long.

5 Follow *figure 2* on page 145 to measure and then cut one 45-degree diagonal dado 3½ inches wide and 1¾ inches deep, 12 inches from what will be the bottom of the upright support (B).

6 Cut one front brace (C) from 4x4 pine, measuring 33½ inches long.

7 Miter both ends of the front brace (C) at opposing 45-degree angles, as shown in *figure 3* on page 145.

8 Cut two opposing diagonal dadoes in the front brace (C), 3½ inches wide and 1¾ inches deep, as shown in *figure 4* on page 145.

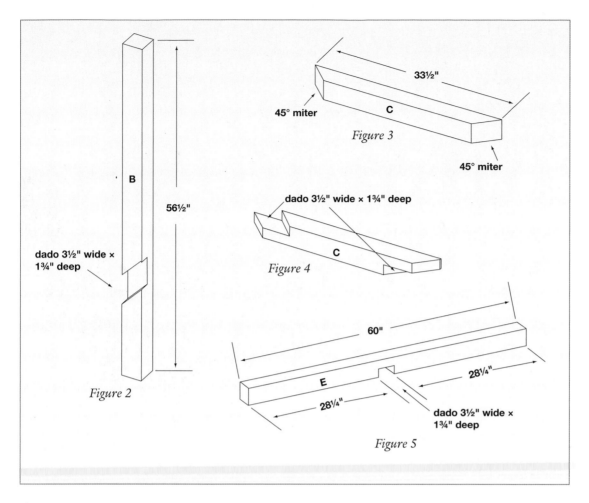

**45° miter**
**33½"**
C
*Figure 3*
**45° miter**

B
**56½"**

**dado 3½" wide × 1¾" deep**

**dado 3½" wide × 1¾" deep**
C
*Figure 4*

*Figure 2*

**60"**
E
**28¼"**
**28¼"**
**dado 3½" wide × 1¾" deep**
*Figure 5*

9 Cut two side braces (D) from 4x4 pine, each measuring 12 inches long.

10 Miter both ends of the side braces (D) at opposing 45-degree angles in the same manner as you did with the front braces (C), shown in *figure 3*.

11 Cut one footing (E) from 4x4 pine, measuring 60 inches long.

12 Follow *figure 5* to cut a $3\frac{1}{2}$-inch-wide dado, $1^3/_4$ inches deep, in the center of the footing (E).

## Assembling the Stand

1 Place the cross tie (A) on a level surface, with the lap dado exposed on the top, as shown in *figure 1* on page 143.

2 Place the footing (E) dado side down, over the lap dado in the cross tie (A). Screw them together by screwing through the footing dado into the cross tie dado. Use four 3-inch-long screws to secure the joint.

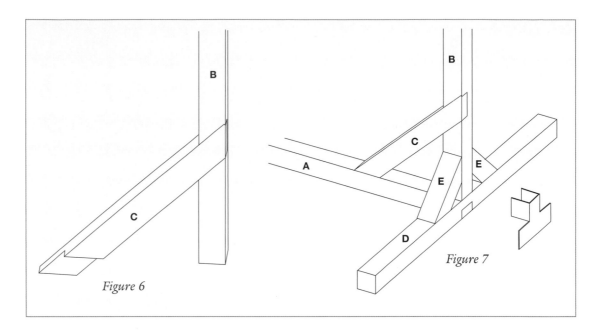

Figure 6

Figure 7

3 Fit the front brace (C) into the diagonal dado cut into the upright (B), as shown in *figure 6*.

4 Refer to *figure 7* to complete the final steps of the assembly. Place the upright (B) directly over the dado joining the footing (E) and the cross-tie (A). Fit the free end of the front brace (C) into the diagonal dado cut in the cross tie (A). Do not secure the joint yet.

5 Place the metal back plate, "T" down, over the joint between the upright (B) and the footing (D), so that the side brackets extend around the upright. Screw the back plate to the footing using 2-inch-long screws through the back plate into the footing.

6 Make certain that the upright is exactly square to both the footing and the cross tie. First, screw through the metal back plate to secure the upright in place. Then, screw through the dado joint in the cross tie (A) and front brace (C), using four 3-inch-long screws. Finally, screw through the dado joint in the upright (B) and front brace (C), using four 3-inch-long screws.

7 Place one side brace (D), short side down, against the footing (E) and upright (A). Screw through one end of the side brace (D) into the footing (E) and through the other end of the side brace (D) into the upright (A). Use two 3-inch-long screws on each joint.

8 Repeat step 7 to attach the remaining side brace (D) to the opposite side of the upright (A) and footing (E).

9 Repeat all previous steps to make the second stand.

## Finishing

1 Screw a metal hanger into each of the uprights (A), about 5 inches from the top, on the same side as the front brace (C).

2 The ends of the cross ties now must be marked and cut depending upon the size of your hammock. Place the two stands opposite each other, with the ends of the cross ties side by side. Hang your hammock on the hangers between the two stands. Move the two stands closer or farther apart, depending upon the size of your hammock, and how far from the ground you wish the hammock to hang. IT IS NOT SAFE TO GET IN THE HAMMOCK YET!

3 When you have decided what length the cross ties (A) should be, mark the length on the cross ties (A), and then mark a 12-inch length for overlap on each cross tie (A) Cut the cross ties (A) to length.

4 Remember the additional dado shown on the cross tie (A) shown in *figure 1* on page 143? Well, now is the time to cut it. Cut a 12-inch-long dado 1$^3/_4$ inch deep in both cross ties, making certain that they are mirror images of each other.

5 Clamp the two dadoes together, and 3 inches from each end of the joint, drill two holes through both dadoes, large enough to accommodate your 4-inch bolts.

6 Place a washer on each bolt, fit the bolts through the drilled holes, add a second washer and a nut, and tighten the nuts.

7 Mark the center of the top of each upright, and screw in a decorative fencepost finial.

8 We left our hammock stand unfinished, but if you wish a more formal look, fill any cracks, crevices, or screw holes with wood filler, and thoroughly sand all surfaces.

9 Paint or stain the finished project the color of your choice, or simply seal it with a clear sealer.

10 Climb in your hammock and take a nap.

# Lattice Bower

*This romantic bower will become your own personal hideaway. Place it in a quiet corner of the yard, and it's perfect for early morning coffee or late afternoon lounging. The frame is constructed of 2x4s, so this beauty is very sturdy.*

### Special Tools & Techniques

- Router
- Rabbet bit

### Materials

- 140 linear feet of 2x4 pine
- 12 linear feet of 1x2 pine
- 35 linear feet of 1x4 pine
- 3 sheets of lattice, 4'x8'*

*premade lattice can be purchased at lumber-supply outlets*

### Hardware

- 200 $2^{1}/_{2}$" screws
- 25 $1^{1}/_{2}$" screws
- 200 4dx$1^{1}/_{2}$" nails
- 14 lag bolts, 3" long

### Cutting List

| Code | Description | Qty. | Materials | Dimensions |
|------|-------------|------|-----------|------------|
| A | Vertical | 6 | 2x4 pine | 72" long |
| B | Horizontal Side | 6 | 2x4 pine | $21^{1}/_{2}$" long |
| C | Slats | 19 | 2x4 pine | $23^{1}/_{2}$" long |
| D | Side Panel | 2 | lattice | 23"x$34^{1}/_{2}$" |
| E | Horizontal Back | 3 | 2x4 pine | 57" long |
| F | Back Panel | 1 | lattice | $58^{1}/_{2}$"x$34^{1}/_{2}$" |
| G | Long Bench Support | 2 | 2x4 pine | 64" long |
| H | Short Bench Support | 2 | 2x4 pine | 24" long |
| I | Inner Supports | 2 | 1x2 pine | 61" long |
| J | Bench Slat | 16 | 1x4 pine | 24" long |
| K | Long Top Support | 2 | 2x4 pine | 64" long |
| L | Short Top Support | 2 | 2x4 pine | 24" long |
| M | Top Panel | 1 | lattice | $62^{1}/_{2}$"x$25^{1}/_{2}$" |

## Making the Sides

1 Cut two verticals (A) from 2x4 pine, each measuring 72 inches long.

2 Cut three horizontal sides (B) from 2x4 pine, each measuring $21^{1}/_{2}$ inches long.

3 Place the two verticals (A) on a level surface, wide face up, $21^{1}/_{2}$ inches apart and parallel to each other. Fit the three horizontal sides (B) between the two verticals, spacing them as shown in *figure 1* on page 150. The inside of the top two horizontal sides (B) will later be

routed ³/₄ inch deep to accommodate the lattice. Because of this, we need to avoid placing screws where they will interfere with the routing. Mark what will be the inside of the assembly, and avoid placing screws within ³/₄ inch of that side. Then apply glue to the meeting surfaces, clamp the assembly together securely, and toenail through each side of the horizontal sides (B) into the verticals (A) using two 2¹/₂-inch-long screws on each joint.

4 Cut four slats (C) from 2x4 pine, each measuring 23¹/₂ inches long.

5 Fit the four slats (C) between the two lower horizontal sides (B), as shown in *figure 2* on page 151. Toenail through each side of the slats (C) into each of the two lower horizontal sides (B), using two 2¹/₂-inch-long screws on each joint.

6 The upper opening between the two upper horizontal side (B) and the two verticals (A) must be routed to accommodate the lattice panel. Place the assembly with the side you designated as the "inside" face up. Use a rabbet bit to rout the edges ³/₄ inch deep and ³/₄ inch wide where the lattice will fit, as shown in *figure 2* on page 151.

7 Before cutting any of your lattice, carefully plan exactly how to position the pieces that you need to cut. Lattice is a little tricky, since it looks like the same design whichever way you look at it. But this is not true. Be sure that you cut it so that the over-and-under lattice panels are the same. Cut the lattice with the grain each time, or, when you place the pieces together, the differences will be obvious. Cut a side panel (D) from lattice, measuring 23x34¹/₂ inches. Save any lattice slats that are left over from the cutting. These will be used as trim.

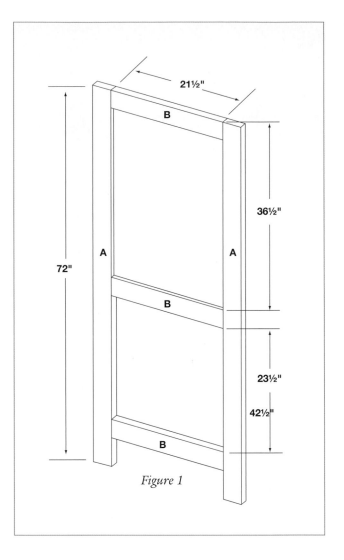

Figure 1

8 Apply glue to the meeting surfaces, and fit the side panel (D) into the routed opening on the upper section of the assembled side panel. Use 1¹/₂-inch-long finishing nails to attach the lattice to the verticals (A) and horizontal sides (B).

9 Repeat steps 1 through 8 to assemble the other side.

## Making the Back

1 Cut two verticals (A) from 2x4 pine, each measuring 72 inches long.

2 Cut three horizontal backs (E) from 2x4 pine, each measuring 57 inches long.

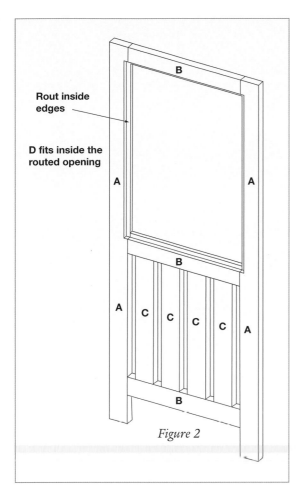

**Rout inside edges**

**D fits inside the routed opening**

B

A        A

B

A     C   C   C   C   A

B

*Figure 2*

3 Place the two verticals (A) on a level surface, wide face up, 57 inches apart and parallel to each other. Fit the three horizontal backs (E) between the two verticals (A), spacing them as shown in *figure 1* on page 150. Here, too, the inside edges of the top two horizontal backs (E) will later be routed ³/₄ inch deep to accommodate the lattice. Because of this, we need to avoid placing screws where they will interfere with the routing. Mark what will be the inside of the assembly, and avoid placing screws within ³/₄ inch of that side. Then apply glue to the meeting surfaces, clamp the assembly together securely, and toenail through each side of the horizontal backs (E) into the verticals (A), using two 2¹/₂-inch-long screws on each joint.

4 Cut 11 slats (C) from 2x4 pine, each measuring 23¹/₂ inches long.

5 Fit the 11 slats (C) between the two lower horizontal backs (E) in the same manner you used to assemble the sides. Space the slats 1¹/₂ inches apart. When you have the spacing correct, toenail through each side of the slats (C) into each of the two lower horizontal backs (E), using two 2¹/₂-inch-long screws on each joint.

6 Now the upper opening between the two upper horizontal backs (E) and the two verticals (A) must be routed to accommodate the lattice panel. Place the assembly with the side you designated as the "inside" face up. Use a rabbet bit to rout the edges ³/₄ inch deep and ³/₄ inch wide where the lattice will fit.

7 Cut a back panel (F) from lattice, measuring 58¹/₂x34¹/₂ inches. Save the leftover lattice slats for the trim.

8 Fit the back panel (F) into the routed opening on the upper section of the assembled back. Use 1¹/₂-inch-long finishing nails to attach the lattice to the verticals (A) and horizontal backs (E).

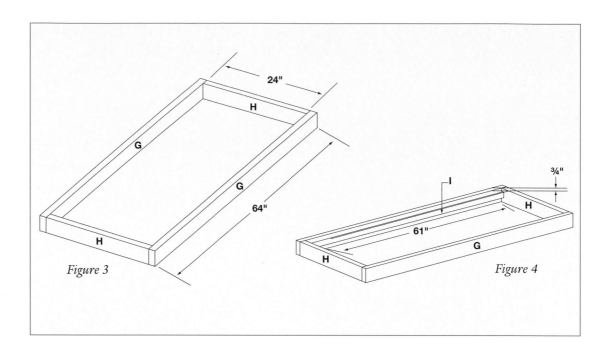

24"

H

G

G

64"

H

Figure 3

I

¾"

H

61"

H

G

Figure 4

## Connecting the Sides and Back

1 You will probably want to enlist the assistance of a helper for this next maneuver. If one is not available, use bar clamps to hold the pieces in place while you join them. Place the back assembly on a level work surface, with the "inside" surface facing up. Place one side assembly, edge up, next to the back assembly. Predrill and countersink holes, and use three 3-inch-long lag bolts to-secure the joint. Place each of the lag bolts opposite each of the horizontal backs (E).

2 Repeat the procedure to attach the other side assembly to the opposite side of the back assembly.

## Constructing the Bench

1 Cut two long bench supports (G) from 2x4 pine, each measuring 64 inches long.

2 Cut two short bench supports (H) from 2x4 pine, each measuring 24 inches long.

3 Place the two long bench supports (G) on a level surface, parallel to each other, and 24 inches apart. Fit the two short bench supports (H) between the two long bench supports (G), as shown in *figure 3*. Screw through the long bench supports (G) into the ends of the short bench supports (H). Use two 2¹/₂-inch-long screws on each of the joints.

4 Cut two inner supports (I) from 1x2 pine, each measuring 61 inches long.

5 Apply glue to the meeting surfaces and screw one inner support (I) to the inner side of one long bench support (G), ³/₄ inch from the top edge, as shown in *figure 4* on page 152. Use 1¹/₂-inch-long screws about every 5 inches.

6 Repeat step 5 to attach the other inner support (I) to the opposite long bench support (G).

7 Cut 16 bench slats (J) from 1x4 pine, each measuring 24 inches long.

8 Fit the 16 bench slats (J) over the two inner supports (I), leaving approximately ¹/₄ inch between bench slats (J), as shown in *figure 5*. When you are satisfied with the placement, nail through each bench slat (J) into the inner supports (I), using two 1¹/₂-inch-long nails on each joint.

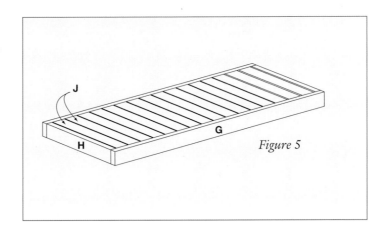

*Figure 5*

9 Place the back assembly, with attached side assemblies, on its back. Fit the bench assembly inside, with its bottom 14 inches from the lower ends of the verticals (A). Predrill holes for 3-inch lag bolts through the front verticals into the ends of the long bench supports (G). Insert the lag bolts and tighten them securely. Repeat this procedure to insert two more lag bolts through the verticals (A) into the ends of the other long bench supports (G).

## Making the Top

1 Cut two long top supports (K) from 2x4 pine, each measuring 64 inches long.

2 Cut two short top supports (L) from 2x4 pine, each measuring 24 inches long.

3 Place the two long Top supports (K) on a level surface, parallel to each other and 24 inches apart, similar to the arrangement shown in *figure 3* on page 152. Fit the two short top supports (L) between the two long top supports (K). Screw through the long top supports (K) into the ends of the short top supports (L), using two 2¹/₂-inch-long screws on each joint.

4 The top also contains a recessed lattice panel. To accommodate the panel, use a rabbet bit to rout the inner edges of one side of the top assembly, ³/₄x³/₄ inches.

5 Cut a top panel (M) from lattice, measuring 62¹/₂x25¹/₂ inches.

6 Fit the top panel (M) into the routed groove in the top assembly. Nail through the top panel (M) into the long top supports (K) and short top supports (L), using $1^{1}/_{2}$-inch-long finishing nails.

7 Place the back assembly, with attached side and bench assemblies, on its back. Fit the top assembly inside, flush with the top edge of the verticals (A). Predrill holes for 3-inch lag bolts through the front verticals into the ends of the long top supports (K). Insert the lag bolts and tighten them securely. Repeat this procedure to insert two more lag bolts through the verticals (A) into the ends of the other long top supports (K).

## Finishing

1 Cover any exposed edges of the lattice panels with leftover slats from the unused lattice panels. To secure them, use glue and $1^{1}/_{2}$-inch- long nails spaced about every 5 inches.

2 Fill any cracks, crevices, or screw holes with wood filler, and thoroughly sand all surfaces of the completed project.

3 Seal and paint or stain your lattice bower the color of your choice.

# Accessories

# Wooden Doormat

*This oversized striped doormat is not only attractive but extremely practical. Debris can easily be scraped off the soles of shoes, and the weather-resistant wood can be hosed off with water. The doormat also provides sure footing during rain because water runs into the spaces between the wooden strips.*

## Materials

- 50 linear feet of 1x2 pine
- 10 linear feet of 1x4 pine

## Hardware

- 300 3dx1¼" nails

## Cutting List

| Code | Description | Qty. | Materials | Dimensions |
|------|-------------|------|-----------|------------|
| A | Long Side | 2 | 1x2 pine | 34½" long |
| B | Short Side | 2 | 1x2 pine | 24½" long |
| C | Narrow Support | 6 | 1x2 pine | 23" long |
| D | Wide Support | 2 | 1x4 pine | 23" long |
| E | Narrow Slat | 9 | 1x2 pine | 34½" long |
| F | Wide Slat | 2 | 1x4 pine | 34½" long |

## Making the Frame

1 Cut two long sides (A) from 1x2 pine, each measuring 34½ inches long.

2 Cut two short sides (B) from 1x2 pine, each measuring 24½ inches long.

3 Place the two short sides (B) on a level surface, parallel to each other and 34½ inches apart. Fit the two long sides (A) between the two short sides (B), as shown in *figure 1*. Nail through the short sides (B) into the ends of the long sides (A), using two 1½-inch-long nails on each joint.

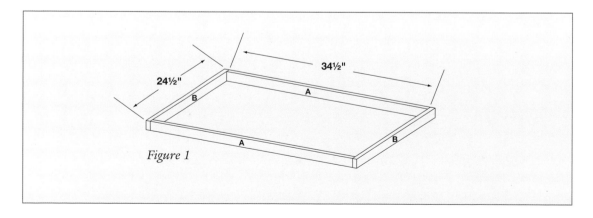

*Figure 1*

## Adding the Support Boards

1 Cut six narrow supports (C) from 1x2 pine, each measuring 23 inches long.

2 Cut two wide supports (D) from 1x4 pine, each measuring 23 inches long.

3 Place the frame assembly on a level surface. Refer to *figure 2* to fit the narrow and wide supports (C and D) inside the frame assembly, placing the two wide supports (D) in the center of the frame, and three narrow supports (C) on each side of the wide supports (D). All the supports should be flush with the bottom of the frame assembly, ³/₄ inch from the top of the frame assembly, and approximately 2¹/₂ inches apart. The exact spacing is not critical. Nail through the long sides (A) into the ends of the narrow and wide supports (C and D).

## Adding the Top Slats

1 Cut nine narrow slats (E) from 1x2 pine, each measuring 34¹/₂ inches long.

2 Cut two wide slats (F) from 1x4 pine, each measuring 34¹/₂ inches long.

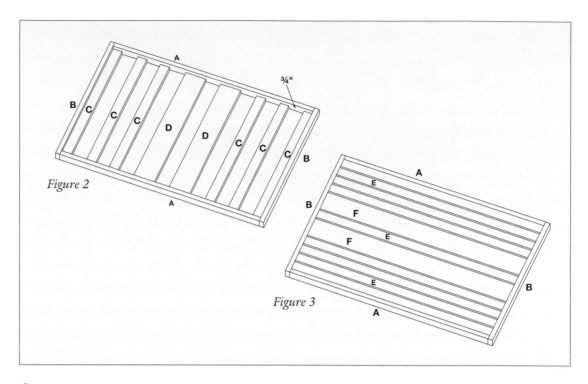

*Figure 2*

*Figure 3*

3 Place the frame assembly on a level surface. Refer to *figure 3* to position the narrow and wide slats (E and F) inside the frame assembly. First, place one narrow slat (E) in the center, then two wide slats (F) on either side, then four more narrow slats (E) on each side. All the supports should be flush with the top of the frame assembly and $\frac{1}{2}$ inch apart. The outer two narrow slats (E) should be flush with the long sides (A). Apply glue to the meeting surfaces, and nail through the long sides (A) into the ends of the narrow and wide slats (E and F). Then nail through each of the narrow and wide slats (E and F) into each of the narrow and wide supports (C and D).

## Finishing

1 Fill any cracks, crevices, or screw holes with wood filler, and thoroughly sand all surfaces of the completed doormat.

2 Seal or stain your doormat the color of your choice.

# Footstool

*This simple footstool has been put to many uses in our backyard. We have used it to accompany our Garden Sofa (page 95) and our Adirondack Chair (page 78). Great as a footrest, it also provides a handy surface for a stack of magazines or a pitcher of iced tea. And if things get crowded, this nifty footstool can double as an extra seat.*

| Materials | Hardware |
|-----------|----------|
| ■ 11 linear feet of 2x4 pine<br>■ 14 linear feet of 1x4 pine | ■ 10 2½" screws<br>■ 15 3dx1¼" nails |

## Cutting List

| Code | Description | Qty. | Materials | Dimensions |
|------|-------------|------|-----------|------------|
| A | Long Horizontal | 2 | 2x4 pine | 21" long |
| B | Leg | 4 | 2x4 pine | 12" long |
| C | Short Horizontal | 2 | 2x4 pine | 13" long |
| D | Slat | 8 | 1x4 pine | 18" long |

## Constructing the Base

1 Cut two long horizontals (A) from 2x4 pine, each measuring 21 inches long.

2 Cut four legs (B) from 2x4 pine, each measuring 12 inches long.

3 Place two legs (B) on a level surface, parallel to each other and 20 inches apart. Fit one long horizontal (A) between the two legs (B), flush with the ends of the legs (B), as shown in *figure 1*. Toenail through the ends of the long horizontals (A) into the legs (B). Use two 2½-inch-long screws on each joint.

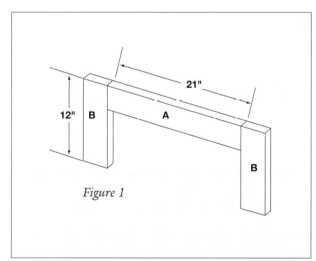

*Figure 1*

4 Repeat step 3 to attach the remaining long horizontal (A) to the other two legs (B).

5 Cut two short horizontals (C) from 2x4 pine, each measuring 13 inches long.

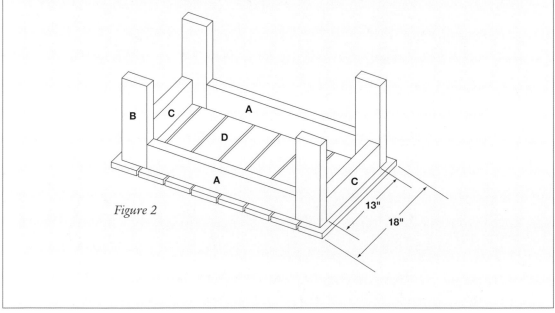

Figure 2

13"

18"

B    C         A

D

A              C

6 Place the two leg assemblies upside down on a level surface, parallel to each other and 13 inches apart, as shown in *figure 2* on page 160. Fit the short horizontals (C) between the two leg assemblies, flush with the outer legs (B). Screw through the legs (B) into the ends of the short horizontals. Use two 2$^1$/$_2$-inch-long screws on each joint.

## Adding the Slats

1 Cut eight slats (D) from 1x4 pine, each measuring 18 inches long.

2 Center the eight slats (D) over the base assembly, spacing them $^1$/$_4$ inch apart. The slats (D) should overhang each of the short horizontals (C) by $^7$/$_8$ inch, and overhang each of the long horizontals (A) by 1 inch, as shown in *figure 2* on page 160. Apply glue to the meeting surfaces, and nail through each of the eight slats (D) into the horizontals (A and C) and legs (B).

## Finishing

1 Fill any cracks, crevices, or nail and screw holes with wood filler, and thoroughly sand all surfaces of the completed footstool.

2 Seal and paint or stain your completed footstool the color of your choice. Here, we painted the footstool to match the Adirondack Chair, seen on page 78.

# Cottage Mailbox

*When we bought our house it came complete with a standard boring mailbox. When we shopped for a new one we discovered that all the good-looking mailboxes had a very healthy price tag attached to them. So we covered our standard boring mailbox with inexpensive plywood and, we think, a few delightful details. We're very happy with the result, and the mailbox brings smiles to people passing by.*

### Special Tools & Techniques

- Beveling

### Materials

- ½ sheet of ⅜"-thick exterior plywood, measuring 4'x4'
- 2 linear feet of 2x4 pine
- 11 picket fence sections*
- 6-10 plants in 3" pots (optional)
- Premade numbers for your address
- Standard size mailbox

*\*Premade pickets are available at most hobby and craft-supply stores, or you can construct your own (see Adding the Fencing on page 166).*

### Hardware

- 60 3dx1" nails
- 10 1½" screws

### Cutting List

| Code | Description | Qty. | Materials | Dimensions |
|------|-------------|------|-----------|------------|
| A | Front | 1 | ⅜" plywood | 11¼"x13" |
| B | Back | 1 | ⅜" plywood | 11¼"x13" |
| C | Sides | 2 | ⅜" plywood | 18¾"x9¾" |
| D | Roof | 2 | ⅜" plywood | 9¼"x23½" |
| E | Chimney | 1 | 2x4 pine | 14" long |
| F | Base | 2 | ⅜" plywood | 9¾"x6½" |

## Making the Front, Back & Sides

1 Cut one front (A) from ⅜-inch-thick plywood, measuring 11¼x13 inches.

2 Refer to *figure 1* on page 164 to cut a curved doorway and a peaked roof on the front (A). Double-check to make certain that the curved doorway is sized to accommodate your mailbox.

3 Cut one back (B) from ⅜-inch-thick plywood, measuring 11¼x13 inches.

4 Use the front (A) as a pattern to cut a peaked roof on the back (B). Do not cut the curved doorway on the back (B).

5 Cut two sides (C) from $^3/_8$-inch-thick plywood, each measuring $18^3/_4$x$9^3/_4$ inches.

6 Place the two sides (C) on a level surface, parallel to each other and $11^1/_4$ inches apart. The

18³/₄-inch-long edge of the sides should face down. Fit the front (A) and back (B) between the two sides (D), as shown in *figure 2*. Note that the sides (C) will be slightly shorter at the top edges than the front (A) and back (B). That distance will allow for the angle of the roof peak. Apply glue to the meeting surfaces and use four 1-inch-long nails on each joint.

## Adding the Roof

1 Cut two roofs (D) from ³/₈-inch-thick plywood, each measuring 9¹/₄x23¹/₄ inches.

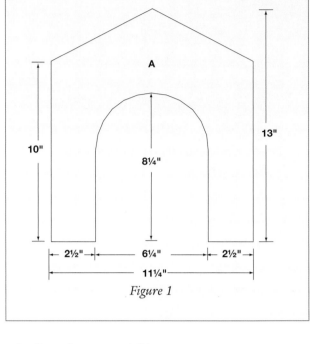

*Figure 1*

2 Bevel one 23¹/₄-inch edge of each of the roofs (D) at a 30-degree angle, as shown in *figure 3* on page 165.

3 Fit the two roofs (D) over the sides (C), front (A), and back (B), matching the bevels. The roofs (D) should overhang the front (A) and back (B) an equal amount. Nail through the roof (D) into the front, back, and sides (A, B, and C), using 1-inch-long nails.

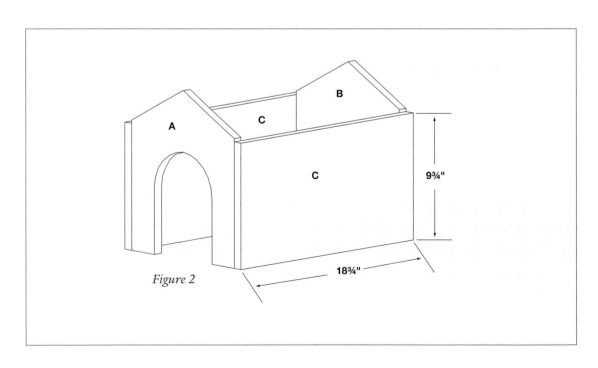

*Figure 2*

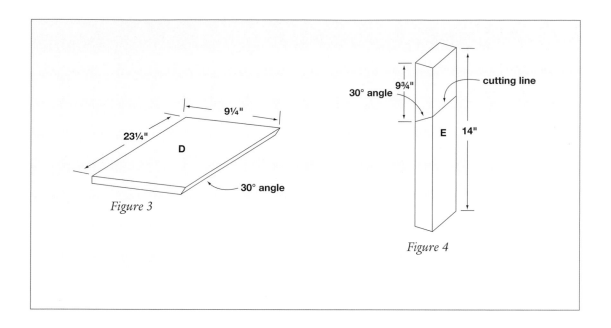

Figure 3

Figure 4

## Adding the Chimney

1 Cut one chimney (E) from 2x4 pine, measuring 14 inches long.

2 Measure 9³/₄ inches from one end of the chimney (E), mark the spot, and cut across the width of the chimney (E) at a 30-degree angle, as shown in *figure 4*.

3 Fit the shorter portion of the chimney (E) on top of the roof (D), just above where the longer portion of the chimney will fit. Screw through the underside of the roof (D) into the short chimney, using two 112-inch-long screws. Countersink the screws.

4 Fit the longer portion of the chimney (E) under the roof against one side of the house. Screw through the inside of the side (C) into the chimney (E), using two 1¹/₂-inch long screws. (Note: The longer portion of the chimney is not visible in the project photograph.)

## Adding the Base

1 Cut two bases (F) from 5³/₈-inch-thick plywood, each measuring 19³/₄x6¹/₂ inches.

2 Attach one base (F) to the right bottom of the house assembly, flush with the inside with the front door and extending 1 inch from the house front. Apply glue to the meeting surfaces and nail through the base (F) into the edges of the front, back, and side (A, B, and C), using 1-inch-long nails spaced every three inches.

3 Repeat step 2 to attach the remaining base (F) to the left side of the house.

## Adding the Fencing

1 We purchased premade sections of white picket fence at a hobby store. Each section is 6¹/₂ inches long.

 If you prefer to make your own picket fence, simply cut two ⁵/₈-inch-wide strips, each measuring 6¹/₂ inches long. These will be the fence rails. Then cut eight pickets from ⁵/₈-inch-wide strips, each measuring 4 inches long. Space the pickets evenly over the two fence rails and glue and nail together using small brads.

2 Cut and fit the picket fence sections to fit all the way around both of the bases.

## Finishing

1 Remove the flag from the old mailbox and attach it to the top of the chimney.

2 Fill any cracks, crevices, or screw holes with wood filler, and thoroughly sand all surfaces of the completed mailbox.

3 Seal and paint or stain your mailbox the colors of your choice.

4 Attach the numbers for your address on the side of the mailbox.

5 Slip the cottage mailbox over your purchased mailbox.

6 As a final decorative touch, we placed several live plants in 3-inch containers in our mailbox "yard."

# Privacy Screen

*No matter where you live, it seems outdoor privacy is always needed. This screen is portable enough to be moved occasionally but sturdy enough to avoid blowing over. Use it to define an outdoor living space or to screen out an undesirable view.*

## Materials

- 65 linear feet of 2x4 pine
- 120 linear feet of 1x1 pine
- 4'x8' sheet of privacy lattice

## Hardware

- 35 3" wood screws
- 350 1¼" (3d) finish nails
- 9 3" hinges

## Cutting List

| Code | Description | Qty. | Materials | Dimensions |
|------|-------------|------|-----------|------------|
| A | Long Side | 8 | 2x4 pine | 75" long |
| B | Short Side | 8 | 2x4 pine | 12" long |
| C | Long Trim | 16 | 1x1 pine | 72" long |
| D | Short Trim | 16 | 1x1 pine | 10½" long |
| E | Lattice Inserts | 4 | Privacy lattice | 12"x72" |

## Building the Frames

1 Cut eight Long Sides (A) from 2x4 pine, each measuring 75 inches.

2 Cut eight Short Sides (B) from 2x4 pine, each measuring 12 inches.

3 Position two of the Short Sides (B) on edge, parallel to each other and 72 inches apart. Place the Long Sides (A) over the ends of the Short Sides (B), as shown in *figure 1*. Apply glue to the meeting surfaces, and screw through the Long Sides (A) into the ends of the Short Sides (B), using two 3-inch wood screws on each joint.

4 Repeat step 3 to build three more frames.

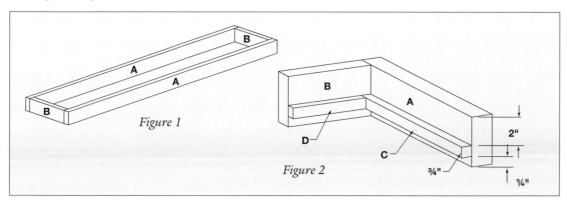

*Figure 1*

*Figure 2*

## Adding the Lattice

1 Cut 16 Long Trims (C) from lxl pine, each measuring 72 inches.

2 Cut 16 Short Trims (D) from lxl pine, each measuring 10$^{1}/_{2}$ inches.

3 Attach one of the Long Trims (C) to the inside of one Long Side (A) $^{3}/_{4}$ inch from the edge, as shown in *figure 2* on page 167. Apply glue to the meeting surfaces, nail through the Long Trims (C) into the face of the Long Side (A), using 1$^{1}/_{4}$-inch finish nails spaced every 4 inches.

4 Repeat step 3 for the remaining Long Sides (A).

5 Attach one of the Short Trims (D) to the inside of the Short Side (B), again $^{3}/_{4}$ inch in from the edge. Apply glue to the meeting surfaces, and nail through the Short Trim into the face of the Short Side (B), using 1$^{1}/_{4}$-inch finish nails spaced every 4 inches.

6 Repeat step 5 for the remaining Short Sides (B).

7 Cut four Lattice Inserts (E) from a 4-x8-foot sheet of privacy lattice, each measuring 1 2x72 inches.

8 Place the Lattice Inserts (E) inside the assembled frames, on top of the Long and Short Trims (C and D), as shown in *figure 3*.

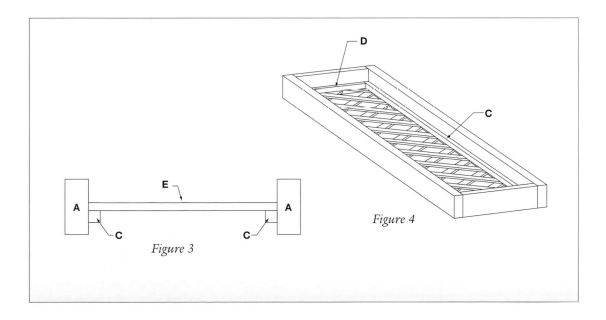

Figure 3

Figure 4

**9** Repeat steps 3 through 5 to add two Short Trims (D) and two Long Trims (C) on the opposite side of the lattice insert (E), as shown in *figure 4* on page 169, then assemble three more identical screen sections.

### Finishing

**1** We used three hinges between each of the main panels. Remember when attaching the hinges to alternate them so the screen will fold properly. The hinge peg faces the back of the screen between the two middle panels and faces the front of the screen on the outer panels.

**2** Fill any screw or nail holes with wood filler.

**3** Sand screen thoroughly.

**4** Paint or stain the screen the color of your choice, or leave natural.

# Mini Gazebo

*Since a traditional gazebo has eight sides and this one has four, Mark suggested that the proper name for this project should be either a "Gaz" or an "Ebo." Whatever you call it, it is a pretty addition to any yard, and provides a quiet nook for reading, drinking lemonade, or just enjoying the day. The gazebo is easy to build if you take it one step at a time. It is built in sections from the ground up, beginning with the bottom frame.*

## Special Tools & Techniques

- Miter
- Level

## Materials

- 32 linear feet of 2x6 pine
- 4 8' 4x4 pine posts
- 4 concrete footings
- 1 package shims
- 90 linear feet of $5/4$x6 pine decking
- 34 linear feet of 2x4 pine
- 4'x4' sheet of $1/4$" plywood
- 4 4'x8' sheets of $1/2$" plywood
- Shingles, enough to cover 75 square feet
- 14 linear feet of 1x4 pine
- 58 linear feet of 1x1 pine
- 3 4'x8' sheets of lattice

## Hardware

- 100 $3^1/2$" wood screws
- 16 $3^1/2$" lag screws
- 120 $2^1/2$" wood screws
- 220 $1^5/8$" wood screws
- 70 2" wood screws
- 500 1" roofing nails
- 50 2" (6d) finish nails
- 300 $1^1/4$" (3d) finish nails

## Cutting List

| Code | Description | Qty. | Materials | Dimensions |
|------|-------------|------|-----------|------------|
| A | Front/Back | 2 | 2x6 pine | $57^1/2$" long |
| B | Sides | 2 | 2x6 pine | $60^1/2$" long |
| C | Center Support | 1 | 2x6 pine | $57^1/2$" long |
| D | Corner Post | 4 | 4x4 pine post | 96" long |
| E | Floorboards | 11 | $5/4$x6 pine | $60^1/2$" long |
| F | Roof Supports | 2 | 2x4 pine | 85" long |
| G | Roof Rafter | 2 | 2x4 pine | 59" long |
| H | Rafter Connector | 2 | $1/4$" plywood | see figure |
| I | Rafter Brace | 2 | 2x4 pine | 58" long |
| J | Roof | 4 | $1/2$" plywood | 47"x74" |
| K | Peak Cover Sides | 4 | 2x6 pine | 16" long |
| L | Planter Outer Side | 3 | $5/4$x6 pine | $58^3/4$" long |
| M | Planter Inner Side | 2 | $5/4$x6 pine | 54" long |
| N | Planter Middle | 1 | $5/4$x6 pine | $49^3/4$" long |
| O | Planter End | 2 | $5/4$x6 pine | $5^1/2$" long |
| P | Planter Bottom | 3 | 1x4 pine | $49^1/2$" long |
| Q | Vertical Support | 12 | 1x1 pine | 32" long |
| R | Horizontal Support | 6 | 1x1 pine | 48" long |
| S | Trellis Panel | 3 | lattice | 32"x$49^1/2$" |

## Building the Bottom Frame

1 Cut two Back/Fronts (A) from 2x6 pine, each measuring 57½ inches.

2 Cut two Sides (B) from 2x6 pine, each measuring 60½ inches.

3 Position the two Back/Fronts (A) on a level surface, parallel to each other and 57½ inches apart.

4 Place one Side (B) against the ends of the two Back/Fronts (A) to form a 60½-inch square, as shown in *figure 1*. Screw through the ends of the Side (B) into the Back/Fronts (A), using two 3½-inch wood screws on each joint.

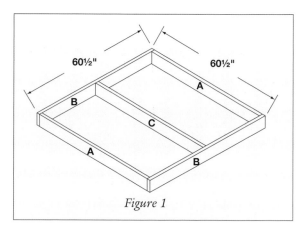

*Figure 1*

5 Cut one Center Support (C) from 2x6 pine, measuring 57½ inches long.

6 Place the Center Support (C) between the two Front/Backs (A), centered between the Sides (B) inside the bottom frame, as shown in *figure 1*. Screw through the two Front/Backs (A) into the ends of the Center Support (C), using three 3½-inch wood screws on each joint.

## Adding the Posts

1 Place four concrete footings on the ground to form a square. The distance between the four outer corners of the post openings in the concrete footings should measure exactly 57½ inches, as shown in *figure 2*. When the footings are exactly square, the measurement between opposing corners should be exactly the same.

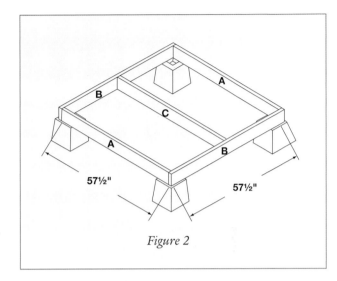

*Figure 2*

2 Place the assembled bottom frame over the concrete footings, as shown in *figure 2*. To level the bottom frame, it is a good idea to enlist the assistance of a helper. Beginning at the highest corner, level each of the remaining three corners, working in rotation around the bottom frame. Use shims to level the frame. Insert the thin end of the shim underneath the Corner Post (D) until that edge of the Corner Post (D) is level.

3 Cut about 1 inch off the end of the four Corner Posts (D) so that one end of each Corner Post (D) is square.

4 When you are satisfied that the bottom frame is exactly level and square, insert a Corner Post (D) inside the bottom frame (squared end down) on one corner of the structure. Use a level vertically to make certain that the Corner Post (D) is plumb. Temporarily hold the post in place by screwing through the bottom frame into the Corner Post (D), using two 3½-inch wood screws (one on each side of the post).

5 Repeat steps 3 and 4 three times to add the remaining three Corner Posts (D) to the structure.

6 Recheck the level and squareness of the structure, and when it is perfect, predrill holes and insert a 3½-inch lag screw through the bottom frame into the each side of each Corner Post (D).

## Adding the Floorboards

1 Cut 11 Floorboards (E) from ⁵/₄x6 decking, each measuring 60½ inches.

2 Since the Floorboards (E) must be cut to fit around the Corner Posts (D), follow the cutout measurements and the placement sequence, as shown in *figure 3* to add the Floorboards (E) to the structure. Cut and place one Floorboard (E) at a time, beginning with number 1 and ending with number 11. Because of variations in lumber sizes, it may be necessary to retrim some of the Floorboards (E). Make certain that each of your Floorboards (E) fits correctly before cutting the next one. The Floorboards (E) will overhang the Front/Back (A) and Sides (B) by 1³/₄ inches. Screw through each Floorboard (E) into the Sides (B) and Center Support (C), using two 2¹/₂-inch wood screws on each joint.

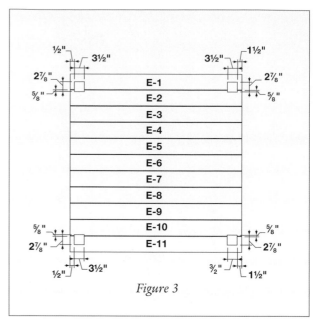

Figure 3

## Adding the Top Frame

1 Repeat the section Building the Bottom Frame (steps 1 through 5) to assemble a top frame that is identical to the bottom frame. To make certain that the top and bottom frames are identical, we suggest that you assemble the top frame around the existing posts on top of the Floorboards (E).

2 You will need a trusty helper for this step. Mark the desired height of the lower edge of the top frame on each of the four Corner Posts (D). We attached ours 6¹/₂ feet above the Floorboards (E). Raise the top frame to the height desired, and make certain it is level on all four sides. We used an extra board to prop the top frame in place until we had it leveled and could secure it.

3 When you are satisfied that the top frame and all four Corner Posts (D) are exactly level and square, hold the assembly in place temporarily by screwing through the Front/Backs (A) and Sides (B) into the Corner Post (D), using one 3¹/₂-inch wood screw. To hold it securely, predrill holes and insert one 3¹/₂-inch lag screw through each Front/Back (A) and Side (B) into the each Corner Post (D).

4 Cut off the top of each of the Corner Posts (D) flush with the upper edge of the top frame.

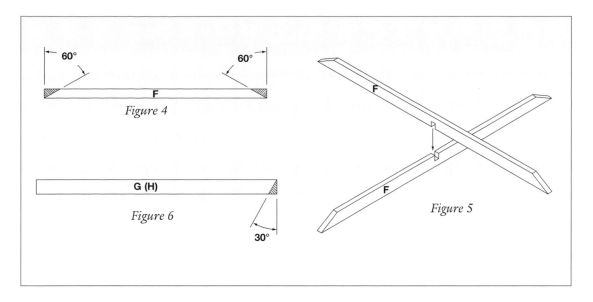

Figure 4

G (H)

Figure 6

30°

Figure 5

## Adding the Rafters

1 Cut two Roof Supports (F) from 2x4 pine, each measuring 85 inches.

2 Miter each end of both Roof Supports (F) at opposing 60° angles, as shown in *figure 4*.

3 The two Roof Supports (F) fit together by means of a slot system (see *figure 5*). Cut a notch measuring 1½ inches wide and 1¾ inches deep in the exact center of both Roof Supports (F). Make certain that you make these cuts very carefully (watching the direction of your mitered ends), or the Roof Supports (F) will not fit together correctly. The two Roof Supports (F) will be joined in a later step.

4 Cut two Roof Rafters (G) from 2x4 pine, each measuring 59 inches.

5 Miter one end of each Roof Rafter (G) at a 30° angle, as shown in *figure 6*.

6 Cut two Rafter Connectors (H) from ¼-inch plywood, following the measurements given in *figure 7*.

7 Place two Roof Rafters (G), mitered ends together, on a level surface. Place one Rafter Connector (H) over the mitered joint, as shown in *figure 8* on page 176. Apply glue to the meeting surfaces, and screw through the Rafter Connector (H) into both Roof Rafters (G), using 1½-inch wood screws spaced every 3 inches.

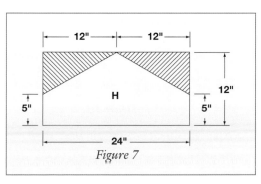

Figure 7

## Adding the Peak Cover

1 Cut four Peak Cover Sides (K) from 2x6 pine, each measuring 16 inches.

2 Miter each end of the four Peak Cover Sides (K) at opposing 45° angles, as shown in *figure 13* on page 179

3 Position two Peak Cover Sides (K) on a level surface, parallel to each other and 13 inches apart, with miters facing each other. Fit the remaining two Peak Cover Sides (K) between the first two, matching miters, to form a 16-inch square. Apply glue to the meeting surfaces, and screw through each side of all four corners, using two $2^1/_2$-inch wood screws on each joint.

4 Place the assembled peak cover over the roof peak. Center and level the peak cover on all four sides. Secure the peak cover to the roof by screwing at an angle through the peak cover into the roof, at least once on each of the four sides of the roof, using $3^1/_2$-inch wood screws.

## Adding the Planter Boxes

1 Cut three Planter Outer Sides (L), from $^5/_4$x6 deck boards, each measuring $58^3/_4$ inches.

2 Cut two Planter Inner Sides (M) from $^5/_4$x6 deck boards, each measuring 54 inches.

3 Cut one Planter Middle (N) from $^5/_4$x6 deck boards, measuring $49^3/_4$ inches.

4 Cut two Planter Ends (O) from $^5/_4$x6 deck boards, each measuring $5^1/_2$ inches.

5 The planter boxes are built around the four Corner Posts (D). Measure and mark each of the four Corner Posts (D) at a height of 32 inches above the Floorboards (E). Each of the six planter pieces (L, M, N, and O) is mitered on both ends. The ends of the three Planter Outer Sides (L), Planter Middle (N), and Planter Ends (O) are mitered at opposing 45" angles. The two Planter Inner Sides (M) are mitered at the same 45° angle. Refer to *figure 13* to be certain that your 45° miter is cut properly.

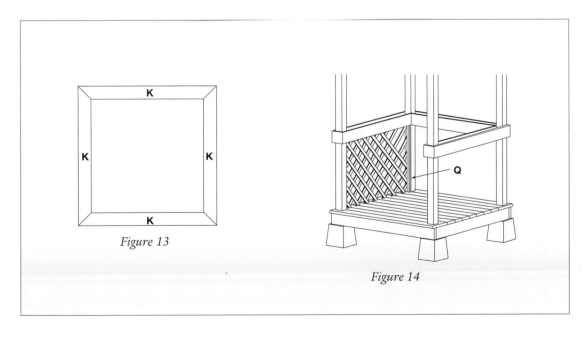

Figure 13

Figure 14

6 Measure your structure carefully and work in rotation around the Corner Posts (D). First add the three Planter Outer Sides (L), one at a time, then add one Planter Inner Side (M), then the Planter Middle (N), the remaining Inner Side (M), and finally the Planter Ends (O). Apply glue to the meeting surfaces, and use two 2$^1/_2$-inch wood screws on each joint.

7 Cut three Planter Bottoms (P) from 1x4 pine, each measuring 49$^1/_2$ inches.

8 Insert one Planter Bottom (P) flush with the bottom edge of the Outer and Inner Planter Sides (L and M). Nail through the Outer and Inner Planter Sides (L and M) into the edges of the Planter Bottom (P), using 2-inch finish nails spaced every 5 inches.

9 Repeat step 8 to add the remaining Planter Bottoms (P) to the opposite side and back of the structure.

## Adding the Trellis

1 Cut 12 Vertical Supports (Q) from 1x1 pine, each measuring 32 inches.

2 Cut six Horizontal Supports (R) from 1x1 pine, each measuring 48 inches. Attach one of the Vertical Supports (Q) under the planter to the inside of one Corner Post (D), $^3/_4$ inch from the edge, as shown in *figure 14* on page 179. Apply glue to the meeting surfaces, and nail through the Vertical Support (Q) into the face of the Corner Post (D), using 1$^1/_4$-inch finish nails spaced every 4 inches.

3 Repeat step 2 five times to attach the remaining Vertical Supports (Q) to the remaining three Corner Posts (D).

4 Attach one of the Horizontal Supports (R) to one Planter Bottom (P), between the two Vertical Supports (Q), again $^3/_4$ inch in from the edge. Apply glue to the meeting surfaces, and nail through the Horizontal Support (R) into the face of the Planter Bottom (P), using 1$^1/_4$-inch finish nails spaced every 4 inches.

5 Repeat step 4 twice to attach the remaining Horizontal Supports (R) to the two remaining Planter Bottoms (P).

6 Cut three Trellis Panels (S) from lattice, each measuring 32x49$^1/_2$ inches.

7 Place one Trellis Panel (S) over the Horizontal and Vertical Supports (Q and R), as shown in *figure 13* on page 179.

8 Nail through the Trellis Panel (S) into the Horizontal and Vertical Supports (Q and R), using 1¼-inch finish nails spaced 6 inches apart.

9 Repeat step 8 twice to add the remaining two Trellis Panels (S) under the Planter Bottoms (P).

10 Repeat steps 3 through 6 to add one Horizontal and two Vertical Supports (Q and R) on the opposite side of each Trellis Panel (S). Horizontal supports have not been added to the bottom of the lattice, to make it easier to hose debris off the completed structure.

## Finishing

1 We backfilled with extra dirt around our gazebo, then added sod over the dirt to hold it in place.

2 Sand off any rough edges on the structure.

3 Paint or stain the gazebo the color of your choice, or leave it the natural wood color.

# Portable Deck

*If you have always wanted an outdoor deck but are renting or not planning to live in your house very long, this portable deck is the answer. It also has the advantage of being built in squares that can be arranged, rearranged, or moved. So when you leave that apartment or rental house, this handy deck goes on the moving truck with you!*

### Materials

- 22 linear feet of 2x6 pine
- 35 linear feet of ⁵/₄x6 pine decking
- 3 linear feet of 4x4 pine

### Hardware

- 28 3¹/₂" wood screws
- 55 2¹/₂" wood screws

### Cutting List (for one square)

| Code | Description | Qty. | Materials | Dimensions |
|------|-------------|------|-----------|------------|
| A | Short Side | 3 | 2x6 pine | 43" long |
| B | Long Side | 2 | 2x6 pine | 46" long |
| C | Top | 8 | ⁵/₄x6 pine | 46" long |
| D | Leg | 4 | 4x4 pine | 7¹/₂" long |

## Building the Frame

1 Cut three Short Sides (A) from 2x6 pine, each measuring 43 inches.

2 Cut two Long Sides (B) from 2x6 pine, each measuring 46 inches.

3 Position two of the Short Sides (A) on edge, parallel to each other and 43 inches apart. Place the two Long Sides (B) over the ends of the Short Sides (A), as shown in *figure 1*. Apply glue to the meeting surfaces, and nail through the Long Sides (B) into the ends of the Short Sides (A), using two 3¹/₂-inch wood screws on each joint.

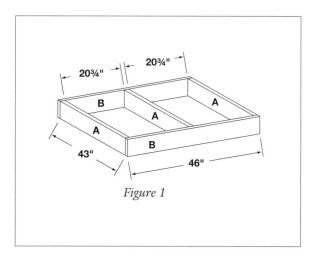

*Figure 1*

4 Place the third Short Side (A) between the two Long Sides (b) and parallel to the Short Sides (A), as shown in *figure 1*. Apply glue to the meeting surfaces, and screw through the face of the Long Side (B) into the end of the Short Side (A), using two 3¹/₂-inch wood screws on each joint.

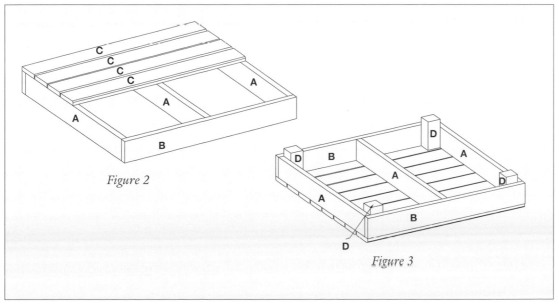

Figure 2

Figure 3

## Adding the Decking

1 Cut eight Tops (C) from $^5/_4$x6 pine decking, each measuring 46 inches.

2 Place the Tops (C) over one side of the assembled frame so that the boards lay perpendicular to the Short Sides (A), as shown in *figure 2* on page 183. Screw through the face of the deck boards into the edges of all three Short Sides (A), using two $2^1/_2$-inch wood screws per joint.

## Adding the Legs

1 Cut four Legs (D) from 4x4 pine, each measuring $7^1/_2$ inches.

2 Turn the assembled frame and decking over so that the decking is on the bottom. Place the four Legs (D) in each corner, as shown in *figure 3* on page 183, and secure each in place, using two $3^1/_2$-inch wood screws in each Short Side (A) and each Long Side (B).

## Finishing

1 Sand the edges of your deck square.

2 Paint, stain, or seal square as desired.

# Deck Canopy

*Until we built this canopy, we could not use most of our deck during the heat of the day. Now we can enjoy the outdoor space all day. The canvas panels shade the entire deck or can be pulled back if you want to feel more of the warmth of the sun.*

## Special Tools & Techniques

- Miter (optional)

## Materials

- 32 linear feet of 4x4 pressure-treated pine
- 2 50-pound bags of concrete
- 65 linear feet of 2x6 pine
- 4 6' lengths of ³/₄"-diameter galvanized pipe, threaded on both ends*
- 8 1" lengths of ³/₄"-diameter galvanized pipe, threaded on both ends*
- 8 galvanized pipe flanges to fit ³/₄"-diameter pipe
- 8 90°- pipe angles to fit ³/₄"-diameter pipe
- 2 canvas panels, each 54"x72", hemmed on all four sides, with grommets inserted every foot along the 72" lengths

## Hardware

- 10 2¹/₂" wood screws
- 4 3¹/₂" lag bolts
- 6 galvanized metal tie-down braces
- 40 1¹/₄" wood screws
- 32 metal shower curtain rings

## *Notes on Construction & Materials

We suggest that, before starting this project, you consult local building codes. We also suggest obtaining the appropriate construction permits before you begin, since this project will be attached to your home. Because every house is different, make certain that the chosen height and distance from the house will work with your structure. Also, the pitch of your roof may make a difference in how some of the project pieces are attached.

This project will require a professional to cut the pipe to length and thread the ends. Most home centers will do this for a minimal charge.

## Cutting List

| Code | Description | Qty. | Materials | Dimensions |
|------|-------------|------|-----------|------------|
| A | Post | 2 | 4x4 pine | 16' long |
| B | Roof Supports | 2 | 2x6 pine | 143" long |
| C | Tops | 3 | 2x6 pine | 144" long |

## Building the Frame

1 Dig two holes approximately 116 inches apart from the center of the hole and 118 inches away from your house to the depth of about 3 feet or to the depth your local building code specifies.

2 Cut two Posts (A) from 4x4 pressure treated pine, each measuring 16 feet. Place one Post (A) in each hole and set in place, using a bag of mixed concrete for each Post (A). Make sure that both posts are plumb. Secure Posts (A) temporarily by using a bracing board on two sides of the posts. Let cement set up overnight.

3 Cut 2 Roof Supports (B) from 2x6 pine, each measuring 143 inches long. For a decorative (but optional) touch, miter both ends of the Roof Supports (B) at opposing 30° angles, as shown in *figure 1*.

4 This step requires the use of two ladders or two really tall people. Mark the distance to the required height to match the shingled edge of your roof from the ground or deck. Place one Roof Support (B) over one side of the Posts (A), as shown in *figure 2*. Screw through the Roof Support (B) into the Posts (A). Temporarily hold the pieces together with two 2¹/₂-inch wood screws in each post, then install one 3¹/₂-inch lag bolt on each Post (A).

5 Repeat step 4 to attach the remaining Roof Support (B) to the other side of the Posts (A). This will sandwich the two Posts (A) between the two Roof Supports (B).

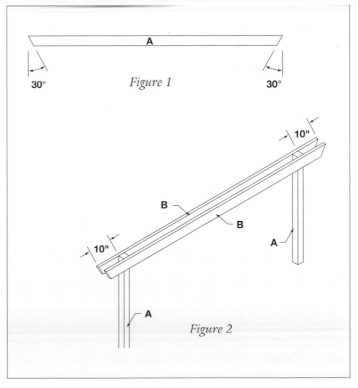

Figure 1

Figure 2

## Adding the Tops

1 Cut three Tops (C) from 2x6 pine, each measuring 144 inches long. If desired, use a miter to make a 30° cut on one end of each of the Tops (C).

2 Place the three Tops (C) on edge over the Roof Supports (B), with the mitered end away from the house, as shown in *figure 3* on page 189. Attach the Tops (C) to the Roof Supports (B) with metal tie-down braces. Make sure that the Tops (C) are level before installing the braces.

3 Attach the ends of the Tops (C) on top of the roof in the same manner, making sure that any relevant code requirements are followed explicitly. Use the same braces as used to connect the Tops (C) to the Roof Support (B).

## Adding the Pipe

1 Attach, in the following order, the 90° pipe corner to the long pipe, then the 1-inch-long pipe to the other side of the 90° corner, then the flange to the 1-inch-long pipe, which will allow you to screw the flange to the Top (C).

2 Repeat step 2 with the opposite end and the remaining pipes.

## Installation

1 Install the pipes 10 inches away from the end of the Tops (C), as shown in *figure 4*.

2 Attach the canvas to the pipes, using shower curtain rings.

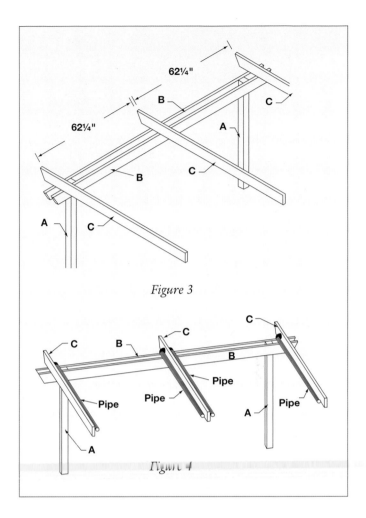

*Figure 3*

*Figure 4*

# Trash Container

*It is nice to have a trash container that is pretty enough to place near the outdoor eating area. We developed this simple, yet attractive—not to mention easy-to-construct—project when we got tired of having to walk our trash around the house to the back of the garage.*

## Materials

- 28 linear feet of 1x4 pine
- 12 linear feet of 2x2 pine
- 4'x4' sheet of privacy lattice
- 10 linear feet of 1½" L-shaped molding
- 2'x2' sheet of ¾" plywood
- Fence-post finial

## Hardware

- 50 1⅝" wood screws
- 340 1¼" (3d) finish nails

## Cutting List

| Code | Description | Qty. | Materials | Dimensions |
|------|-------------|------|-----------|------------|
| A | Long Side | 4 | 1x4 pine | 24½" long |
| B | Short Side | 4 | 1x4 pine | 23" long |
| C | Support | 4 | 2x2 pine | 28" long |
| D | Sides | 4 | Lattice | 24"x21" |
| E | Corner Trim | 4 | L-molding | 24" long |
| F | Short Trim | 2 | 1x4 pine | 17½" long |
| G | Long Trim | 2 | 1x4 pine | 24½" long |
| H | Lid | 1 | ¾" plywood | 22½"x22½" |
| I | Lid Center | 1 | 1x4 pine | 3½"x3½" |

## Building the Frame

1  Cut four Long Sides (A) from 1x4 pine, each measuring 24½ inches.

2  Cut four Short Sides (B) from 1x4 pine, each measuring 23 inches.

3  Cut four Supports (C) from 2x2 pine, each measuring 28 inches.

4  Position two of the Short Sides (B), parallel to each other on edge and 23 inches apart. Place two of the Long Sides (A) over the ends of Short Sides (B), as shown in *figure 1*, to form a square. Apply glue to the meeting surfaces, and screw through the Long Sides (A) into the Short Sides (B), using two 1⅝-inch wood screws in each joint.

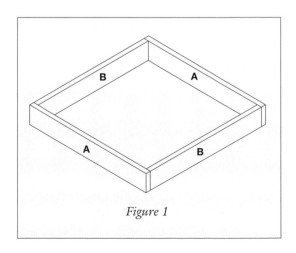

*Figure 1*

**5** Repeat step 4 to assemble another square, using the remaining Short (A) and Long (B) Sides. Designate one as "Top" and one as "Bottom."

**6** Place the Bottom square flat on a level surface and attach the Supports (C) to the inside corners of the Bottom square, as shown in *figure 2* on page 192. Apply glue to the meeting surfaces, and screw through the Short and Long sides (A and B) into the Supports (C), using four 1⅝ inch wood screws in each joint.

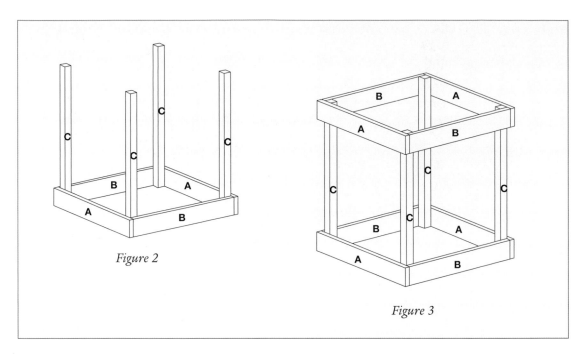

*Figure 2*

*Figure 3*

7 Repeat step 6 to attach the Top square to the exposed supports, as shown in *figure 3*.

## Adding the Lattice

1 Cut four Sides (D) from privacy lattice, each measuring 24x21 inches.

2 Attach the Sides (D) by laying the assembly on its side and placing the Sides (D) between the Top and Bottom squares and over the Supports (C). Nail through the Sides (D) into the Supports (C), using about five $1^{1}/_{4}$-inch finish nails per Support (C).

3 Cut four Corner Trims (E) from $1^{1}/_{2}$-inch L-Shaped molding, each measuring 24 inches.

4 Place the Corner Trims (E) over the corners of the frame, and nail through the Corner Trims (E) and through the lattice into the Supports (C), using about five $1^{1}/_{4}$-inch nails per Side (D).

## Making the Top

1 Cut two Short Trims (F) from 1x4 pine, each measuring $17^{1}/_{2}$ inches.

2 Cut two Long Trims (G) from 1x4 pine, each measuring $24^{1}/_{2}$ inches.

3 Cut one Lid (H) from $^{3}/_{4}$-inch plywood, measuring $22^{1}/_{2}$x$22^{1}/_{2}$ inches.

**4** Position the two Short Trims (F) flat on a level surface, parallel to each other and 17½ inches apart. Place the Long Trims (G) against the ends of the Short Trims (F), as shown in *figure 4*. Position the Lid (H), centered over the Trims (F and G) so that they extend 1 inch beyond the Lid (H), as shown in *figure 5*. Apply glue to the meeting surfaces, and nail through the Lid (H) into the Trims (F and G), using 1¼-inch finish nails spaced about every 4 inches.

**5** Cut one Lid Center (I) from 1x4 pine, measuring 3½x3½ inches.

**6** Turn the assembled lid over, so that Lid (H) is on the bottom and the Trims (F and G) are facing up. Using *figure 6* on page 194 as a guide, place the Lid Center

(I) on the Lid (H). Apply glue to the meeting surfaces, and nail through the Lid Center (I) into the Lid (H), using four 1¼-inch finish nails. *Note:* Do not nail into the center of the Lid Center (I), but rather nail an inch inside the corners of the Lid Center (I). The finial will be attached to the Lid Center (I) in the next step.

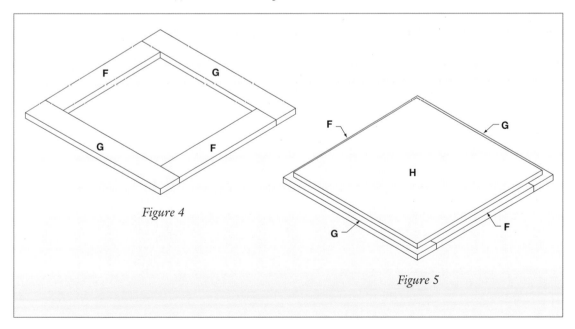

Figure 4

Figure 5

**7** Drill into the Lid Center (I), using an $1/8$-inch drill bit, making sure to center the hole in the Lid Center (H). Screw the finial into the Lid Center (I).

## Finishing

**1** Sand the container thoroughly and fill any cracks or crevices with wood filler.

**2** Paint or stain the container the color of your choice, or leave it natural.

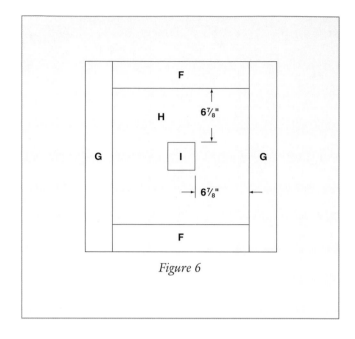

*Figure 6*

# Outdoor Storage Center

*When you entertain outside, where do you put all the crummy-looking supplies that you use to maintain your outdoor room? Here's a simple solution: Store them behind the door of this great-looking storage shed. Your supplies will be out of sight, but close at hand.*

## Special Tools & Techniques

- Sabre saw

## Materials

- 12 linear feet of 2x4 pine
- 4'x 8' sheet of ¹/₂" exterior grooved plywood paneling
- 4'x4' sheet of ¹/₂" exterior plywood
- ¹/₂" bundle of cedar shingles
- 3 linear feet of 1¹/₂"-wide lath
- 7 linear feet of 2x2 pine

## Hardware

- 20 3¹/₂" wood screws
- 150 1¹/₄" (3d) finish nails
- 100 1" wire brads
- 20 2" (6d) finish nails
- 3 exterior hinges
- 1 exterior door latch

## Cutting List

| Code | Description | Qty. | Materials | Dimensions |
|------|-------------|------|-----------|------------|
| A | Long Inner Supports | 4 | 2x4 pine | 22¹/₂" long |
| B | Short Inner Supports | 4 | 2x4 pine | 8¹/₂" long |
| C | Front/Back | 2 | ¹/₂" paneling | 23¹/₂"x80" |
| D | Side | 2 | ¹/₂" paneling | 11¹/₂"x72" |
| E | Roof | 2 | ¹/₂" plywood | 13¹/₂"x17" |
| F | Roof Trim | 2 | 1¹/₂" lath | 17" long |
| G | Shelf | 4 | ¹/₂" plywood | 11¹/₂"x22¹/₂" |
| H | Shelf Support | 9 | 2x2 pine | 8¹/₂" long |

## Building the Frame

1 Cut four Long Inner Supports (A) from 2x4 pine, each measuring 22¹/₂ inches.

2 Cut four Short Inner Supports (B) from 2x4 pine, each measuring 8¹/₂ inches.

3 Position two of the Short Inner Supports (B) on edge, parallel to each other and 19¹/₂ inches apart. Place two of the Long Inner Supports (A) over the ends of the Short Inner Supports (B) to form a rectangle measuring 22¹/₂x11¹/₂ inches. Apply glue to the meeting surfaces, and screw through the Long Inner Supports (A) into the ends of the

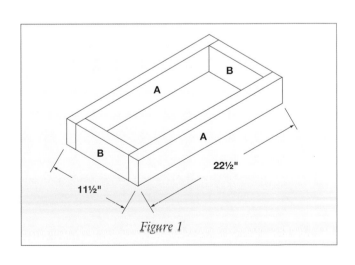

*Figure 1*

Short Inner Supports (B), using two 3½-inch wood screws on each joint. See *figure 1* on page 195.

4 Repeat step 3 to assemble a second rectangle. Designate one rectangle as "Top" and one as "Bottom."

5 Cut two Front/Backs (C) from ½-inch-thick exterior grooved plywood, each measuring 23½x80 inches. Because you will use the grooves in the paneling as guides to create the door, place one of the paneling grooves down the exact vertical center of one Front/Back (C), and label that piece "Front."

6 Using *figure 2* as a guide, cut the door portion out of the Front (C). Since our plywood paneling was grooved every 3½ inches, we simply used the grooves as a guide to cut the door. Mark the cutting lines, and use a sabre saw to cut vertically up one groove, across the top, and down the groove on the opposite side.

7 Using *figure 2* as a guide, trim off the top two corners of the Front/Backs (A), eliminating the shaded portions.

8 Cut two Sides (D) from ½-inch-thick grooved plywood, each measuring 11½x72 inches.

9 Position the two assembled Top and Bottom rectangles, parallel to each other and 64 inches apart, placing the Long Inner Supports (A) against the work surface. Place the Sides (D) against the Short Inner Supports (B), as shown in *figure 3*. Apply glue to the meeting surfaces, and nail through the Sides (D) into the Short Inner Supports (B), using 1¼-inch finish nails about every 4 inches.

10 Place the Front (C) against the Long Inner Supports (A), as shown in *figure 4*. Apply glue to the meeting surfaces, and nail through the Front (C) into the Long Inner Supports (A), using 1¼-inch finish nails spaced every 4 inches.

11 Turn the assembly over, and repeat step 10 to attach the Back (C) to the assembly, using the same procedure you used to attach the Front (C).

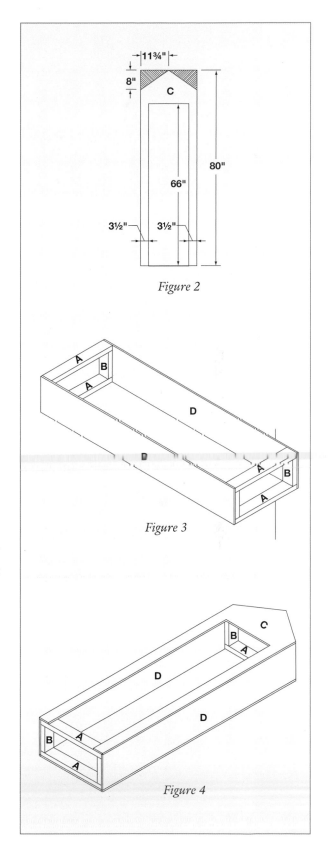

Figure 2

Figure 3

Figure 4

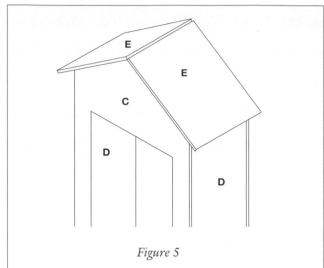

*Figure 5*

## Adding the Roof

1 Cut two Roofs (E) from ¹/₂-inch plywood, each measuring 13¹/₂x17 inches.

2 Position the two Roofs (E) over the top of the assembly, so that they meet at the peak, as shown in *figure 5*. Note that the Roofs (E) are flush with the Back (C) and overhang the Front (C). Do not worry about the resulting gap at the roof peak; it will be covered with shingles in the next step. Apply glue to the meeting surfaces, and nail through the Roofs (E) into the edges of the Front (C), Back (C), and Sides (D), using 1¹/₄-inch finish nails spaced about every 3 inches.

## Adding the Shingles

1 Use three rows of shingles to cover each side of the roof of the storage center. On the second and third rows, trim regular-size shingles to the appropriate length, so they do not extend past the roof peak. It is better to work with the top portion of the original shingle, since it is thinner than the bottom edge. It is not difficult to shingle, and since the finished project should look somewhat rustic, this job is even easier. Begin attaching the first row

of shingles with 1-inch wire brads, just overlapping the bottom edge of one Roof (D). Each shingle should be nailed twice to prevent shifting. Choose varying widths of shingles as you work. Continue the row across the bottom edge.

2  Next, add a second row overlapping the first row, about 6 inches higher. Then add a third row, overlapping the second row, again about 6 inches higher.

3  Repeat the application of shingles on the remaining Roof (D). Try to match the rows of shingles on the two Roofs (D).

4  To cover the roof peak, cut the shingles to $1^1/_2$ inches wide, and attach the resulting narrow shingles to both sides of the peak, working from the front to the back of the roof. Add three rows, trimming the shingles to length so they do not extend past the back edges of the roof.

## Adding the Roof Trims

1  Cut two Roof Trims (F) from $1^1/_2$-inch-wide lath, each measuring 17 inches.

2  Refer to the photograph on page 200 of the finished project to miter the ends of the trim to cover the front exposed edges of the Roofs (E). Apply glue to the meeting surfaces, and nail through the Roof Trims (F) into the edge of the Roofs (E), using 1-inch wire brads spaced about 2 inches apart.

## Adding the Shelves

1  Cut four Shelves (G) from $^1/_2$-inch plywood, each measuring $11^1/_2$x$22^1/_2$ inches.

2  Fit one Shelf (G) over the Bottom rectangle inside the storage center. Apply glue to the meeting surfaces, and nail through the Shelf (G) into the Long and Short Inner Supports (A and B), using $1^1/_4$-inch finish nails spaced every 4 inches.

3  Cut nine Shelf Supports (H), each measuring $8^1/_2$ inches. These will be attached to the Sides (D), Front (C), and Back (C) to support the three upper shelves. The exact positioning of the three additional shelves is a matter of personal preference. We installed the lower of these shelves 12 inches above the bottom shelf, the next one 12 inches above that shelf, and the top shelf 18 inches above the middle shelf.

4  When you have decided on the placement of the shelves, mark the position of each shelf on the Back (C) and the Sides (D). Next, install three Shelf Supports (H) for each shelf: one in the center of the Back (C) and one in the center of each Side (D). Make certain that the Shelf

Supports (H) are perfectly level, or your contents will end up in a heap on one side of the shelf. Apply glue to the meeting surfaces, and nail through the Shelf Support (H) into the Back (C) or Side (D), using two 2-inch finish nails on each Shelf Support (H). Do not countersink the nail, or it will show up on the outside of the storage center.

5 Install the Shelves (G) on top of the Shelf Supports (H).

## Finishing

1 Install the door, using three exterior hinges.

2 Install the door latch.

3 Very little sanding is required on this project, as the paneling is supposed to keep its rustic look. Simply remove any obvious splinters or rough edges.

4 You can either paint or stain the storage center the color of your choice, or leave it natural. Here, the storage center has been painted light blue and the roof painted black.

# Yard Light

*If you entertain outside a lot, you'll appreciate adding a soft glow to an unlit portion of the yard. Add this yard light to a previously dark and unused corner, and you'll increase your useable entertaining space considerably.*

## Materials

- 2 linear feet of 2x8 pine
- 13 linear feet of 1x6 pine

## Hardware

- 36 1¼" wood screws
- 16 2½" wood screws
- Exterior light kit and exterior-rated electrical wire*

## *Notes on Materials

*Before beginning this project, check local codes concerning exterior electrical wiring. Make certain that all of the materials you use meet these codes and that a licensed electrician is not required for this project.

## Cutting List

| Code | Description | Qty. | Materials | Dimensions |
|------|-------------|------|-----------|------------|
| A | Side | 4 | 1x6 pine | 36" long |
| B | Top/Bottom | 2 | 2x8 pine | 7¼" long |

## Making the Sides

1 Cut four Sides (A) from 1x6 pine, each measuring 36 inches.

2 Assemble the four Sides (A), overlapping each piece in rotation, as shown in *figure 1*. With the four sides in position, the assembly measures 6¼ inches wide on all sides. Apply glue to the meeting surfaces, and screw all four Sides (A) along their entire length, using 1¼-inch wood screws spaced about 6 inches apart.

## Adding the Top and Bottom

1 Cut two Top and Bottoms (B) from 2x8 pine, each measuring 7¼ inches. Label one piece "Top" and one piece "Bottom."

2 Drill a ½-inch-diameter hole through the center of the Bottom (B) to accommodate the electrical wire. Then cut a ½-x½-inch groove from the hole to one edge of the Bottom (B), as shown in *figure 2* on page 202. The groove will also accommodate the electrical wire and allow the finished project to sit flat.

*Figure 1*

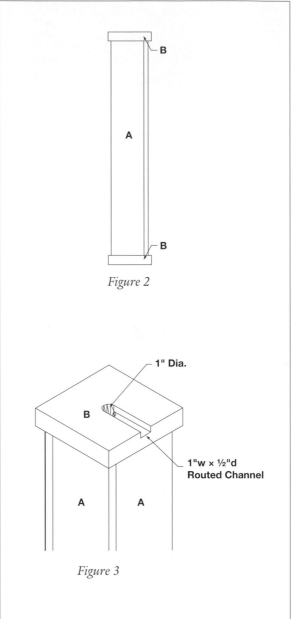

*Figure 2*

1" Dia.

B

1"w × ½"d
Routed Channel

A      A

*Figure 3*

3 Drill a hole in the center of the Top (B), and attach the exterior lamp fixture to the Top (B), following the manufacturer's directions. The size of the center hole will be determined by the type of exterior light and the installation requirements.

4 When the lamp fixture is installed, center the Top (B) over the Sides (A), making sure to place the electrical wiring inside the four Sides (A). The Top (B) should overhang the Sides (A) by ½ inch on all sides. Apply glue to the meeting surfaces, and screw through the Top (B) into the Sides (A), using two 2½-inch wood screws on each side. (See *figure 3*.)

5 Insert the free end of the electrical wire through the hole on the ungrooved side of the Bottom (B), and tie a loose knot on the grooved side to make sure the wire stays in place. Center the Bottom (B) over the open end of the Sides (A). Again, the Bottom (B) should overhang the Sides (A) by $1/2$ inch on all sides. Apply glue to the meeting surfaces, and screw through the Bottom (B) into the Sides (A), using two $2^1/_2$-inch wood screws on each side.

6 Attach a plug to the end of the electrical wire, and use exterior construction glue to secure the wire inside the groove. Let the glue set up overnight.

## Finishing

1 Fill all cracks, crevices, and screw holes with wood filler.

2 Stain or paint the yard light the color of your choice, or simply leave it the natural color and seal it with a waterproof finish.

# Hurricane Lamps

*These easy-to-make lamps provide terrific lighting for outdoor evening meals, and they cost next to nothing to make. We painted our pair white, and stamped on a vine pattern. Combine them with your favorite candles, and they will add light and charm to backyard entertaining.*

## Materials
**(for one lamp)**

- linear feet of 1x4 pine
- linear foot of 1x6 pine
- One hurricane glass globe
- Primer
- Base paint
- Trim paint
- Paintbrushes
- Stamp in a motif of your choice
- Clear, waterproof sealer

## Hardware

20 3dx1¼" nails

## Cutting List

| Code | Description | Qty. | Materials | Dimensions |
|------|-------------|------|-----------|------------|
| A | Side | 4 | 1x4 pine | 12" long |
| B | Top/Bottom | 2 | 1x6 pine | 5½" long |
| C | Candle Holder | 1 | 1x4 pine | 2" long |

## Constructing the Lamp

1 Cut four sides (A) from 1x4 pine, each measuring 12 inches long.

2 Assemble the four sides (A), overlapping each piece in rotation, as shown in *figure 1*. With the four sides (A) in position, the stand measures 4¼ inches wide on all sides. Apply glue to the meeting surfaces, and nail all four sides (A) along their entire length. Use 1¼-inch-long nails spaced about four inches apart.

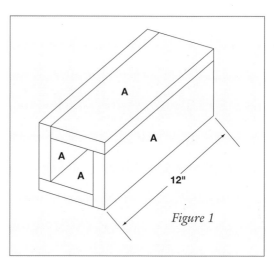

*Figure 1*

3 Cut two top/bottoms (B) from 1x6 pine, measuring 5½ inches long.

4 Center one top/bottom (B) over the assembled sides (A). Nail through the top/bottom (B) into the sides (A).

5 Cut one candle holder (C) from 1x4 pine, 2x2 inches square. Drill a candle-sized hole (ours was ³/₄ inch in diameter) in the center of the 2-inch square. Trim the corners of the square, as shown in *figure 2*, so that the candle holder fits inside the bottom of the hurricane glass.

6 Center the candle holder (C) over the remaining top/bottom (B). Apply glue to the meeting surfaces, and nail through the candle holder (C) into the top/bottom (B). Use four 1¹/₄-inch-long nails (one in each corner).

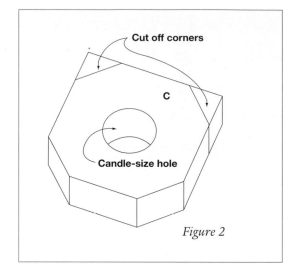

Figure 2

7 Turn the assembled sides (A) right side up. Center the top/bottom (B) with the attached candle holder (C) over the assembled sides (A). Nail through the top/bottom (B) into the sides (A).

## Finishing

1 Fill any cracks, crevices, or nail holes with wood filler, and thoroughly sand all surfaces of the completed lamp.

2 We primed and painted our lamps white, then stamped on an ivy pattern. There are many different types of stamps available in craft-and hobby-supply stores, so you should be able to find an ivy motif like this one, or choose a pattern to match your own table decor. Be sure that your trim paint is compatible with your base paint.

3 When the paint is dry, seal your completed lamp to protect it from the elements.

# Hurricane Lamp Shelf

*This simple project solves the problem of keeping candles lit out-of-doors. Constructed of one sturdy shelf and two ornamental gingerbread shelf brackets, it holds a hurricane globe and a generous-sized candle.*

## Materials
### (for one lamp)

- 1 linear foot of 2x8 pine
- 5 linear feet of 1x1 pine
- Glass hurricane globe, measuring just less than 5" in diameter and 11½" high*

## Hardware

- 20 1⅝" finish nails
- Premade ornamental shelf brackets, 5"x8"

## *Notes on Materials & Hardware

Any size glass hurricane globe up to 5 inches in diameter will work for this project, but the dimensions of the Front/Backs (B) and the Sides (C) will have to be altered to accommodate a smaller size. The premade ornamental shelf brackets are available at most hardware and building supply stores. They already have a metal hanger installed in the back and come in a variety of designs.

## Cutting List

| Code | Description | Qty. | Materials | Dimensions |
|------|-------------|------|-----------|------------|
| A | Base | 1 | 2x8 pine | 10" long |
| B | Front/Back | 2 | 1x1 pine | 5" long |
| C | Sides | 2 | 1x1 pine | 6½" long |

## Cutting the Pieces

1  Cut one Base (A) from 2x8 pine, measuring 10 inches.

2  Cut two Back/Fronts (B) from 1x1 pine, each measuring 5 inches.

3  Cut two Sides (C) from 1x1 pine, each measuring 6½ inches.

## Assembling the Lamp

1  Place the Base (A) on a level surface. Position one Back/Front (B) lengthwise against one edge of the Base (A), 2½ inches from each end, as shown in *figure 1*. Apply glue to the meeting surfaces, and nail through the Back/Front (B) into the Base (A), using two 1⅝-inch finish nails.

2  Repeat step 1 to attach the second Front/Back (A) to the base, parallel to and 5 inches from the first, as shown in *figure 2* on page 210.

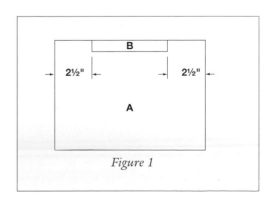

*Figure 1*

3 Place the Sides (C) over the ends of the Front/Backs (A), to form a 6½-inch square (outside measurement), as shown in *figure 2*. Apply glue to the meeting surfaces, and nail through the Sides (C) into the Base (A), using two 1⅝-inch finish nails on each piece.

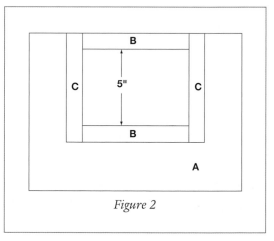

*Figure 2*

4 Turn the base assembly upside down, and attach the 6-inch edge of the ornamental shelf brackets to each end of the Base (A) so that the back of the bracket, which has a metal hanger, is flush with the back of the base assembly. Apply glue to the meeting surfaces, and nail through the sides of the ornamental shelf brackets into the Base (A), using six 1⅝-inch finish nails on each bracket.

## Finishing

1 Fill any cracks, crevices, and nail holes with wood filler, and sand the lamp thoroughly.

2 Paint or stain the shelf the color of your choice—we chose seafoam green.

3 Hang the completed base on your wall or fence, utilizing the metal hangers on the back of the shelf bracket.

4 Install the candle and glass hurricane globe.

# Arbor

*Every garden needs an arbor. This one is positioned over a walkway in the yard to serve as a pleasant transition from one outdoor living area to another; it would also be at home over a entryway gate or in a corner of the yard. Plant a fast-growing vine at the base of the arbor, and you'll have a beautiful addition to your garden.*

**Special Tools & Techniques**

- Dado

**Materials**

- 32 linear feet of 2x2 pine
- 4'x8' sheet of privacy lattice
- 10 linear feet of 1x6 pine
- 15 linear feet of 2x4 pine

**Hardware**

- 80 $1^{1}/_{4}$" (3d) finish nails
- 15 $1^{5}/_{8}$" wood screws
- 12 2" wood screws

**Cutting List**

| Code | Description | Qty. | Materials | Dimensions |
|------|-------------|------|-----------|------------|
| A | Side | 4 | 2x2 pine | 90" long |
| B | Panel | 2 | Privacy Lattice | 12"x80" |
| C | Support | 2 | 1x6 pine | 48" long |
| D | Top | 5 | 2x4 pine | 33" long |

## Building the Side Frames

1 Cut four Sides (A) from 2x2 pine, each measuring 90 inches long.

2 Cut two Panels (B) from lattice, each measuring 12x80 inches.

3 Cut a dado, $^{3}/_{4}$ inch wide and $^{1}/_{2}$ inch deep, down the length of the Sides (A), as shown in *figure 1*.

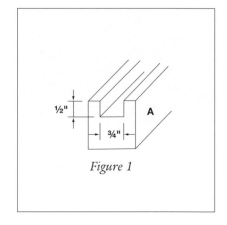

*Figure 1*

4 Place one Panel (B) inside one Side (A) dado. The Panel (B) should be even with one end of the Side (A), as shown in *figure 2* on page 214. Apply glue to the dado, and toenail through the Panel (B) into the Side (A), using $1^{1}/_{4}$-inch finish nails spaced about every 5 inches.

5 Repeat step 4 to attach the other Side (A) to the opposite edge of the Panel (B).

6 Assemble a second frame, using the remaining two Sides (A) and the remaining Panel (B).

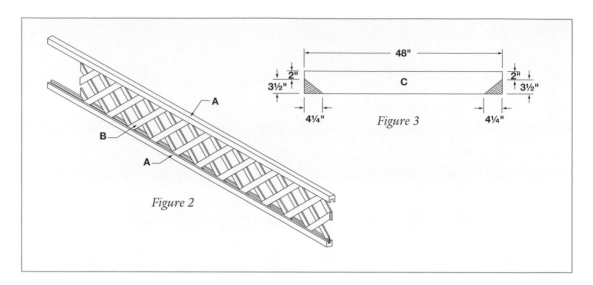

Figure 2

Figure 3

## Adding the Top

1 Cut two Supports (C) from 1x6 pine, each measuring 48 inches long.

2 Using *figure 3* as a guide, cut off two of the corners on both Supports (C).

3 Cut five Tops (D) from 2x4 pine, each measuring 33 inches long. Using *figure 4* as a guide, cut the ends of the Tops (D) at an angle.

4 Place the two assembled frames on edge, parallel to each other, and 34 inches apart. Place one Support (C) over the flush ends of the assembled frames, as shown in *figure 5*. The edge of the Support (C) should be even with the ends of the Sides (A). Apply glue to the meeting surfaces, and screw through the Support (C), using three 1⅝-inch screws on each joint.

5 Repeat step 4 to attach the remaining Support (C).

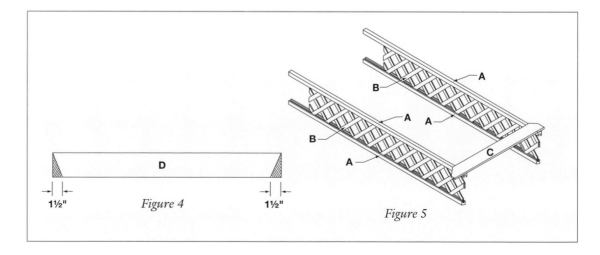

Figure 4

Figure 5

6 Install the arbor in its final spot outside, making sure that the legs are level and plumb. The Sides (A) that extend beyond the Panel (B) should be below ground level.

7 Position the five Tops (D) in place, perpendicular to the Supports (C), as shown in *figure 6*. Screw through the Supports (C) at an angle into the Tops (D), using 2-inch screws.

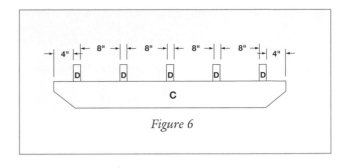

*Figure 6*

## Finishing

1 Sand the completed arbor thoroughly.

2 Either paint or stain the arbor the color of your choice or simply leave it natural.

# Fence Planter Box

*This project transforms a plain fence into a fabulous decorative element. It's quick to make, and, with the addition of some charming (albeit premade and readily available) ornamental gingerbread, it will certainly perk up any uninteresting space in your yard.*

## Materials

- 10 linear feet of 1x6 pine
- 2 premade wooden gingerbread ornaments, approximately 6"x8" inches each

## Hardware

- 50 1⅝" wood screws
- 20 1" (2d) finish nails
- 3 3½" wood screws (optional)

## Cutting List

| Code | Description | Qty. | Materials | Dimensions |
|------|-------------|------|-----------|------------|
| A | Front/Back | 2 | 1x6 pine | 36" long |
| B | Side | 2 | 1x6 pine | 5½"long |
| C | Bottom | 1 | 1x6 pine | 34½" long |

## Making the Planter Box

1 Cut two Front/Backs (A) from 1x6 pine, each measuring 36 inches.

2 Cut two Sides (B) from 1x6 pine, each measuring 5½ inches.

3 Position the two Front/Backs (A) on a level surface, parallel to each other and 5½ inches apart. Fit the two Sides (B) between the two Front/Backs (A) to form a rectangle measuring 36x7 inches, as shown in *figure 1* on page 217.

Apply glue to the meeting surfaces, and nail through the Front/Backs (A) into the Sides (B), using three evenly spaced 1⅝-inch screws on each joint.

4 Cut one Bottom (C) from 1x6 pine, measuring 34½ inches.

5 Insert the Bottom (C) inside the assembled rectangle, flush with the bottom edges of the Front/Backs (A) and Sides (B). Nail through the Front/Backs (A) and Sides (B) into the bottom, using 1⅜-inch screws spaced every 2 inches.

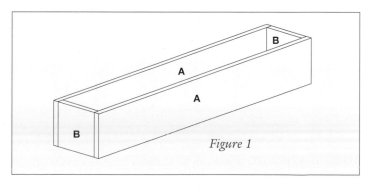

*Figure 1*

## Finishing

1 Sand the assembled fence planter thoroughly. An optional step is to drill several holes through the bottom of the planter, to allow the plants to drain properly.

2 Paint or stain the planter and gingerbread ornaments the colors of your choice—or leave the planter its natural color. (If you decide to paint or stain the planter and ornaments the same color, you may do so after the project is completely assembled.)

3 Attach the gingerbread ornament to the front corners of the planter, using 1-inch finish nails.

4 Attach the planter to the fence. It is a good idea to use $3^{1}/_{2}$-inch wood screws, and attach the planter to both the fence and the fence post. (When the planter is full of dirt and flowers, it may be too heavy for some fences.)

# Plant Pedestal

*We had fun designing a simple and easy-to-build pedestal that was attractive and substantial enough to support a healthy fern. Then we finished it to look like marble. The pedestal looks great on a porch or in a corner of a deck.*

## Materials

- 17 linear feet of 1x6 pine
- 2 linear feet of 1x8 pine
- 2 linear feet of 1x10 pine
- Marbleizing paint kit (comes in several different colors, and includes instructions)

## Hardware

- 50 3dx1¼" nails
- 15 6dx2" nails

## Cutting List

| Code | Description | Qty. | Materials | Dimensions |
|------|-------------|------|-----------|------------|
| A | Side | 4 | 1x6 pine | 48" long |
| B | Small Base | 2 | 1x8 pine | 7¼" long |
| C | Large Base | 2 | 1x10 pine | 9¼" long |

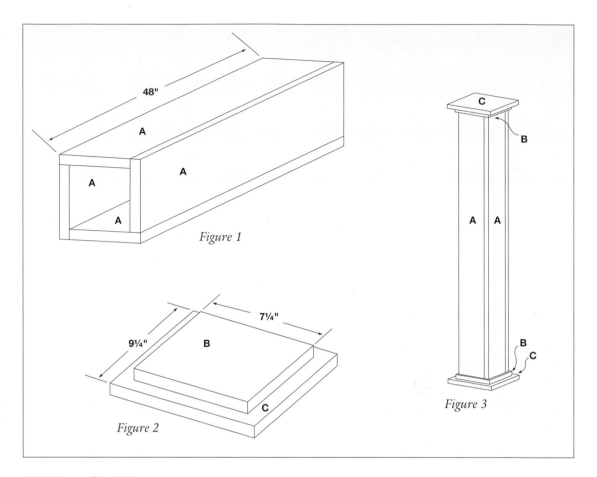

Figure 1

Figure 2

Figure 3

## Cutting the Pieces

1 Cut four sides (A) from 1x6 pine, each 48 inches long. It's essential that you cut the ends perfectly square to avoid creating a tower that leans like the famous one we all know about.

2 Cut two small base pieces (B) from 1x8 pine, each 7¼ inches long.

3 Cut two large base pieces (C) from 1x10 pine, each 9¼ inches long.

## Assembly

1 Assemble the four side pieces (A), overlapping each piece in rotation, as shown in *figure 1*. With the four sides (A) in position, the stand measures 6¼ inches wide on all sides. Nail all four sides (A) along their entire length, using the 3d nails, spaced about 6 inches apart. Countersink the nails.

2 Center one small base (B) over one large base (C), as shown in *figure 2*. Nail the two pieces together using 3d nails.

3 Repeat step 2 on page 220 using the other small base (B) and large base (C).

4 Center one base assembly on top of the stand. The large base should be facing up (see *figure 3* on page 220). Attach the base to the stand using the larger nails. Countersink the nails.

5 Turn the stand over and repeat step 4 to attach the remaining base assembly.

## Finishing

1 Fill any cracks, crevices, or nail holes with wood filler, and thoroughly sand all surfaces of the completed pedestal.

2 We finished our plant stand using a purchased marbleizing kit. It was fun to do, and the results are impressive.

# Planter Trio

*These attractive and handy planters are at home either inside or out. We finished ours to place on a covered porch, but they would look terrific on a deck or indoors in front of a picture window. We made two small planters and one large one, but you can make any combination you wish and either attach them to one another or use them individually.*

## Materials

**Large Planter Box**

- 6 linear feet of 1x8 pine
- 18 linear feet of 1x2 pine
- 12 linear feet of 2x2 pine

**Small Planter Box**
**(remember to double this amount if you intend to make two)**

- 4 linear feet of 1x8 pine
- 10 linear feet of 1x2 pine
- 10 linear feet of 2x2 pine

## Hardware
### (for each planter box)

- 25 4dx1½" nails
- 20 1⅝" screws

## Cutting List
### Large Planter Box

| Code | Description | Qty. | Materials | Dimensions |
|------|-------------|------|-----------|------------|
| A | Side | 2 | 1x8 pine | 7¼" long |
| B | Front/Back | 2 | 1x8 pine | 22" long |
| C | Long Leg | 4 | 2x2 pine | 32½" long |
| D | Shelf Side | 2 | 1x2 pine | 7¼" long |
| E | Shelf Front/Back | 2 | 1x2 pine | 22" long |
| F | Slat | 18 | 1x2 pine | 7¼" long |

### Small Planter Box

| Code | Description | Qty. | Materials | Dimensions |
|------|-------------|------|-----------|------------|
| A | Side | 2 | 1x8 pine | 7¼" long |
| G | Small Front/Back | 2 | 1x8 pine | 1¼" long |
| H | Short Leg | 4 | 2x2 pine | 27½" long |
| D | Shelf Side | 2 | 1x2 pine | 7¼" long |
| I | Small Shelf Front/Back | 2 | 1x2 pine | 12" long |
| F | Slat | 8 | 1x2 pine | 7¼" long |

## Making the Large Planter Box

1 Cut two sides (A) from 1x8 pine, each measuring 7¼ inches long.

2 Cut two long front/backs (B) from 1x8 pine, each measuring 22 inches long.

3 Place the two sides (A) on a flat surface, parallel to each other and 20¹/₂ inches apart. Place the two front/backs (B) over the ends of the sides (A), as shown in *figure 1* on page 225. Screw through the ends of the front/backs (B) into the ends of the sides (A).

## Adding the Legs

1 Cut four planter legs (C) from 2x2 pine, each measuring 32¹/₂ inches long.

**2** Fit one planter leg (C) in each corner of the open-ended planter box, 1 inch from what will be the top of the planter (decision time!), as shown in *figure 2*. Screw through the front/back (B) and side (A) into each leg (C), using 1⅝-inch-long screws. Use two screws on each joint.

## Adding the Lower Shelf

**1** Cut two shelf sides (D) from 1x2 pine, each measuring 7¼ inches long.

**2** Attach one shelf side (D) 7½ inches from the bottom of the two legs (C), as shown in *figure 3*. Screw through the shelf side (D) into each leg (C), using a 1⅝-inch-long screw. Repeat this procedure to attach the other shelf side (D) to the opposite legs (C).

**3** Cut two shelf front/backs (E) from 1x2 pine, each measuring 22 inches long.

**4** Fit one shelf front/back (E) over the ends of the two shelf sides (D), as shown in *figure 3*. Screw through the shelf front/back (E) into the legs (C), using a 1⅝-inch-long screw. Repeat this procedure to attach the other shelf front/back (E) over the opposite ends of the two shelf sides (D).

## Adding the Slats

**1** Cut 18 slats (F) from 1x2 pine, each measuring 7¼ inches long. Nine slats will be used to make the bottom of the planter box, and nine will be used to make the lower shelf.

**2** To fashion the lower shelf, attach the first slat (F) between the shelf front/backs (E), flush with the inside of the legs (C) and with one face even with the top edge of the shelf front/backs (E). Nail through the shelf front/backs (E) into the end of the slat (F), using two 1½-inch-long nails on each joint.

**3** Attach the second slat (F) to the opposite side of the shelf.

**4** Attach seven more slats (F) between the shelf front/backs (E), spacing them ½ inch apart.

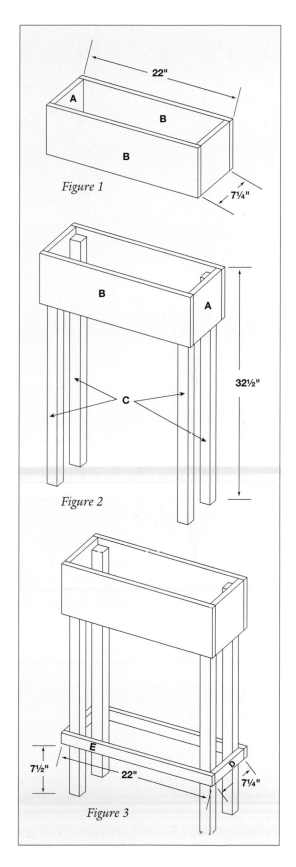

Figure 1

Figure 2

Figure 3

5 Attach the remaining nine slats (F) between the front/back (A) at the bottom of the planter box. The lower surface of the slats (F) should be flush with the bottom of the planter box, as shown in *figure 4*.

## Making the Small Planter Box

1 Cut two sides (A) from 1x8 pine, each measuring $7^1/_4$ inches long.

2 Cut two small front/backs (C) from 1x8 pine, each measuring 12 inches long.

3 Place the two sides (A) on a flat surface, parallel to each other and $10^1/_2$ inches apart. Place the two small front/backs (G) over the ends of the sides (A). Screw through the ends of the small front/backs (G) into the ends of the sides (A).

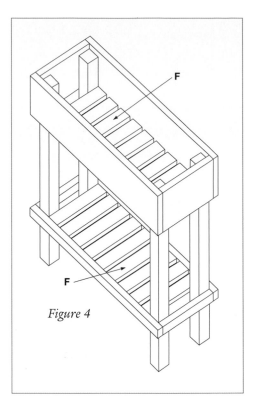

*Figure 4*

## Adding the Legs

1 Cut four short legs (H) from 2x2 pine, each measuring $27^1/_2$ inches long.

2 Fit one short leg (H) in each corner of the open-ended planter box, 1 inch from what will be the top of the planter, as shown in *figure 1* on page 225. Screw through the small front/back (G) and side (A) into the short leg (H), using $1^5/_8$ inch-long screws. Use two screws on each joint.

## Adding the Lower Shelf

1 Cut two shelf sides (D) from 1x2 pine, each measuring $7^1/_4$ inches long.

2 Attach one shelf side (D) $7^1/_2$ inches from the bottom of the two short legs (H), as shown in *figure 2* on page 225. Screw through the shelf side (D) into each short leg (H), using a $1^5/_8$- inch-long screw. Repeat to attach the other shelf side (D) to the two opposite short legs (H).

3 Cut two small shelf front/backs (I) from 1x2 pine, each measuring 12 inches long.

4 Fit one small shelf front/back (I) over the ends of the shelf sides (D), as shown in *figure 3* on page 225. Screw through the small shelf front/back (I) into the short legs (H), using a $1^5/_8$-inch-long screw. Repeat to attach the other shelf front/back (I).

## Adding the Slats

1 Cut eight slats (F) from 1x2 pine, each measuring $7^{1}/_{4}$ inches long. Four slats will be used to make the bottom of the planter box, and four will be used to make the lower shelf.

2 To make the lower shelf, attach the first slat (F) between the small shelf front/backs (I), flush with the inside of the short legs (H), as shown in *figure 4* on page 226. Nail through each small shelf front/back (I) into the end of the slat (F), using two $1^{1}/_{2}$-inch-long nails on each joint.

3 Attach the second slat (F) to the opposite side of the shelf.

4 Attach two more slats (F) between the first and second slats (F), spacing them $^{1}/_{2}$ inch apart.

5 Attach the remaining four slats (F) between the small front/back (C) at the bottom of the planter box. The lower surface of the slats (F) should be flush with the bottom of the planter box.

## Finishing

1 Fill any cracks, crevices, or screw holes with wood filler, and thoroughly sand all surfaces of the completed planters.

2 Paint or stain the finished project the color of your choice, or simply seal it with a waterproof sealer for a natural look.

# Picket Window Box

*This pretty window box really comes alive when filled with colorful flowers. Not only does it look attractive mounted outside on a window ledge, but it also brightens up your window when admired from inside the house. The box is constructed around an inexpensive pre-made plastic planter. The size can be adjusted to fit any window.*

## Materials

- 30 linear feet of 1x2 pine
- 2 linear feet of 2x2 pine
- ¹/₂ linear foot of 1x4 pine
- Plastic planter box*

## Hardware

- 150 3dx1¹/₄" nails
- 42" screws

## *Notes on Materials

We purchased a plastic planter box measuring 29 inches long, 5¹/₄ inches deep, and 8¹/₄ inches wide. It has a lip on the top that rests on the wooden supports we built. You can use this design for any size box you wish, but you need to adjust the dimensions accordingly. The support assemblies fit just under the top lip of the planter.

## Cutting List

| Code | Description | Qty. | Materials | Dimensions |
|------|-------------|------|-----------|------------|
| A | Long Supports | 4 | 1x2 pine | 29¹/₂" long |
| B | Short Supports | 4 | 1x2 pine | 7¹/₂" long |
| C | Pickets | 23 | 1x2 pine | 8" long |
| D | Posts | 2 | 2x2 pine | 8¹/₂" long |
| E | Post Cap | 2 | 1x4 pine | 2"x2" long |

## Constructing the Planter Supports

1 Cut four long supports (A) from 1x2 pine, each measuring 29¹/₂ inches long.

2 Cut four short supports (B) from 1x2 pine, each measuring 7¹/₂ inches long.

3 Place two long supports (A) on a level surface, parallel to each other and 7¹/₂ inches apart. Fit two short supports (B) between the long supports (A), as shown in *figure 1*. Nail through the long supports (A) into the ends of the short supports (B). Use two 1¹/₄-inch-long nails on each joint.

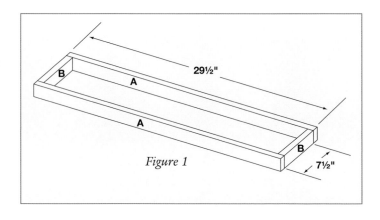

*Figure 1*

## Adding the Pickets

1 Cut 23 pickets (C) from 1x2 pine, each measuring 8 inches long.

2 Cut the corners off each of the 23 pickets (C), as shown in *figure 2*.

3 Lay the two support assemblies on a level surface, parallel to each other, 1½ inches apart, with the long supports (A) on the top and bottom, and the short supports (B) on the sides. Attach all 15 pickets (C) to the top of both support assemblies, starting with the outer pickets, as shown in *figure 3* on page 230. These outer pickets should be exactly flush with the ends of the long supports (A). Space the pickets ½ inch apart. Note that the square ends of the pickets are flush with the bottom edge of one long support (A), and the pointed end is 3½ inches higher than the top edge of the other long support (A). Apply glue to the meeting surfaces, and nail through the pickets into both of the long supports (A), using two 1¼-inch long nails on each joint.

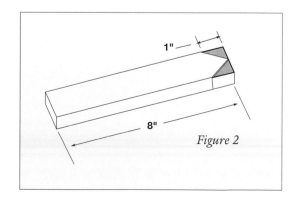

1"

8"

*Figure 2*

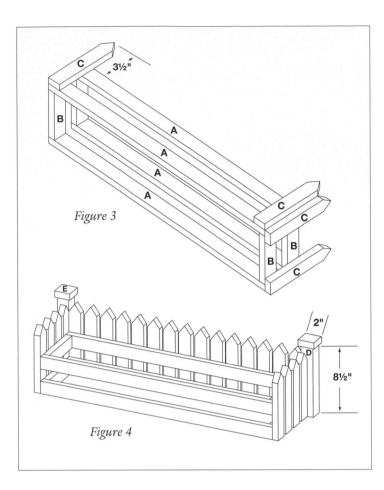

*Figure 3*

*Figure 4*

4 Follow the procedure in step 3 to attach four pickets to each of the short supports (B).

## Adding the End Posts

1 Cut two posts (D) from 2x2 pine, each measuring 8¹⁄₂ inches long.

2 Cut two post caps (E) from 1x4 pine, each measuring 2x2 inches.

3 Center one post cap (E) over the end of one post (D). Apply glue to the meeting surfaces and nail through the post cap (E) into the end of the post (D), using two 1¹⁄₄-inch-long nails. Repeat this procedure to attach the remaining post cap (E) to the second post (D).

4 Fit the posts on each end of the window box, filling in the exposed corner between the side and front pickets (C), as shown in *figure 4*. Screw through the inside corner of each of the support assemblies into the post (D), using a 2-inch-long screw on each joint.

## Finishing

1 Fill any cracks, crevices, or screw holes with wood filler, and thoroughly sand all surfaces of the completed window box.

2 Seal and paint or stain your window box the color of your choice.

# Rectangular Planter

*This good-looking planter measures 18x20 inches, and will accommodate very large plants. It's also a quick-and-easy project to build. If you have ever priced large planter boxes in a garden store, then you will really appreciate how economical this one is to make.*

## Materials

- 14 linear feet of 1x2 pine
- 8 linear feet of 1x4 pine
- 28 linear feet of 1x6 pine
- 1 piece of $1/2$"-thick exterior plywood, measuring $16^1/2$"x$20^1/2$"

## Hardware

- 120 $1^1/4$" screws

## Cutting List

| Code | Description | Qty. | Materials | Dimensions |
|------|-------------|------|-----------|------------|
| A | Long Inner Support | 4 | 1x2 pine | $20^1/2$" long |
| B | Short Inner Support | 4 | 1x2 pine | 15" long |
| C | Bottom | 1 | $1/2$" plywood | $16^1/2$"x$20^1/2$" |
| D | Side Panel | 14 | 1x6 pine | 18" long |
| E | Short Trim | 2 | 1x4 pine | 19" long |
| F | Long Trim | 2 | 1x4 pine | 22" long |

## Making the Inner Supports

1 Cut four long inner supports (A) from 1x2 pine, each measuring $20^1/2$ inches long.

2 Cut four short inner support (B) from 1x2 pine, each measuring 15 inches long.

3 Place two long inner supports (A) parallel to each other and 15 inches apart. Fit two short inner supports (B) between the ends of the long inner supports (A), as shown in *figure 1* on page 233. Screw through the ends of the long inner supports (A) into the short inner supports (B), using two $1^1/4$-inch-long screws on each of the joints.

4 Repeat step 3 to form a second assembly using the remaining two long inner supports (A) and two short inner supports (B).

## Adding the Bottom

1 Cut one bottom (C) from $1/2$-inch-thick plywood, measuring $16^1/2$x$20^1/2$ inches.

2 Drill six 1-inch holes through the bottom (C) to allow for drainage. The exact placement is not critical, but they should be well distributed across the bottom (C).

3 Attach the bottom (C) to one inner assembly, as shown in *figure 1* on page 233. Apply glue to the meeting surfaces, and screw through the bottom (C) into the edges of the long inner supports (A) and short inner supports (B).

## Adding the Sides

1 Cut 14 side panels (D) from 1x6 pine, each measuring 18 inches long.

2 Working on a level surface, place three side panels (D) next to each other, wide sides up. Place one 16½-inch-long side of the inner support assembly—with bottom (C) attached—

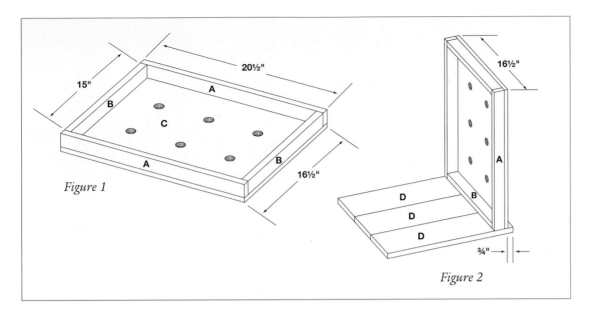

Figure 1

Figure 2

$^3/_4$ inch from one end of the three panels, as shown in *figure 2*. Apply glue to the meeting surfaces, and screw through the short inner supports (B) into each of the three side panels (D). Use two $1^1/_4$-inch-long screws on each of the side panels (D). Repeat this process to attach the other support assembly to the same three side panels (D), flush with the opposite ends of the side panels (D).

3 Repeat step 2 to attach three side panels (D) to the opposite side of the two support assemblies, as shown in *figure 3* on page 234.

4 Repeat step 2 to attach four side panels (D) to one long side of the two support assemblies, as shown in *figure 3*. Note that these four side panels (D) will overlap the three side panels (D) that you previously attached.

5 Repeat step 4 to attach the remaining four side panels (D) to the remaining long side of the two support assemblies.

## Adding the Trim

1 Cut two short trims (E) from 1x4 pine, each measuring 19 inches long.

2 Cut two long trims (F) from 1x4 pine, each measuring 22 inches long.

3 As shown in *figure 4* on page 234, position the short trims (E) so that their inside edges are flush with the inside faces of the long inner supports (A). The ends of the short trims (E) must be even with the inside edges of the short inner supports (B). The trims will overlap the planter by 2 inches. Apply glue to the top edge of each long inner support (A) and each side

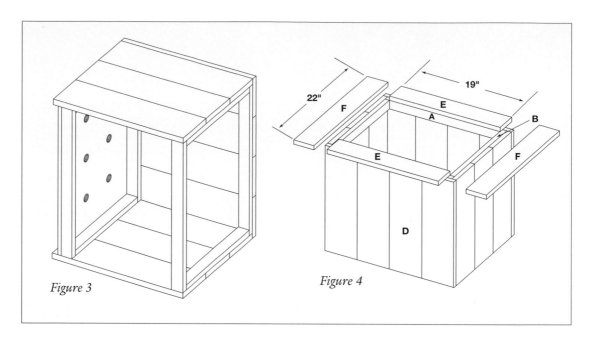

*Figure 3*

*Figure 4*

panel (D); then screw through each short trim (E) into the long inner support (A), using four 1¼-inch-long screws for each trim.

4 Position each long trim (F) with its inside edge flush with the inside face of a short inner support (B) and its ends even with the outside edges of the short trims (E), as shown in *figure 4*. Apply glue to the top edge of each short inner support (B) and each side panel (D); then screw through each long trim (F) into the short inner support (B), using four 1¼-inch-long screws for each trim.

## Finishing

1 We left our planter unfinished, but if you wish a more formal look, fill any cracks, crevices, or screw holes with wood filler, and thoroughly sand all surfaces of the completed planter.

2 Paint or stain the finished project the color of your choice, or simply seal it with a waterproof sealer for a natural look.

# Cupola Birdhouse

*This whimsical birdhouse is mounted on our deck. It's such a treat watching the birds carry twigs into their house to build the nest! Even if you're not a bird watcher, you'll enjoy seeing this birdhouse in your garden or on your patio.*

## Materials

- 1 piece of $\frac{1}{2}$"-thick exterior plywood, measuring 12"x24"
- 1 piece of $\frac{3}{8}$"-thick exterior plywood, measuring 12"x36"
- 3 linear feet of 1x8 pine
- 15 linear feet of 1x4 pine
- 1 linear foot of 1x2 pine
- 1 decorative curtain rod finial
- 3 linear feet of 2"-wide canvas fabric strips
- Staple gun and staples
- Paneling adhesive

## Hardware

- 20 4dx1$\frac{1}{2}$" nails
- 20 1$\frac{1}{4}$" screws

## Cutting List

| Code | Description | Qty. | Materials | Dimensions |
|------|-------------|------|-----------|------------|
| A | Top/Bottom | 2 | $\frac{1}{2}$" plywood | 11$\frac{1}{4}$" diameter circle |
| B | Wide Side | 10 | 1x4 pine | 11" long |
| C | Narrow Side | 1 | 1x2 pine | 11" long |
| D | Base Side | 4 | 1x4 pine | 14$\frac{1}{2}$" long |
| E | Base | 2 | 1x8 pine | 16" long |
| F | Roof Panel | 8 | $\frac{3}{8}$" plywood | 12"x12"x7" triangle |

## Making the House

1 Cut two top/bottoms (A) from $\frac{1}{2}$-inch-thick plywood, each a circle measuring 11$\frac{1}{4}$ inches in diameter.

2 Cut 10 wide sides (B) from 1x4 pine, each measuring 11 inches long.

3 Cut a 1$\frac{1}{2}$-inch-diameter hole in one wide side (B), 4 inches from one end, and centered on the width, as shown in *figure 1*. (Note: Different birds require different size openings. Refer to a book on building

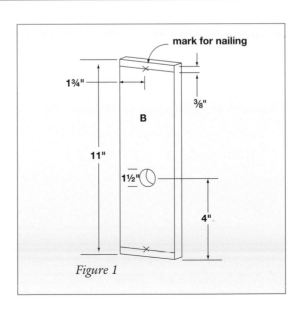

*Figure 1*

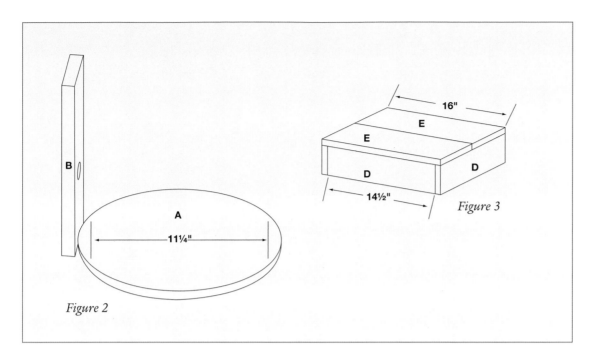

Figure 3

Figure 2

birdhouses to help you determine what size hole to drill. The hole size used here is a good match for flycatchers, wrens, nuthatches, and tree swallows.)

4 Measure carefully and mark the center of the 1x4 width of each of the wide sides (B), ³/₈ inch from each end, as shown in *figure 1* on page 235.

5 Place one top/bottom (A) on a level surface. Attach one wide side (B) to the top/bottom (A). Nail through the mark on the wide side (B) into the edge of the top/bottom (A) using a 1¹/₂-inch-long nail, as shown in *figure 2*.

6 Place a second wide side (B) next to the first one, so that the inner edges meet. Nail through the wide side (B) into the edge of the top/bottom (A). Continue this procedure to attach the remaining eight wide sides (B) to the top/bottom (A).

7 Cut one narrow side (C) from 1x2 pine, measuring 11 inches long. Mark the exact center of the width, ³/₈ inch from each end.

8 Attach the narrow side (C) to the top/bottom (A) in the space remaining between the first and last wide sides (B). Nail through the mark in the narrow side (C) into the top/bottom (A).

9 Place the remaining top/bottom (A) on a level surface. Turn the house assembly upside down, and fit the narrow and wide sides (B and C) over the remaining top/bottom (A). Nail through the marks to attach each of the sides (B and C) to the top/bottom (A).

## Making the Base

1 Cut four base sides (D) from 1x4 pine, each measuring 14$\frac{1}{2}$ inches long.

2 Place two bases (D) on a level surface, parallel to each other and 14$\frac{1}{2}$ inches apart. Fit the remaining two base sides (D) between the first two base sides (D), as shown in *figure 3* on page 237. Nail through the overlapping base sides (D) into the ends of the inner base sides (D), using two 1$\frac{1}{2}$ inch-long nails on each of the joints.

3 Cut two bases (E) from 1x8 pine, each measuring 16 inches long.

4 Fit the two bases (E) over the base sides (D), as shown in *figure 3* on page 237. Apply glue to the meeting surfaces, and nail through the edges of the two bases (E) into the base sides (D). Use four or five 1$\frac{1}{2}$-inch-long nails on each side.

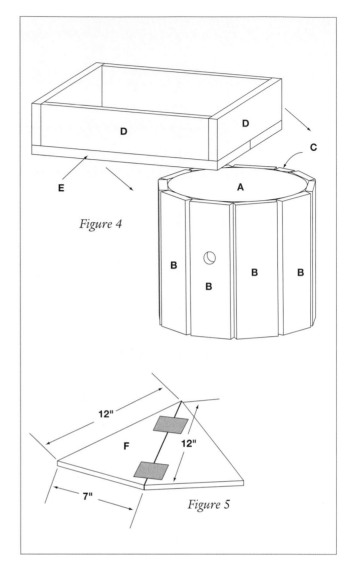

*Figure 4*

*Figure 5*

5 Place the house assembly on a level surface, with the drilled hole closer to the top.

6 Turn the base assembly upside down and center it over the house assembly, as shown in *figure 4*. Apply glue to the meeting surfaces, and screw through both bases (E) into the top/bottom (A), using five or six 1$\frac{1}{4}$-inch screws.

## Making the Roof

1 Cut eight triangular roof panels (F) from $\frac{3}{8}$-inch thick plywood, each panel measuring 12x12x7 inches. These will be joined together to form an eight-sided cone for the roof.

2 To hold the pieces together temporarily, we used small strips of canvas fabric and a staple gun.

3 Begin by placing two roof panels (F) on a flat surface, with their 12 inch sides exactly matching, as shown in *figure 5* on page 238. Cut two 2-inch-long strips of canvas fabric. Place one strip about 2 inches from the top, and one strip about 1 inch from the bottom of the panels. Use a staple gun to staple the fabric to each of the two roof panels (F). Repeat until you have attached the remaining six roof panels (F) to the first two.

4 Now comes the awkward part. You may wish to enlist the assistance of a friend for this step. Have someone hold the assembly so that you can connect the first roof panel to the eighth roof panel. Again use two fabric strips to connect the panels.

5 Place the connected roof right side up on a level surface. Adjust the panels so that the assembly is even on all sides. Then apply paneling adhesive into each of the joints to form a smooth surface. Let the assembly dry overnight.

## Finishing

1 As a finishing touch, we glued a curtain rod finial to the top of the roof.

2 If you plan to have visitors to your new birdhouse, it's best to attach the roof to the house assembly with a hinge so that you can clean it out after one family of birds has come and gone. If you plan to use the birdhouse as an outdoor ornament, simply nail through the roof into the house assembly.

3 Fill any cracks, crevices, or screw holes with wood filler, and thoroughly sand all surfaces of the completed birdhouse.

4 Seal and paint or stain your birdhouse the colors of your choice.

# Tuteur

*Modeled after the vine trellises in Europe, this tuteur not only looks great, but provides a place for vines to grow and be protected. The unique shape will add interest to your garden, without taking up much space.*

### Special Tools & Techniques

- Miter

### Materials

- 50 linear feet of 1x4 pine
- 23 linear feet of 1x1 pine
- 10"x10" square of ³/₄" exterior plywood
- Fence-post finial

### Hardware

- 50 1¼" wood screws
- 30 1¼" (3d) finish nails
- 50 1⁵/₈" wood screws

### Cutting List

| Code | Description | Qty. | Materials | Dimensions |
|------|-------------|------|-----------|------------|
| A | Vertical | 8 | 1x4 pine | 51" long |
| B | Center Vertical | 4 | 1x1 pine | 51" long |
| C | Short Top Support | 2 | 1x4 pine | 7³/₄" long |
| D | Short Middle Support | 2 | 1x4 pine | 11¼" long ' |
| E | Short Bottom Support | 2 | 1x4 pine | 13½" long |
| F | Long Top Support | 2 | 1x4 pine | 9¼" long |
| G | Long Middle Support | 2 | 1x4 pine | 12³/₄" long |
| H | Long Bottom Support | 2 | 1x4 pine | 15" long |
| I | Top | 1 | ³/₄" plywood | 10½" square |
| J | Top Trim | 4 | 1x1 pine | 12" long |

## Cutting the Wide Side Pieces

1 Cut eight Verticals (A) from 1x4 pine, each measuring 51 inches.

2 Miter each end of each Vertical (A) at a 5° angle, as shown in *figure 1*.

3 Cut four Center Verticals (B) from 1x1 pine, each measuring 51 inches.

4 Cut two Short Top Supports (C) from 1x4 pine, each measuring 7³/₄ inches.

5 Miter each of the Short Top Supports (C) at opposing 5° angles, as shown in *figure 2* on page 242.

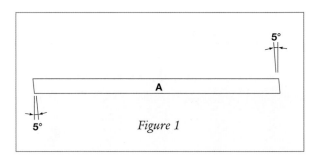

Figure 1

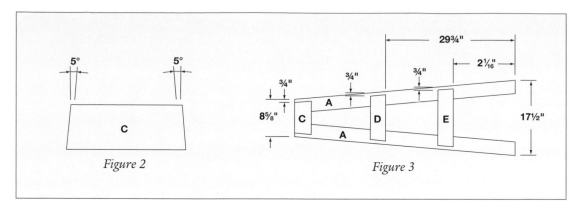

Figure 2

Figure 3

6 Cut two Short Middle Supports (D) from 1x4 pine, each measuring 11¼ inches.

7 Miter the ends of each of the two Short Middle Supports (D) at opposing 5° angles, as shown in *figure 2*.

8 Cut two Short Bottom Supports (E) from 1x4 pine, each measuring 13½-inches.

9 Miter the ends of each of the two Short Bottom Supports (E) at opposing 5° angles, as shown in *figure 2*.

## Assembling the Wide Sides

1 Position two Verticals (A) on a level work surface so that they form an upside-down V-shape that is open at the top (see *figure 3*). The Verticals (A) should be 8⅝ inches apart at the top, and 17½ inches apart at the bottom.

2 The sides of the finished tuteur should slope in at the top and out at the bottom. Each of the sides has three horizontal supports that determine the angle of the slope. Place all of the Supports (C, D, and E) on the Verticals (A) to make certain that the side is properly assembled before attaching any of the supports to the Verticals (A). Refer to *figure 3* to check your measurements.

3 Position one Short Top Support (C) on top of the two Verticals (A), flush with the top of the assembly. Position one Short Bottom Support (E) over the two Verticals (A), flush with the bottom of the assembly. Position one Short Middle Support (D) over the Verticals (A) in the middle of the assembly, as shown in *figure 3*. Once all the supports are positioned correctly, apply glue to the meeting surfaces, and screw through the Short Top, Middle, and Bottom Supports (C, D, and E) into the Verticals (A), using two 1¼-inch wood screws on each joint.

4 Turn the side assembly upside down, so that the Verticals (A) are on the top. Place one

Center Vertical (B) between the two Verticals (A), on top of the Short Top, Middle, and Bottom Supports (C, D, and E), as shown in *figure 4*. Apply glue to the meeting surfaces, and nail through the Center Vertical (B) into the Short Top, Middle, and Bottom Supports (C, D, and E), using a 1¼-inch finish nail on each joint.

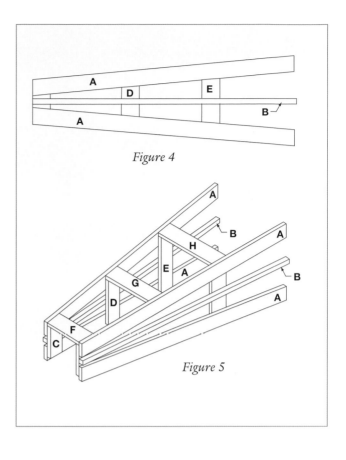

*Figure 4*

*Figure 5*

5 Repeat steps 1 through 4 to form a second wide side. There should be four Verticals (A) and two Center Verticals (B) remaining. Set them aside for use in the next assemblies.

## Cutting the Narrow Sides

1 Cut two Long Top Supports (F) from 1x4 pine, each measuring 9¼ inches.

2 Miter each of the Long Top Supports (F) at opposing 5° angles, as shown in *figure 2* on page 242.

3 Cut two Long Middle Supports (G) from 1x4 pine, each measuring 11¼ inches.

4 Miter the ends of each of the two Long Middle Supports (G) at opposing 5° angles, as shown in *figure 2* on page 242.

5 Cut two Long Bottom Supports (H) from 1x4 pine, each measuring 15 inches.

6 Miter the ends of each of the two Long Bottom Supports (H) at opposing 5° angles, as shown in *figure 2* on page 242.

## Connecting the Frame

1 Position the two vertical assemblies (pieces A through E) opposite each other, as shown in *figure 5*.

2 Place one Long Top Support (F) over the ends of the Short Top Supports (C), as shown in *figure 5*. Apply glue to the meeting surfaces, and screw through the Long Top Support (F) into the end of the Short Top Supports (C), using 1¼-inch wood screws spaced about 6 inches apart.

3 Repeat step 2 to attach the remaining Long Middle and Top Supports (G and H), as shown in *figure 5*.

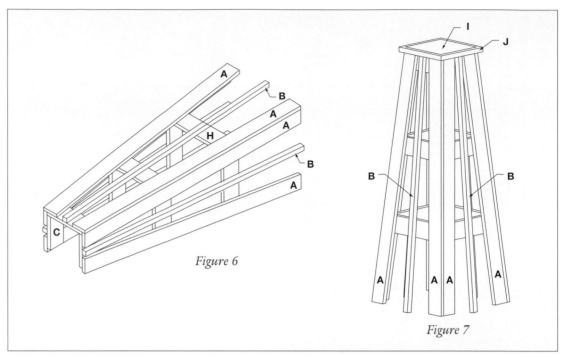

*Figure 6*

*Figure 7*

4 Turn the assembly over and repeat steps 2 and 3 to attach the remaining Long Top, Middle, and Bottom Supports (F, G, and H).

5 Place one Vertical (A) against the edge of another Vertical (A) and Long Top, Middle, and Bottom Supports (F, G, and H), as shown in *figure 6*. Apply glue to the meeting surfaces, and screw through the Vertical (A) into the Long Top, Middle, and Bottom Supports (F, G, and H) and into the Vertical (A), using two 1¼-inch wood screws in each joint spaced every 6 inches along the Vertical (A).

6 Repeat step 5 to attach another Vertical (A).

7 Turn the assembly over and repeat steps 5 and 6 to attach the remaining two Verticals (A).

8 Position one Center Vertical (B) between the two Verticals (A), over the Long Top, Middle, and Bottom Supports (F, G, and H), as shown in *figure 6* on page 244. Apply glue to the meeting surfaces, and nail through the Center Vertical (B) into the Long Top, Middle, and Bottom Supports (F, G, and H), using a 1¼-inch finish nail on each joint.

9 Repeat step 8 for the remaining Center Vertical (B).

## Finishing

1 Cut one Top (I) from ¾-inch-thick plywood, measuring 10½ inches square.

2 Stand the tuteur upright, and center the Top (I) over the ends of the Verticals (A). Apply

glue to the meeting surfaces, and screw through the Top (I) into the Verticals (A), using two 1⅝-inch wood screws on each side.

3 Locate and mark the center of the Top (I). Predrill a starter hole, then screw the fence-post finial to the Top (I).

4 Cut four Top Trims (J) from 1x1 pine, each measuring 12 inches.

5 Miter the ends of each of the Top Trims (J) at opposing 45° angles.

6 Working around the Top (I) in rotation, glue and nail each of the Top Trims (J) over the edges of the Top (I), matching miters on all four corners. Use three 1¼-inch finish nails on each Top Trim (J). (See *figure 7* on page 244.)

7 Stain or paint the finished tuteur the color of your choice, or simply leave it natural.

# Trellis & Fountain

*Ah, the sound of water on a summer's day seems to cool everything down while also soothing the soul. The combination of trellis and fountain is an easy way to add a water feature to your outdoor living area without huge expense. Choose a statuary that fits in your garden and build the trellis yourself.*

## Special Tools & Techniques

- Miter

## Materials

- 26 linear feet of 4x4 pine
- 17 linear feet of 2x2 pine
- 18 linear feet of 1x4 pine
- 4'x 8'sheet of privacy lattice
- 6 linear feet of 2x4 pine

## Hardware

- 50 2½" wood screws
- 20 1⅝" wood screws
- 30 1" wire brads
- 2 5" lag screws
- Fountain statuary piece"
- Fountain pump
- Plastic hose (sized to connect the statuary piece to the pump)
- Galvanized bucket, approximately 3'x4'x2'

## *Notes on Materials

This trellis will work with any statuary fountain piece. Most lawn and garden stores sell a variety of designs. Or you can convert a wall plaque into a fountain piece by drilling a hole through the plaque to accommodate the plastic pump hose. Be sure to purchase a pump large enough to pump the water from the tank up the height of your fountain piece. Check the pump manufacturer's specifications to be sure.

## Cutting List

| Code | Description | Qty. | Materials | Dimensions |
|------|-------------|------|-----------|------------|
| A | Side | 2 | 4x4 | 120" long |
| B | Side Supports | 2 | 2x2 | 96" long |
| C | Connectors | 4 | 1x4 | 48" long |
| D | Trellis | 1 | Lattice | 4'x8' sheet |
| E | Top | 2 | 2x4 | 26" long |
| F | Ledge | 1 | 4x4 | 55" long |

## Building the Frame

1 Cut two Sides (A) from 4x4 pine, each measuring 120 inches.

2 Cut two Side Supports (B) from 2x2 pine, each measuring 96 inches.

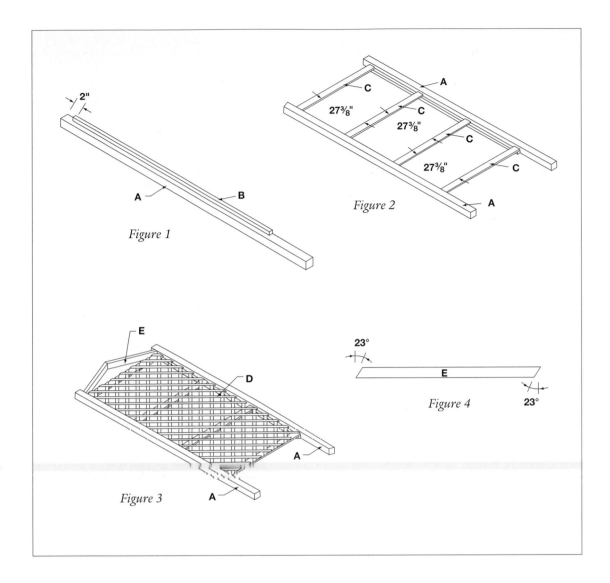

Figure 1

Figure 2

Figure 3

Figure 4

3 Position one Side Support (B) flush with one edge of one Side (A), as shown in *figure 1*. Note that the Side (A) is 4 inches from one end of the Side Support (B), and extends past the Side Support (B) 20 inches on the opposite end. Apply glue to the meeting surfaces, and screw through the Side Support (B) into the Side (A), using $2^{1}/_{2}$-inch-long nails spaced every 5 inches.

4 Repeat step 3 to assemble a mirror image, using the remaining Side (A) and Side Support (B).

5 Cut four Connectors (C) from 1x4 pine, each measuring 48 inches.

6 Position the side assemblies on a level surface, 45 inches apart and parallel to each other, with the Side Supports (B) facing each other.

7 Place the one Connector (C) over the Side Supports (B), flush with the upper ends of the topmost Side Support (B), as shown in *figure 2* on page 249. Apply glue to the meeting surfaces, and screw through the Connector (C) into the Side Supports (B), using two 1⁵/₈-inch wood screws on each joint.

8 Repeat step 7 three times to attach the remaining Connectors (C), one flush with the lower end of the Side Supports (B), and the two remaining Connectors (C) in the center of the assembly, 27³/₈ inches apart.

## Adding the Lattice, Top & Ledge

1 Place the 4-x8-foot Trellis (D) on top of the four Connectors (C), as shown in *figure 3* on page 249. Nail through the Trellis (D) into the three connectors, using 1-inch wire brads spaced every 4 inches.

2 Cut two Tops (E) from 2x4 pine, each measuring 26 inches.

3 Position the Tops (E) on edge, and miter both ends of the Tops (E) at a 23° angle, as shown in *figure 4* on page 249.

4 Place the two Tops (E) on a flat work surface with the mitered ends together. Apply glue to the meeting surfaces, and screw through each of the Tops (E) into the opposing Top (E), using two 2¹/₂-inch finish nails on each side.

5 Using *figure 3* on page 249 as a guide, position the top assembly on top of the Trellis (D). Apply glue to the meeting surfaces, and screw through the ends of the Tops into the Sides (A), using two 2¹/₂-inch wood screws on each joint.

6 Cut one Ledge (F) from 4x4 pine, measuring 55 inches.

7 The Ledge (F) will be attached to the Sides (A) with two 5-inch lag screws. Predrill holes on each end of the Ledge (F) to accommodate the screws, then screw through the Ledge (F) into the Sides (A).

8 Center the fountain piece on top of the ledge, and secure the top of the fountain piece to one of the four Connectors (C). If the Connector (C) is not in the proper position for the height of your particular fountain piece, secure it to a shorter scrap piece of board placed on the opposite side of the trellis.

## Finishing

1 Place the galvanized bucket on the ground beneath the fountain, then position the pump inside the bucket. Attach the plastic hose to the fountain piece. Guide the plastic hose down the back side of the Trellis (D), then back through the Trellis (D) to the front of the trellis behind the galvanized bucket.

2 Set the completed trellis in the desired outdoor location, taking care to stabilize the structure against strong winds. We placed our trellis in a corner of the yard and secured it to both sides of the fence.

3 Set the galvanized bucket at the bottom center of the trellis, fill it with water. Then connect the free end of the plastic hose to the pump.

# Metric Conversion Chart

| Inches | CM | Inches | CM |
|---|---|---|---|
| 1/8 | 0.3 | 20 | 50.8 |
| 1/4 | 0.6 | 21 | 53.3 |
| 3/8 | 1.0 | 22 | 55.9 |
| 1/2 | 1.3 | 23 | 58.4 |
| 5/8 | 1.6 | 24 | 61.0. |
| 3/4 | 1.9 | 25 | 63.5 |
| 7/8 | 2.2 | 26 | 66.0 |
| 1 | 2.5 | 27 | 68.6 |
| 1 1/4 | 3.2 | 28 | 71.1 |
| 1 1/2 | 3.8 | 29 | 73.7 |
| 1 3/4 | 4.4 | 30 | 76.2 |
| 2 | 5.1 | 31 | 78.7 |
| 2 1/2 | 6.4 | 32 | 81.3 |
| 3 | 7.6 | 33 | 83.8 |
| 3 1/2 | 8.9 | 34 | 86.4 |
| 4 | 10.2 | 35 | 88.9 |
| 4 1/2 | 11.4 | 36 | 91.4 |
| 5 | 12.7 | 37 | 94.0 |
| 6 | 15.2 | 38 | 96.5 |
| 7 | 17.8 | 39 | 99.1 |
| 8 | 20.3 | 40 | 101.6 |
| 9 | 22.9 | 41 | 104.1 |
| 10 | 25.4 | 42 | 106.7 |
| 11 | 27.9 | 43 | 109.2 |
| 12 | 30.5 | 44 | 111.8 |
| 13 | 33.0 | 45 | 114.3 |
| 14 | 35.6 | 46 | 116.8 |
| 15 | 38.1 | 47 | 119.4 |
| 16 | 40.6 | 48 | 121.9 |
| 17 | 43.2 | 49 | 124.5 |
| 18 | 45.7 | 50 | 127.0 |
| 19 | 48.3 | | |

# Acknowledgments From Previous Editions:

## Great 2x4 Projects for Outdoor Living

**Editor:** Laura Dover Doran
**Book and Cover Design:** Dana Irwin
**Photostylist:** Chris Bryant
**Photographer:** Evan Bracken
**Illustrator:** Todd Jarrett
**Editorial Assistance:** Catharine Sutherland
**Production Assistance:** Hannes Charen

As always, there are many people who spent many hours making this book better. We would like to take this opportunity to thank them.

Our gratitude to:
**Laura Dover Doran** (Lark Books, Asheville, North Carolina), our editor, who tirelessly sorted through our manuscript and drawings and contributed so very much to the final book.
**Chris Bryant** (Lark Books, Asheville, North Carolina), art director, who suffered through heat exhaustion and temporary tattoos to make sure we "got the shot".
**Evan Bracken** (Light Reflections, Hendersonville, North Carolina), who made it through yet another shoot with professionalism, humor, and patience.
**Todd Jarrett** (Sarasota, Florida), illustrator, who put together excellent illustrations in very short order.

Special thanks also to the following companies for helping with the production of this book: Intermatic, Inc. (Intermatic Plaza, Spring Grove, Illinois 60081-9698, www.intermatic.com) provided the wonderful outdoor lighting fixtures and Stanley Tools (New Britain, Connecticut 06053, www.stanleyworks.com) helped us cut, measure, and shape the projects.

## Great Outdoor 2x4 Furniture

For the gang at Cannons!
**Editor:** Deborah Morgenthal
**Art Director and Production:** Kathleen Holmes
**Computer Illustrations and Technical Support:** Thomas Stender
**Line Drawings:** Orrin Lundgren
**Photography:** Evan Bracken

We gratefully acknowledge the assistance of many people who deserve credit for the successful production of this book.

Many thanks to:
**Evan Bracken** (Light Reflections, Hendersonville, NC), who once again triumphed over a four-day photography shoot. Thanks for your talent and patience!
**Deborah Morgenthal** (Lark Books, Asheville, NC), our editor, whose skill, patience, and kindness got us through this project.
**Kathy Holmes** (Lark Books, Asheville, NC), our art director, for designing a beautiful and user-friendly book.
**Thomas Stender** (Chicago, IL) for turning our sketches into professional-looking illustrations, and for catching our mistakes.

To the following people who assisted with photography and let us tramp around and through their property and lives; they are (in alphabetical order) Jack Bergbom, Jessica Diehl, Debbie and Maurice Droulers, Charlene Foy, Phil Goldman, Patti Kertz, Benny and Becky Parrish, Carrie and Marty Shindler, and Phil Winkelspecht. Thanks for giving up your sanity and your space to make this book better!

# Index

## Subject Index

## Project Index